SACRED CAPITAL

JEFFERSONIAN AMERICA

Charlene M. Boyer Lewis, Annette Gordon-Reed, Peter S. Onuf,
Andrew J. O'Shaughnessy, and Robert G. Parkinson, Editors

SACRED CAPITAL

Methodism and Settler Colonialism
in the Empire of Liberty

Hunter Price

University of Virginia Press
CHARLOTTESVILLE AND LONDON

The University of Virginia Press is situated on the traditional lands of the Monacan Nation, and the Commonwealth of Virginia was and is home to many other Indigenous people. We pay our respect to all of them, past and present. We also honor the enslaved African and African American people who built the University of Virginia, and we recognize their descendants. We commit to fostering voices from these communities through our publications and to deepening our collective understanding of their histories and contributions.

University of Virginia Press
© 2024 by the Rector and Visitors of the University of Virginia
All rights reserved
Printed in the United States of America on acid-free paper

First published 2024

9 8 7 6 5 4 3 2 1

978-0-8139-5132-4 (cloth)
978-0-8139-5133-1 (paper)
978-0-8139-5134-8 (ebook)

Library of Congress Cataloging-in-Publication data is available for this title.

Cover art: Pictorial Map of the United States, published by Ensigns & Thayer, 1847. (iStock.com/sergeyussr)
Cover design: David Drummond

For my mother, a one-time Methodist and all-time parent

And to the memory of my grandfathers, Percy Cummings Osteen Jr. and Bruce Walker Price Sr., exemplary gentlemen

CONTENTS

Acknowledgments ix

Introduction: The Methodist Age and the Empire of Liberty 1

1 The Structures of Western Methodism in the Empire of Liberty 15

2 Pilgrims and Settlers: The Culture of Methodist Travel in the West 55

3 The Social Principle: Settlement Networks and Sacred Capital in the Trans-Appalachian West 86

4 The Traveling Life of John Littlejohn: Mobility, Exchange, and Settling in the Empire of Liberty 131

5 The Settling and Unsettling of Ann Hulme Price: Women and the Limits of Methodist Sacred Capital 156

Conclusion: Love Thy Neighbor as Thyself 181

Notes 191

Bibliography 231

Index 259

ACKNOWLEDGMENTS

It's a humbling experience to recount the people who have invested their labor into this book, but it is also a joy to reflect on their substantial generosity.

The book began under the guidance of the inimitable dissertation committee of Alan Gallay, John L. Brooke, and Randolph A. Roth, making Ohio State University the best program in the country for me to learn the work of history. Alan is my dear friend but, thankfully, never tires of being my mentor. By instruction and example, he has led me to trust my own questions, care less for trends, and write with empathy and clarity. John generously bought lunches and asked hard questions, while also encouraging and helping me think of religion in a creative historiographical tradition. Randy taught me to think about nonhuman primates and bees and thus humans in unconventional ways. I'd had summer jobs in construction and stonemasonry, but it was from these three that I learned to work and work hard. Before graduate school, four other scholars inspired and supported me: political scientists Michael Bressler, Brent Nelsen, Aristide Tessitore, Steve Wainscott; philosopher Todd May; and historians Paul C. Anderson and Ronald Granieri.

At Ohio State, many friends and colleagues supported me and this project. Matt Foulds lent his knowledge of Methodism and his ear for story and argument. He has continued to do so at every stage of this work. I am grateful for Matt's excellent taste in edits, music, whiskey, and beer. Mark Boonshoft has read several parts of the manuscript and offered characteristically smart and witty feedback and friendship. Brian and Carrie Feltman, Lawrence Bowdish, Greg Kupsky, and Dustin Kemper provided the best company for not writing a dissertation. For keen advice

ACKNOWLEDGMENTS

and questions, I am grateful to Paula Baker, Kenneth Andrien, Mitchell Snay, and the late Andrew Cayton.

Much work on this book was completed at Western Washington University. Working as an adjunct my first three and a half years there made progress on the book difficult, but supportive colleagues offered great help along the way. Particularly impactful were History Department chairs Kevin Leonard, Steven Garfinkle, Johann Neem, and Susan Costanzo. From our first days at WWU, Jared Hardesty has been a great friend and colleague, always ready to read a draft, discuss the field, or catch a ball game. Steven Garfinkle has been a wise and exceedingly generous colleague and friend. I am grateful to Steven and Johann for helping to organize a manuscript workshop for *Sacred Capital* in 2018, sponsored by the College of Humanities and Social Sciences. I thank them and my coworkers Chris Friday and Jennifer Seltz for participating in that workshop. I am especially indebted to Patrick Griffin, Beth Barton Schweiger, and Randolph Scully for traveling to Bellingham for the occasion. These seven historians closely read and critiqued a work that I was unsure warranted their talents. They helped me to clarify my argument and amplify my voice. The workshop will certainly remain among the most rewarding experiences of my career. My colleagues in the History Department, through our works-in-progress meetings, shared valuable thoughts on the final chapter, especially my friend and office neighbor Emi Bushelle. I am also indebted to members of the Pacific Northwest Early American Seminar, and I must specifically credit the contributions of former host Richard Johnson and the late Bill Rorabaugh.

Outside the Pacific Northwest, a number of groups and institutions supported this book. Glenn Crothers and Kelly Ryan provided helpful readings of a chapter for a meeting of the Kentucky Early American Seminar. Glenn has been a boon to this project at several points, commenting on conference papers and arranging fellowship support at the Filson Historical Society. I am also grateful to the following organizations for financial support: the American Antiquarian Society (my thanks to Paul Erickson and the fellows), the Tennessee Historical Society (my thanks to Kristofer Ray), the University of Chicago Library, the History Department and Graduate School at Ohio State University, and the Office of Research and Sponsored Programs at Western Washington University. A version of one chapter appeared as "The Traveling Life of John Littlejohn: Methodism, Mobility, and Social Exchange from Revolutionary Virginia to Early Republican Kentucky," *Journal of Southern History* 82, no. 2 (May 2016): 237–68, and I am grateful to the editors for permission to reprint it.

This book emerged, in varying degrees, from research at twenty-four repositories across fifteen states, and I am in the debt of the archivists at those organizations. I must say a special thank you to Carol Holliger at the Archives of Ohio United Methodism at Ohio Wesleyan University, who kindly helped at the origins of this book, and to Richard Weiss of Kentucky Wesleyan College.

Working with the University of Virginia Press has been a true pleasure. My great thanks to Peter Onuf for reading and recommending the manuscript to Richard Holway. Holway retired soon thereafter, and I thank him for his support. Nadine Zimmerli took over as editor, and I can imagine no better guide for a first-time book author. She has given excellent practical advice on writing and production and, perhaps most importantly, enthusiasm and encouragement. She also recruited two anonymous readers who helped me to emphasize the book's main purpose, and I thank them.

I dedicate this book to my mother, Many Ann Mills. Ever devoted, she has given constant and unquestioning support as I have walked my own path. And to the memory of my grandfathers, Percy Cummings Osteen Jr., generous, hardworking, and kind, and Bruce Walker Price Sr., who was humorous and curious and took me on trips into the past.

SACRED CAPITAL

INTRODUCTION

The Methodist Age and the Empire of Liberty

American Methodism's growth was one of the great developments of the early American republic. What began as an English sect with a few, small American outposts in the 1760s was by 1830 the new nation's largest religious organization. By midcentury, the Methodist Episcopal Church (MEC) was among the nation's largest organizations, public or private. The early republic was known for economic and territorial expansion. It was also known for major religious expansion. No general account of the period is complete without consideration of the Second Great Awakening, and Methodism was the primary driver of that bout of religious growth. Historians have gone so far as to say that the Second Great Awakening was essentially a Methodist event, calling the period "the Methodist Age."[1] Methodism's influence came from its organizational power. After the American Revolution, Methodism swelled in numbers as it stretched over great distances, following the contours of the US settler explosion. In the West and South especially, Methodists deployed institutions like preaching circuits and events like camp meetings that perfected techniques originating with Presbyterians and radical European sects. Methodism not only led the nation's religious landscape in numerical and geographical expansion but exemplified for Baptists and Presbyterians, including the famous evangelist Charles Grandison Finney, how to spread revivalism and help turn the United States into one of the world's most Christian nations.

This book asks how this rise of Methodism related to the "Empire of Liberty." Specifically, it examines how the young republic's largest religious movement—perhaps the era's largest social movement—worked in the lives of white settlers who sought prosperity and stability in an expansive settler nation. Although no longer a favorite of American historians, Frederick Jackson Turner was correct when he wrote, "The multiplication of rival churches in the little frontier towns had deep and lasting social effects."[2] Religious and social spheres were closely tied in settler life, but later generations misunderstood the significance, searching instead for the progress of Anglo-American civilization. That position is epitomized in the words of western Methodism's main historian, William Warren Sweet: "Yet no single force had more to do with bringing order out of frontier chaos than the Methodist circuit-rider, and among no other class of men was the heroic element more 'finely displayed.'" Sweet also claimed that Methodism's success stemmed from preachers' "self-sacrificing devotion," rather than the network's "mechanical perfection."[3] In fact, the social mechanisms enabled by Methodist itinerancy produced much less self-sacrificing than historians have assumed and a fair amount more self-serving. Because much of religion is a quotidian affair, understanding the social effects of religion requires attention to the manifold, subtle, quasi-secular acts that constituted settler life.[4] Understanding the daily acts connecting religion to settlement can be difficult when we treat the Second Great Awakening as either a market-like democratization of religion or a program of social control. Methodism was too complex and too adaptable for that, but the interpretive dichotomy of democratization and social control persists, especially in classrooms.[5] The challenge is to understand Methodism's social importance without categorizing too neatly an aspect of human life as complex and malleable as religion. Early American Methodism was less a church than a movement, a missionary enterprise driving toward the goal of saving the souls of the white settler population.[6]

That insight has allowed historians to see its dynamism and growth, but Methodism was also a network. As such, it was full of relationships and exchanges that defy description as democratization or social control. Methodism's mission was the raison d'être for those relationships, but as a network, they could be put to any use individuals found valuable. In that social way, Methodism was like a technology, adaptable beyond its original design intention. What is clear is that those relationships and exchanges were the kinds of linkages that made settler society, and the significance of Methodism was that it amplified them with a power that few other organizations could at the time.

INTRODUCTION

The reasons for Methodist growth are better known than its social impacts. Methodists used a variety of tools to attract large numbers of members and hearers. Young male preachers traveled circuits of four to six weeks, stopping on regular schedules to deliver the Gospel in homes and meetinghouses and to minister to a flock arranged in small bands and classes. At each stop, preachers sold or gave away books. They carried testaments and hymnals that embedded the rhythms and words of Protestant religion into the minds of Americans. Preachers performed sermons, baptisms, weddings, and funerals for a population of white settlers on the move like few times in history. Methodism was a missionary endeavor in the American West, but the mission was to gather believers and convert white settlers who had outpaced church institutions. All of those activities had social, worldly aspects, all occurring by way of social networks. This book cuts through the dichotomy of democratization and social control by arguing that Methodism cannot be neatly defined through democratization or social domination because for every example of consumer choice there is another of class, race, or gender exclusion. The reality is Methodism variously accomplished both of those ends and others. That is the nature of social networks. They are better understood through exchanges producing a variety of outcomes than through overarching categories. The church's connectionalism—to adapt a Methodist term—brought settlers into relationships that helped some, hurt others, swelled hearts and resources at some points, and drained spirits and means at others. To understand Methodism and the Second Great Awakening is not simply to assess them categorically on outcomes such as liberty or the lack thereof but in terms of the array of social functions they encompassed.

Methodism, the Empire of Liberty, and the Social Principle

Methodism has long been associated with the early American West, for which it seemed nearly divinely designed. As *Sacred Capital* shows, the Methodist Age and the Empire of Liberty converged, but this is not "a tale of the heroic age." Older work on western Methodism embraced the romanticism that accompanied the myths of the frontier and formed American histories of settlement first through the widespread Methodist publishing enterprise and later through twentieth-century church history.[7] The genre lionized circuit riders, emphasized the spectacles of camp meetings, and approved the so-called civilizing process, notions that reverberate still in American culture.

This book offers a different view of western Methodism by exploring Methodism's ordinary functions within settlement. Methodism's expansion west was a key part of the much celebrated, much critiqued "Empire of Liberty" that Thomas Jefferson envisioned—"an expanding union of republics held together by ties of interest and affection."[8] Settler colonial studies typically focus on institutional destruction and dispossession of Indigenous populations and new claims of sovereignty. Within works on settler colonialism, discussion of religion and colonization typically hews, productively, to promotional discourses or to missionary outreach to Native Americans. Relatively few Methodists, however, participated directly in missionary work, Indian removal, ethnic cleansing, or genocide, but as settlers Methodists broadly benefited from those acts. Further, the practices in Methodist networks can be thought of as among the "other tools that aid in both the destruction of the old and the creation of the new." At the disposal of white Methodists was a network easily adapted to core settler concerns—land, work, marriage, money—but Methodists thought of themselves as pilgrims transcending worldly concerns. Their language obscured their daily practices as settlers. As one scholar has argued, this kind of performance "elides ... the *settler* part."[9] This book thus trains its attention on settler practices through Methodism's impact as an institution of white settlement in the long nineteenth century.

This work also takes a broad definition of settlement. Settlers were not simply pioneers. Settlers were those engaged in the varied phases of possessing the country after the American Revolution. Anglo-American settlement of the West was one of the major outcomes of the American Revolution, which initiated a new claim of sovereignty and a new era of military conquest. Colonists clamoring for western lands found themselves stymied by royal proclamation in 1763. After the Revolution, migrants searched out the lands west of the Appalachian Mountains. The inevitable result was diplomatic and military conflict with Native Americans who possessed the land and held opposing claims. Decades passed—along with many lives on both sides—before those military struggles ceased. Although the British colonial era had ended, the colonization of the vast Mississippi River basin continued under the auspices of the United States.[10]

Methodism's main impact was not in the pioneer and conquest phases; rather, it contributed institutionally to the phases of stabilizing and developing settler communities. The conquest of the West was the product of the military power of the state, which brought to a close the "Hobbesian world" born of the French and Indian War.[11] Military force dislodged Native American societies, but force could not construct new societies on those vanquished lands. Within that transition, Methodism complemented the military power of the state in western expansion. Methodism's role was subtle but enduring. It was among the most important organizations connecting far-flung communities, belying the idea that the rural West was a desolate scattering of "island communities."[12] Through its itinerant preaching system, Methodism led the popular Protestant denominations in constructing basic social linkages among settlers and stitching the fabric of an emerging middling society on the newly conquered frontier. Focusing on Methodism and settlement rather than colonial control in the early American West enhances our understanding of the context of Indian removal, ethnic cleansing, and genocide. It ties to that broader context the thousands upon thousands of white Methodists who perceived little connection between their lives and choices and the lives of those who bore the costs of settlement. That failure of perception is a characteristic of settler colonialism.[13] Through removing peoples, settler colonialism obscured its impacts from many who benefited from it.

A specific but broadly practiced form of Indigenous erasure resulted from the everyday acts and statements of common Methodists in the early American West. That is, most western Methodists in the settlement areas covered by this book practiced a tragic and politically charged disregard for the plight of Native peoples in the early American West. Despite Methodist print culture's occasional (and typically distorted) attention to Native cultures, such as conversions at the few Methodist missions and dehumanizing stereotypes about frontier savagery that were routine in contemporary published Methodist memoirs, the key point is that most Methodists in the West rarely (if ever) devoted attention in their manuscript letters to concerns about Native Americans. Those letters are the closest evidence we have to white Methodists' true concerns.

As one scholar writes, "The actions of American citizens in the first half of the nineteenth century helped create and sustain the long era of Indian removal as much as the soldiers acting on the orders of a distant president did."[14] Methodist settlers' insouciance, it must be emphasized, was a political position with powerful knock-on effects for Americans' denialism of major aspects of Indigenous history.

Despite this erasure, Methodism's contribution to settlement, or what we might think of as the social production of the Empire of Liberty, is clearly visible. All one needs is not to be distracted by the language of religion. The average Methodist letter contained the sacred vocabulary of heartfelt theology, everlasting life at the throne of grace, camp-meeting spectacle, and damnable declension of piety and faith. This code of evangelicalism was literally spectacular, focusing one's vision and attention especially in the stories of revival displays. But the average Methodist letter contained two parts. The second part—and it nearly always was accorded second place—was discussion of ordinary life. The significance of the ordinary can be difficult to see. It is especially so when the ordinary and the spectacular are juxtaposed, as spectacular phenomena overshadow ordinary things. The language of the ordinary was the language of settlement. The language of the ordinary was the vocabulary of land, exchange, employment, the stuff of settler life. Methodists were worldly, but they shrouded their worldliness in otherworldly language. Methodists identified as pilgrims while behaving as settlers. That was the value of Methodism—it gave settlers the spectacular language of the sacred and an organizational structure for the ordinary. That combination was powerful because the sacred and the ordinary were continually underpinning and amplifying each other. That combination was advantageous in the Empire of Liberty.

The combination of religion and settlement in ordinary practices had important political stakes, despite being obscured by Methodist language and not following the well-known model of Calvinist, northeastern-headquartered reform and missionary movements. Methodism's pietist political sensibility fixed concern foremost on private settler affairs while also intersecting with the cumulative expulsionary effects of US removal policies from the Revolution onward.[15] *Sacred Capital* focuses on the ground-level settler processes in specific areas of the early American West.

These Methodist settlers were primarily southern and Mid-Atlantic migrants. Among them, Methodism's primary mission was evangelical and Arminian and thus focused on the individual souls of white settlers. Rejecting the Calvinist tenet of perseverance of the saints, Methodists were palpably preoccupied with maintaining belief themselves and among their associates. This Arminian fear of spiritual backsliding and concern for the momentum of holiness tightly focused the MEC's attention on white settlers. This pietist, Arminian worldview framed Methodist priorities and allowed general carelessness about Native lives.

Settlers found social capital especially important because of the era's revolutionary social change. Between the mid-eighteenth century and the mid-nineteenth, demographic and commercial expansion refashioned American lives. In the revolutionary period, the structure of monarchical society was rattled and weakened. Capitalism roiled the social order, a process that continued for nearly a century after the American Revolution.[16] Evangelicalism contributed change by challenging the authority of colonial elites during the Great Awakening. In the years after the Revolution, the revivalism of the Second Great Awakening continued to disturb the social order, and many evangelicals eyed a role in shaping society politically, economically, and otherwise. They became more active in seeking others to join their religious organizations. Paralleling the leveling taking place in politics, common folk took more control of religious life. The growth of popular religion marginalized somewhat the pedigreed ministers who were once persuasive members of the cultural and social elite. Religion thus weakened elite authority in the broader revolutionary age, but this was only the beginning of a longer story. That story is only clear if we follow Methodism past the turn of the nineteenth century, where recent studies have left off, into the 1820s and 1830s.[17] While Methodism helped topple some hierarchies, it contributed to the creation of new ones. For Methodism's institutions to succeed, they had to reflect and promote members' desires for sociability, mutual support, and avenues to prosperity.

Methodism created social capital within a sacred framework. Rather than withdrawing from society to pursue grace and personal piety, or fully engaging the rapidly evolving world around them, Methodists sought a middle way. Ordinary Methodists recognized the social principle of organized religion. In the early republic, no group was better mobilized to turn the multitude from worldliness to holiness, but at the same time few groups could better place common people in the social networks of the world. As migrants settled the western reaches of the Empire of Liberty, those networks had everyday worldly value. This was a tension that Francis Asbury perceived, and lamented, more than anyone. He was not only the leader of early American Methodism; he was one of the most widely traveled and connected men in the new United States.[18] His devotions and travels convinced him that the cares of the world turned the heads of Americans from God and the pursuit of holiness. In that way, the British-born bishop understood the United States well. The nation was expanding, conquering, and settling. Its middling white population was at once galvanized by movement and searching for stability. In this settlement context, Methodism's utility as a social institution became clear.

Asbury and his collaborator Thomas Coke addressed the tension in the *Doctrines and Discipline of the Methodist Episcopal Church*. They wrote of the "social principle"—"one of the grand springs in the soul of man. It was not the design of christianity to annihilate this principle, but the very contrary—to improve it, to spiritualize it, and strengthen it." The social principle was to be "exercised . . . in spiritual intercourse." "Heavenly felicity," they promised, "will flow from friendship and union with our brethren the redeemed of the Lord to all eternity!" By ordering individuals into groups—band meetings, class meetings, quarterly meetings, annual conferences—that were galvanized "under the grace of God," Methodism would turn them to their creator and, for a few, to perfect love. The task was hard. Even as Methodism led American Christians into broad acceptance of the Arminian doctrine of free will, Methodists retained the conviction that within humans was the corrosion of the original sin that occurred in the garden of Eden. Asbury knew, hard as he vied against it, that "the heart of man *by nature* is such a cage of unclean birds."[19]

Asbury routinely worried that local influence would corrupt the Methodist movement. Localism was the core of settlement and the antithesis of his vision. Localism was land, trade, politics—the things of the world and the stuff of settlement. For him, settlement was related to settling in the sense of taking rest and, worse, comfort. Settlement opposed his vision of physical movement, modeled by Paul and the other itinerant apostles, who "had the most powerful tendency to spread the Christian faith." Those preachers who would not move to preach, he intimated, were "imposters and not true ministers"—for those who would not move were likely unmoved by the Holy Spirit and more likely "moved by Satan."[20] He worried that Methodists would "settle in the world . . . getting into trade, and acquiring wealth" and "drink into its spirit." The spirit of settlement led Asbury to think of Zephaniah's curse against Jerusalem and the Kingdom of Judah, which were "settled on their lees" and would not reap the fruits of their worldly endeavors.[21] The spirit of settlement was not confined to the West, but it was powerful there. One preacher railed against it in *Sketches of Western Methodism:* "One Sunday when the brethren met for worship, they gathered around outside the meeting-house, and got to talking about their worldly business—as you know people sometimes do, and it is a mighty bad practice." In this case, what began as an ordinary exchange about crops apparently turned into a churchwide bender with the class leader making a still, most of the men drunk, and "the very devil was raised among them."[22] The sermon was a perfect allegory of Methodist theology—a frontier town that had shed its inebriated past now backsliding into iniquity from a moment's lack of vigilance—but it was also more. It illustrates the power and problem of Methodism's social principle. What seems like a temperance sermon is at root a reminder of Zephaniah's curse and an indictment of settlement. Asbury continually worried about the deleterious effect of settlement. His heirs continued the concern, and it was arguably the root and stuff of all they preached. The nation's largest denomination and voluntary association, devoted to transcending the world, held within it from its first moments the power of society and thus worldliness.

This book examines that connection to the world through Methodism's social organization. One could read Methodists' critiques of the world and longings for heaven as signs of attention to otherworldliness, but Francis Asbury relentlessly banged the drum against worldliness because worldliness was in every crevice of Methodism and always had been. Every Methodist verse, prayer, and exhortation against the world was a mirror reflecting the world.

Everyday Acts and Sacred Capital in Western Methodism

Informal, everyday practices—the socializing, letter-writing, hog-selling, and land-dealing—filled Methodists' lives even more than the eye-catching performances of preaching, barking, and jerking long highlighted in frontier revivalism.[23] Historians of western revivalism have too often overlooked these private, everyday aspects of religious experience that dominated the daily lives of evangelical Protestants. Everyday acts performed in an institutional structure empowered the social principle within Methodism. At the convergence of the Methodist Age and the Empire of Liberty was what I call *sacred capital*. Sacred capital was social capital in a religious context. Social capital is the value—whether individual or communal—within connections or networks.[24] Methodists believed the body of their church was clothed in the spirit, and that the "connections," or what we call networks, were part of that body. Individuals gathered in the Methodist movement often reaped rewards from its connectionalism. Rarely did a Methodist get rich by fellowshipping with other Methodists, but that was also rarely the goal in early American rural life. As settlers—despite their identification as pilgrims—most Methodists aimed for stability and improvement. Methodism was not a bare instrument of capital accumulation. Methodists believed that ordinary exchanges were sacred in that nothing could be separated from the presence and power of God. Why else would a farmer pray for a new horse except that God might provide through the generosity of brethren? Spiritual goods such as the sacrament of baptism often held value in the eyes of the world as a sign of grace and respectability at the same time as holding heavenly value. Why else would Methodist preachers be forbidden to receive payment for the ordinance except that lay persons would pay?[25] And preachers could still accept the important coins of gratitude and esteem.

Although religious itinerants were long associated with charlatanism—consider Chaucer's Pardoner—after the American Revolution traveling Methodist preachers earned the regard of middling white Americans who joined their churches. Itinerancy provided for decades the power of the Methodist social principle. While innovation in print communications propelled the sacred goals of the First and Second Great Awakenings, and forged a religious public sphere that influenced politics and the state, it was local exchanges and manuscripts, linked and carried by itinerants, through which Methodist social capital was built on the ground at least until the 1830s.[26] We can gain fresh perspectives on an institution long studied by denominational historians by borrowing critical questions from sociology and ethnohistory. Comprehending Methodism's sacred capital and its earthly impacts requires examining social resources and transactions, trust, reciprocity, and reputation as much as prayer, grace, salvation, and sanctification. Those social goods, institutionalized in Methodism, were at least as important to Methodism's everyday worldly impact as the work ethics of industry, sobriety, and frugality through which historians have typically explained Methodists' economic pursuits.[27]

In a turbulent nation, access to capital divided those who prospered and those who did not, but there are several forms of capital.[28] The most well known is the struggle for financial capital. Owning enslaved property, inheriting or marrying into wealth, or seizing an opportunity such as cheap western land could secure one's future and deliver the mythical manly independence of republican ideology. Many other Americans struggled mightily to rise above indigence or to put bread to mouth, laboring, for example, in a Kentucky salt mine or dredging Baltimore's harbor for meager wages.[29]

The pursuit of social capital was as prevalent and important as the struggle for financial capital. The basic institution of social capital in early America was the patriarchal household. Methodists enhanced the patriarchal household with their religious associations.[30] Their faithful invocation of *brother, sister, mother,* and *father* in Christ demonstrates the link. The same language is found throughout the records of Baptists, Quakers, and others, but through about 1830 no group was as large or dynamic as Methodism. The point, therefore, is not that Methodism was exceptional. Rather, it was the leading example of a form of interpersonal relations that appealed to evangelicals, a middling faction called the "principal subculture" in the early republic.[31] Americans of all kinds found social value in religion, but this book trains its full attention on the paradigmatic case of Methodism, which by 1850 included one in three American church members and was the largest voluntary association in the early republic.[32] Histories of evangelicalism in the West have searched for the causes of revivalism, chronicled the rise of denominationalism, surveyed the work of missionary outreach, or explained the revitalization of society through national cultural unification.[33] In contrast, *Sacred Capital* highlights the everyday practices of Methodism to show how people thought of themselves as pilgrims while acting as settlers, forming connections and pursuing rewards in the conquering Empire of Liberty.

Sacred Capital is based on the observation that Methodists' ordinary practices had significant value as acts of settlement because they were amplified by the structure of the MEC. As historians of politics and the state write, the institution mattered, and this was as true of religious institutions as agencies of the federal government.[34] As a result, this book presents Methodism as a hierarchy containing a grid of vertical and horizontal connections. A spatial metaphor is helpful for understanding a complex organization and set of institutions like the MEC. Contemporaries tended to conceive of the itinerancy as a set of wheels, emphasizing the flow of preachers and events through concentric circles of circuits and meetings. This metaphor is apt in its way but also flat. A one-dimensional view of Methodism cannot describe the church. One would do better to think of Methodism as a pyramid: three-dimensional, full of levels and varied human actions, and useful to its members. Accordingly, the book begins by laying out the hierarchy in western Methodism. Methodism's early American leader Francis Asbury provided much of the organization's energy and structure through his indefatigable commitment to mission and metrics. A bishop and a man among the people, Asbury's life allows historians to see both Methodism's ideals and its realities. He audited the operations of the nation's circuits and conferences and understood that they were powerful institutions for Methodism's mission but also for the worldly affairs of settlement, especially in the developing West, and he inveighed against the latter in his journals and letters. Asbury and his colleagues did not speak of settler colonization, but that is exactly what they were describing and participating in. The variety of meetings that occurred on circuits and conferences across the expanding American West were effectively opportunities for white settlers to form social networks. Understanding the functions of those meetings and the offices held by traveling preachers, especially presiding elders, shows how Methodism

INTRODUCTION

worked as an institution of settlement as it emerged from the American Revolution poised for growth and expansion.

After describing the structures of western Methodism, the book turns to the work of itinerants on circuits. As an ideal type of the frontier, the circuit rider—often cast in the singular, which is always good for myth-making—developed its own hagiography. Circuit riders were celebrated as long-suffering Protestant pilgrims who braved all kinds of weather and abuse to carry the Gospel for little pay. The reality is that western travel was indeed hard, but the itinerancy was also full of connections and resources and a means of upward mobility for many low and middling settlers during and after their time as traveling preachers.

In both the Old Northwest and Old Southwest, Methodism thrived. The regions were different—the presence of slavery being most significant—but grew through comparable basic settlement processes of the expanding nation. In both, Methodism functioned similarly. Methodist itinerants established the MEC in the West by joining existing settler networks, often those of socially reputable locals. Over time, those networks, containing more Methodist affiliates, connected to other Methodist networks through the linkages of itinerancy. When people gathered at meetinghouses and revivals hosted at Methodist quarterly meetings, the points of contact became clear. Methodists formed networks in Ohio and Mississippi that were largely similar and allowed them access to the resources of information, land, employment, and marriage. Showing the adaptability of Methodist social capital, this led to free-labor opportunities in the North and slaveholding opportunities in the South.

Because everyday acts were as important to Methodist social capital as the church's organizational structure, this book uses short biography, drawing on exceptional sources from ordinary Methodists to examine how Methodist networks worked in individuals' lives. However, Methodist social capital did not work equally for everyone, and so the book describes that reality of unequal access. John Littlejohn, a one-time itinerant and local preacher, accessed the resources of Methodist networks easily. He used that sacred capital to facilitate his family's migration from Virginia to Kentucky. In terms of worldly benefits, Methodism worked for Littlejohn. Methodism worked much less well for Ann Price. She was the wife of a one-time itinerant and pork merchant in Cincinnati. Methodism was at the core of Price's settled life, but after her husband died suddenly, the widow and her daughters had little access to the resources of Methodist networks. Unsurprisingly, race and gender limited access to Methodist social capital. In a nation increasingly ruled by slavery, the boundaries of race were unsurprising and almost entirely excluded Black Methodists in the West from the main springs of Methodist social capital. The issue of gender, which Price's story helps to clarify, is more ironic. Like most contemporary Christian groups, women were the majority of Methodists. Methodists took care to acknowledge the contributions of certain Methodist women, despite the fact that women were barred from authoritative offices in the church.[35] They commemorated the "Mothers in Israel" who hosted preaching and supported preachers. Those women were exceptional. Ordinary Methodist women were deeply devoted to Methodism, but as Price's story shows, Methodism was not always deeply devoted to them.

Sacred Capital is about the value of Methodism for white settlers, but it is not a success story. It is a history of process, not progress. This was not only apparent in the story of Ann Price. The MEC was also believed to be one of the few social institutions strong enough to stave off the divisiveness of the politics of slavery. The assumption was that Methodists north, south, east, and west shared common experiences and commitments. It was not only a national organization but meant to be a nationalist one. But in truth the nationalizing strength of the MEC was superficial. The MEC split in 1844 in part because slavery was so divisive. But at deeper levels, the MEC had expanded in a way that sectionalized the Methodist membership, adhering them more and more to local, regional, and state experiences and interests. When the wedge of slavery struck in 1844, the myriad fissures in the national organization had already weakened it.

1

THE STRUCTURES OF WESTERN METHODISM IN THE EMPIRE OF LIBERTY

"What hath God wrought in America!" Francis Asbury asked his journal. The original phrase was from the book of Numbers, where it exalted the nations of Israel.[1] In 1844, Samuel Morse enshrined the words in American history as he opened the first telegraph line, but in 1807 Asbury wrote in wonder at a movement like few had seen in North America. Like others of the era, he was amazed at the growth of the Methodist Episcopal Church (MEC). As the movement's leader in North America, Asbury was consumed by evangelization. One can imagine him—withering under age and responsibility in his last decade on earth, ground down by constant travel and battling a failing heart, yet persistent and hopeful in spirit—as he poured over the minutes of the Methodists' annual conferences, cataloging the populations and territories of the preaching circuits that constituted Methodist itinerancy. He relished taking stock and planning for growth. With an entrepreneur's anticipation, he wrote to one preacher, "I calculate, if the Lord is with us and we are with Him, we shall have a general and yearly increase of 21,000 in the seven conferences."[2] To another, "God hath given us hundreds in 1800, why not thousands in 1801, yea, why not a million if we had faith."[3] The bishop was reserved compared to other revivalists but not when it came to measuring the expansion of the MEC: "I can see a surprising difference everywhere since the year 1785. Oh, what prospects open in 1805! I am lengthy; I am loving."[4] He had good reason for excitement. The goal was nothing less than "to extend our ministry to the very utmost bounds of the empire of the United States; and the Canadian provinces."[5] And extend it did. "In 45 years," Asbury wrote in 1813, "the poor little daughter mission church, in America has overgrown her mother in Europe of near 70 years standing."[6]

Such impressive growth created an extensive social network that was important to settlers' everyday lives. Even so, the spectacles of frontier religion—the jerking, barking, and falling under the Spirit—have long distracted observers from the significance of one of the largest movements and social organizations in early American history. Methodism's abiding influence was to be found in the everyday, not the spectacular. To be sure, spectacles attracted the curious and the critical, but ordinary relationships made Methodism important in the West. Methodist social capital—its connections—was a product of the denomination's internal structures and their successful symbiosis with the expanding American nation.[7] Methodists were not unique in accessing social capital. From Quakers to Episcopalians, early American Christians found similar resources in their churches, but the dynamism and size of Methodism made it the leading example of this characteristic aspect of white, rural, middling settler life. Methodist leaders understood the importance of religious social capital and called their system of preaching circuits, which was Methodism's signal contribution to American religious organizing, the traveling connection. In their connections, Methodists found benefits other than the hope of eternal life. Everyday, mundane benefits made through social connections were essential in the West, an area undergoing a half-century's bloody transition from Native American to European American control as part of the broader revolutionary era.

The social networks of white Methodists were a powerful means of possessing the early American West. The formation of those networks depended on dispossessing Indigenous people of western lands. Whether or not Methodist settlers served in military units that fought to extend the settler empire or voted for political leaders who promoted programs of "civilization" and removal of Native peoples, they benefited from the expulsion of Indigenous communities from fertile agricultural and hunting lands. In turn, the structure of western Methodists' social institutions helped a large number of white settlers establish footholds and prosper on lands to which groups like the Shawnees and Creeks and their ancestors had attached spiritual and material value for centuries.[8] The ideology of settler colonialism, carried forward into works of modern history, held that the trace of the buffalo and the deer turned into the path of the American Indian and that both converted into the roads of Anglo-American settlement and commerce.[9] There is some truth to that, except the story was not one of Enlightenment progress and the extension of civilization; rather, the story was one of violence-backed dispossession followed by social institutions of settlement. The preaching circuits of Methodism, like the commercial roads, connected the pieces of settler society into a republic.

Through its role in settler colonization, Methodism was a powerful institution of Jefferson's so-called Empire of Liberty. The "very utmost bounds of the empire of the United States," as Asbury had envisioned his church's mission, paralleled the settlement project of the nation. The religious movement's 1796 expansion in the early American West immediately followed US military success after significant losses to Native powers in the 1780s. If the era from 1754 to 1815 was a great contest for the trans-Appalachian West and included the region's general transition from frontier to secure settlement, then Methodist expansion west was a key institutional part of the phase of consolidating settler control.[10] In the mid-1790s, capped by the 1795 Treaty of Greenville, US military power brought enough security to the southern Ohio Valley for settlers to begin arriving in streams rather than trickles. Around the same time, beginning in 1796, the MEC reorganized nationally and turned its attention to what contemporaries called the western waters.

Methodist expansion occurred in a postrevolutionary period of great social change. Two of the most impactful processes of social change in the trans-Appalachian West were migration and settlement. Because Americans often perceived largescale social change as social disorder, many looked to religion for stability. The stability that religion offered was not primarily spiritual or psychological (although this was an era of religious emotionalism). Instead, it was institutional. Here Methodism represented best a major trend in American religion. Historically, churches attempted to moderate the pace and disruptiveness of social disorder. In the colonial period, religious leaders expected civil authorities to stabilize Christian communities, but compulsion proved poorly suited to building social bonds. Over time, churches recognized that voluntarism worked better and thus turned to the emotional bonding of revivalism.

Because emotionalism too invited disorder, it had to be structured into denominations—new inter-congregational organizations that could encourage, educate, and discipline leaders and members.[11] Methodism was one such denomination, but it was also more than that. It was a movement and the paradigmatic force in making the Second Great Awakening an "organizing process" amid the social strains unleashed by the American Revolution.

Historians often marvel at the growth of Methodism in the revolutionary era. In the 1760s, Methodism had only a few small cells in the colonies, unconnected from episcopal organization. During the war, communication and organization were difficult, and some Methodists were suspected of Loyalism. Nevertheless, Methodism was well-poised to succeed in a nation emerging from British imperial control. One of the most important reasons for this was that Methodism offered a significant social and institutional continuity crossing the gap from empire to nation. For a hundred years, colonists had acclimated to a politico-religious system that tolerated Protestant groups which upheld basic British values. This was the empire's mixed establishment, as Katherine Carté has written, which was the more important establishment in the empire, broader and more significant than the Church of England's. While the Church of England was legally and socially the first in this mixed establishment, moderate dissenting Protestants enjoyed increasing protection that allowed their churches to thrive, especially in the colonies. As a blend of magisterial and radical traditions, and specifically originating as a reform society within the Church of England, Methodism contained some of the stability and authority of the core establishment and much of the innovation and ethos of the dissenting traditions of the mixed establishment. The Revolution broke the state ties between the colonies and metropole, but Methodism emerged as the leading denomination linking the fading imperial mixed establishment to the new national Protestant consensus.[12] Although other groups, especially the Baptists, were important denominations, the most extensive organizing in the West was through institutions perfected by the MEC and later embraced by other popular denominations. Just as Charles Grandison Finney, the most famous revivalist in nineteenth-century America, borrowed his techniques from the Methodists, so did other denominations borrow the organizing patterns of Methodism. Especially significant for settlement in the organization was that Methodism offered middling white settlers a multilevel structure that tied together locales and regions.[13]

The Methodist Synthesis, Social Networks, and Anglo-American Empire

Methodism's structure as a social network made it an important institution of settler colonization in the early United States, but it is important to emphasize that this structure was not American in origin. It developed out of British expansiveness in the Atlantic world and out of changes within the Church of England, part of the religious settlement of the late seventeenth and eighteenth centuries. The cooling of religious tension in Britain punctuated the decades after the English Civil War and led to a culture of reform-minded religious societies within Anglicanism. As the state accepted sectarian impulses in the wake of Puritan challenges, religious societies were used to push the Anglican mission out into the empire by groups such as the Society for Promoting Christian Knowledge and the Society for the Propagation of the Gospel in Foreign Parts. Methodism began in the mid-eighteenth century as a small religious society. Its culture was a mix of mild Puritan asceticism among its young founders and of continued respect (for the most part) of Anglican order. It was a synthesis of dissenting and establishment traditions.

That synthesis imparted to Methodism its grid of pious local sociability and episcopal administration. The sources of these were contacts between Anglican clerics and continental pietists in the seventeenth and eighteenth centuries. In the eighteenth century, the link came mostly through John Wesley's experiences with Protestant refugees in England. While the pietists nourished an independent streak, Wesley and other sympathetic Anglican clergy assimilated pietist practices into the Church of England's hierarchy through approved religious societies under the direction of ordained clergy. These borrowers encouraged British Protestants to gather in intimate groups for prayer, hymn-singing, reading, accountability, and preaching. The result was mutual support under the eyes of reform-minded Anglican clergy. American Methodism then carried forth several key features from the long eighteenth century. It combined local societies yearning for and practicing heartfelt religious experience with the evangelical energy coming from an expanding empire and its church.[14]

The institutional advantages that Methodism had accrued in the British Empire survived the American Revolution. By the time American Methodism formed as a denomination formally independent of John Wesley and the Church of England in December 1784, it was well placed to continue its development within the settler empire of the United States. The American Revolution did not lastingly disrupt religion in America. Certainly, many religious groups felt much disruption, especially those that experienced property damage. However, many of the emerging popular religious groups practiced mobility and home-based worship, which weathered the war better. What the Revolution significantly disrupted, in fact destroyed, was "imperial protestantism." American Methodism was born in its late-colonial form as a synthesis of established and "awakened" institutions and networks. The revivalist networks that constituted awakened groups were flexible and durable compared to the bureaucratic networks of the Anglican establishment. That pliancy helped Methodism adapt when many of its earliest itinerants left the rebel colonies under a Loyalist cloud. American Methodism also benefited from John Wesley's controversial slashing of the Gordian knot of ordination in the new nation. The flight of ordained Methodist Loyalists left American Methodists without ministers able to maintain ordinance of the sacraments. It also left this breakaway episcopal church without an episcopate. Wesley, despite his early and infamous opposition to the Revolution, stretched his role as an ordained Anglican minister and consecrated Thomas Coke and, by extension, Francis Asbury as superintendents. As if for good measure, the American preachers gathered at the Christmas Conference of 1784 then elected Coke and Asbury into the role, providing two sources of authority. This solved the ordination problem for the MEC, which converted the title to bishop in time. Network structure and personal charisma left American Methodism poised for success after the American Revolution. Its network structure continued to develop and make the MEC the important settlement institution it became.[15]

While denominational history has long been out of fashion among historians, a critical understanding of the shape and functions of the MEC as an institution helps to explain its role in settlement. Methodism's composite structure can be thought of as a grid containing a vertical line of command and a horizontal plane of pious sociability. The elements of Methodist social networks originated in blending, on the one hand, the apostolic or primitive elements of Christianity, which emphasized personal relationships within small sects, and on the other hand, the ecclesiastical structures of the Church of England. From its Anglican origin Methodism inherited an episcopal form of church government wherein authority descended from a bishop to the lowest ranks of preachers and members. Deference ideally flowed up through the same order of relationships. Methodism borrowed practices of horizontal social network formation from sectarian traditions, most immediately the Moravians. These relationships included real and fictive kinship, prompting Methodists to consider one another "brothers" and "sisters" in Christ. Friendships were grounded in feelings of love and sentimental expressions thereof, in shared experiences of personal salvation and progress toward spiritual perfection, and in common commitments to patterns of individual piety.[16] Methodism's organizational combinations were powerful because they embedded members in a community that offered support for any number of endeavors not restricted to the ultimate goals of spiritual perfection and eternal association with Christ in heaven. In that context, exchanges between individuals created the "norms and networks" of Methodism, a unique and influential religious social structure in which intimacy and administration coursed through connections that were both personal and bureaucratic.[17] Within that structure, individuals participated in the most basic definition of social capital: the proposition that social networks have value.[18]

The organization of Methodism at the end of the eighteenth century was an attempt to conquer space and organize the social complexity in that space. The continent's vast geography was always a blessing to an ambitious nation-state, but it was also a curse to planners and reformers such as George Washington and Benjamin Rush. They feared that centrifugal forces would stretch and weaken the bonds of the republic. The solution was institutions that maintained connections among disparate communities and between East and West. Rush, for example, promoted the postal service because his fundamental concern was shared information. The postal service was the preeminent civil institution of the early American state.[19] It served various ends, creating an informed citizenry, supporting state development, facilitating business, and connecting private individuals. The consolidated MEC was a similar case but as a nonstate institution.

This history is important because the MEC was not only on the way to being the nation's largest religious institution; it was one of the largest institutions of any kind outside of the federal state—having by 1860 as many preachers as the nation had postal workers.[20] Its development was especially significant in the rural West. The significance was not lost on contemporaries. Francis Asbury wrote, "I go like the mail stage in all parts of the continent," and the metaphor extended through the many preachers under his administration.[21] By the 1840s, the northeastern minister and reformer Horace Bushnell clearly grasped the MEC's organizational power when he called for an alliance of northeastern reform with the Methodists in the West to protect the republic from what he deemed Catholic threats to Protestant culture.[22] Bushnell's call for Calvinist reformers to unite with Methodism to defend the Protestant consensus testified to the organizational power of the MEC's "light artillery" of circuit preachers. Asbury's and Bushnell's metaphors were apt. Save the postal service and the US military, no organization equaled the MEC in size or coverage of white settler society in the West. The Methodist synthesis equipped the denomination to execute its main mission of spreading Arminian Christianity to white settlers. So too did it equip Methodists to weave together disparate communities into networks of settlement that overlaid lands taken from Indigenous groups.

Methodist Development in the Age of Revolution and the Empire of Liberty

The Methodist structure reached North America as one of many social and cultural movements within the British Atlantic world. While American Methodism appealed to people from a range of European groups, it originated as a British movement, and its rapid growth in America coincided with the massive migration of British people during the eighteenth and nineteenth centuries. Unexpectedly though, the break with Britain did not significantly retard Methodism's growth in America.[23] Once solidly established in North America, Methodism evolved under the close direction of its first superintendent, or bishop, Francis Asbury. Asbury's vision was continental; like Jefferson's, it was imperial. Succeeding in a migratory world and emerging successfully from the revolutionary era, Methodism spread into the trans-Appalachian West and became an important institution of settler colonization.

Methodism was part of the Anglo world in the long nineteenth century.[24] The Anglo world expanded first over the British Isles and then North America. Many of the migrating English, Scots, Irish, and others were skilled in trades, and they hoped to continue their lives in communities like those where they were born and reared.[25] Increasingly explosive growth began early in the 1700s and carried through the century, propelling British people and aspects of their culture into the larger world. That included Methodism in the middle of the eighteenth century.

Methodism was transferred by migration, and its main institution—itinerancy—was well-suited to a migratory world. Migration defined the British Atlantic world.[26] Migration was also a disordering process. Settlement, then, was the fraught pursuit to reestablish order in one's life. European American settlers filled lands that were new to them, and migration threatened and often disintegrated their social networks. Migration and settlement remained central to the expansion of the American nation during the broader period of the American Revolution. Over time, disorder in settler society turned to order, and for many thousands Methodism was crucial to that process.

By the middle of the eighteenth century, high birth rates and dreams of accessible lands turned the minds of many toward the North American West.[27] The end of the French and Indian War in 1763 opened a contentious chapter of migration and settlement. As soon as British victory weakened France's hold on the Mississippi Valley, the British crown barred colonists from settling it. But imperial policy was little match for the land hunger of settlers.[28] Residents of North Carolina and Pennsylvania crept west. Within eleven years of the royal proclamation, settlers were claiming Kentucky lands. The energy of settlement was such that it again transformed North America, affecting "the entire fabric of American life," as migrants continually arrived on the western shores of the North Atlantic and as those already in residence looked west to the interior.[29] The first permanent European American settlement in Kentucky appeared in 1775. The following year, that coveted land was a county of Virginia.

Kentucky's first settlements were small, scattered, and susceptible to dangers resulting from encroaching on Native lands.[30] Fear and fortifications constrained the lives of men, women, and children. Myths of violence and heroism germinated during this time, and the few Methodists in the West in those years, like the self-styled backwoods preacher Peter Cartwright, became characters in the stories of frontier settlement.

During the 1760s and 1770s, the entire trans-Appalachian West was sparsely populated by European Americans compared to the post-Revolution years. For example, 150 souls were recorded in Kentucky in 1775 (all males); 7,700 counted in Tennessee in 1776. Kentucky did not eclipse that number for another four to six years. But the eight years from 1783 to the first federal census in 1790 revealed the coming trend of the early American West, and especially that of Kentucky, which grew from 12,000 to 73,677. Tennessee's increase was small only in comparison to Kentucky's, as 35,691 called it home in 1790.[31] The end of the American Revolution spurred movement into the western lands of the new United States.[32] In the 1780s, 70,000 settlers arrived in Tennessee, Kentucky, and Ohio. From there, settlement skyrocketed. As of 1810, some 1 million Americans were in the western states.[33] The surge west after the War of 1812 was "one of the great immigrations in the history of the Western world."[34] The western states quickly rivaled their eastern neighbors in size and, increasingly, in important sectors of the national economy.[35] By mid-century, 10 million settlers lived in the trans-Appalachian West, the elder ones perhaps remembering when Native Americans or the odd European garrison controlled those lands.[36] Ten years later, the Old Northwest held 7 million and the Old Southwest another 4.65 million.[37] The first five decades (1780–1830) of major settlement were marked by rapid growth but limited economic and social development. Migrants outran their social networks and institutions but valued order and manly civility.[38] Many who recoiled at the so-called disorder and incivility of hard frontier areas found that the organizational culture of Methodism offered solutions. Culturally elite contemporaries, especially Presbyterians and Congregationalists like Horace Bushnell, often derided Methodist preachers as "rude" and "violent," but the reality in the West in the late eighteenth century was that many white settlers saw the MEC as a defender of respectable community life. Its preachers were not raucous frontiersmen but often exhibited (or pursued) the values and demeanor of bourgeois masculinity.[39] In the early commercializing western communities of southern Ohio, central Kentucky, and central Mississippi, Methodist preachers and the women who supported Methodism through domestic labors represented for settlers the securities they associated with middling life east of the Appalachians.

Early American Methodism has often been described as countercultural in the revolutionary generation of preachers, but the movement attracted ever more Americans during the era. Before Methodism could grow in America, it needed to shed the Loyalist reputation that dogged it at the beginning of the American Revolution.[40] Methodism's founder John Wesley was a committed Anglican and famously rebuked the rebel colonies. Many of the first itinerants in America were also loyal to Britain and fled the colonies early in the revolutionary struggle. The Patriot leadership correctly identified several Methodists who supported the British war effort, but they were few. Replacing Wesley and his earliest itinerants were Francis Asbury and a corps of preachers (many native-born) who were either Patriots or quiet about politics. Some were viewed warily due to suspected Loyalism, their criticism of the patriarchal social structure and culture of honor, or their expression of antislavery sentiments amid the precarities of war, but time reduced suspicions about their commitment to the American cause. The persecution of Methodists targeted suspicious individuals, not the Methodist organization itself. That difference mattered greatly. The movement's organization was not specifically targeted, as an army might target opposition through counterinsurgency efforts. Methodists made the most of the Revolution. Between 1778 and 1782, American Methodism nearly doubled in membership. Methodism "surged forward" during the Revolution. Religious disestablishment provided a greater measure of choice in the regions where Methodism first thrived, but Methodism also capitalized on its historical foundation in the imperial mixed establishment.[41]

The colonial rebellion against Britain confronted Methodists with a crisis of identity, a period of soul-searching, and an opportunity for redefinition. Formed officially in 1784, the MEC was a complex organization, but its leader, Francis Asbury, guided the church as a scrutinizing manager and embodied the ethics of discipline and expansion. Asbury directed the expansion of the Wesleyan system with urgent hope. He came to understand the movement as national and imperial because of its symbiotic relationship to the extending United States.[42] That was a nation-building project for which Asbury retained the word "empire," as he had written a merchant friend in Baltimore in 1804.[43] As President Thomas Jefferson expanded the national state to the west, Asbury dreamed of new fields for his preachers: "When those new lands, discovered by Col. [Meriwether] Lewis shall be peopled, we shall send out to the Pacific Ocean."[44] Asbury measured growth in souls won to Christ, and as a result his dreams resembled Jefferson's settler empire—the Empire of Liberty.[45] Methodism stood ready to follow on the heels of western settlement, which Asbury understood to follow on the heels of US national-imperial increase.

Asbury's enthusiasm for growth is understandable when considering Methodism's geographic coverage during the early republic. Methodists had settled in the American colonies by 1766, but they were few. More than twenty years later in 1790, their number had grown but slightly. They outnumbered other religious groups in only six counties, which were concentrated on the Delmarva Peninsula within the bounds of Delaware and the eastern extremes of Maryland and Virginia. Over the next half-century, Methodists outpaced the competition. By 1830, they had built the most populous church in the United States and extended their reach over much of the West. Methodism predominated in most of the southern states and in those midwestern states that received large numbers of southern migrants. From Pennsylvania and Delaware south to Florida and west to the Arkansas Territory, Missouri, and Illinois, Methodism's coverage was remarkable. That geographic range encompassed seventeen states and one territory, and in all but seven of those Methodists were the largest religious group in more than half the counties. In those seven states where Methodists did not dominate the majority of counties, they held a plurality in three: North Carolina, South Carolina, and Georgia. In Missouri, Methodists and Baptists split the lead with twelve counties each. Baptists led in the counties of Kentucky, and Catholics in the parishes of Louisiana, but Methodists were second in both of those states. Only in Pennsylvania (relevant because of its connections with the Upland South and lower Midwest) did Methodists hold so few counties to rank as low as third, trailing Presbyterians and Lutherans.[46]

That Methodists were spread so thickly across the United States—evidence early Methodist historians read as Methodism's unique fitness to the United States and its frontier—was ironic because the Methodist system was devised not in America but in the mind of an Oxford-educated Anglican cleric who infamously opposed American independence.[47] John Wesley's design of circuits along which a rotating band of traveling preachers proffered a freewill Gospel surpassed all competitors in reaching and converting Americans. Several factors explain Methodism's success in America: the ability of the itinerancy to reach the limits of settlement, its energetic recruitment of youthful preachers, its melodious appeal to the emotions through song, its sometimes cacophonous use of the camp meeting, its doctrinal emphasis on individual choice in the wake of a revolution, and its autocratic relentlessness of purpose. Those factors were well-suited to America's mobility and surging democracy.[48] It did not hurt that many Methodists in the South were probably not deeply opposed to slavery, but Methodism thrived broadly, succeeding in slave states and free states at similar rates and times.

The Language and Organization of Settlement in Methodist Expansion

The institutional factors helped Methodism mix well with the processes of settler colonialism. The term *colonialism* has not traditionally applied to American history after the colonies declared political independence from Great Britain and formed state governments. However, the social processes of colonialism persisted, indeed accelerated, after the Revolution under the new national state and continued through the long nineteenth century.

Anglo-American colonization was founded on Protestant religion as much as desire for wealth. Since the sixteenth century, the language of empire described colonization not only as an economic and political project but also a missionary enterprise. Methodists inherited and extended that discourse, keeping it alive in their print culture, correspondence, and hymns.[49] That discourse provided the intellectual and moral structure—a kind of imaginary *mise-en-scène* of settler colonialism—for everyday acts, even as the great majority of western Methodists exhibited everyday carelessness toward the whereabouts and plights of Native

Americans, as measured by their surviving daily correspondence and journals after 1800. Thus, western Methodism was built on a combination of narrating and erasing Indigenous history, at times garbling Native life and at other times disregarding it.

Pro-settlement propaganda relied especially on two metaphors for land, and these metaphors persisted in the Methodist religious vocabulary after the Revolution. The land was a "wilderness" endowed by God with productive potential but allegedly wasted by its Native inhabitants. Or it was Eden, a "garden," a land blessed by God from which abundance naturally flowed.[50] Both visions were meant to justify Protestant acquisition of the land. The vision of the wilderness in particular persisted beyond the colonial period and fit well the desires of later settlers to describe the trans-Appalachian West. With the surge in western settlement after the American Revolution, the wilderness metaphor helped shape settlers' views of the land as they occupied areas historically claimed and used by Native American communities.

Writing to the editors of the *Methodist Magazine* in 1819, Ezra Booth drew on the wilderness metaphor to describe western settlement as a righteous fulfillment. His was an ordinary voice that shows the link between traditional colonial discourse and the Methodist movement into the West. Like other Methodists, he saw the western country as both a landscape and spirit-scape. Settlement was changing both "the Natural & [Moral] world." He ranked the changes. Those interested in the merely physical changes of settlement could cheer "the sturdy towering trees of the forest falling prostrate before the industrious husbandman." Booth found the clearing of the land "pleasing . . . but it is infinitely more pleasing to behold the prostrate Worshipers of Jehovah." Those worshippers had altered the very sound of the country, making it "[sweet] with the transporting sound of the Gospel & the melodious songs of Zion." Booth celebrated that the new sounds replaced "the horrid yell of the uncivilized savage who was to be heard a few years since." Pleased with decades of Indian removal, Booth wrote that for those who "have found substantial pleasure in the Religion of Jesus . . . the solitary places have been made to rejoice & to them the wilderness has become a delightful [*illegible*] & has blossomed as the rose." Booth's quotation about the wilderness blossoming as the rose would have resonated in the ears of Methodists and other evangelicals. Methodism was a religion of words and ideas set to meter and tune, but the language was not always focused on the New Testament themes of salvation and love typically associated with early Methodism. Methodism drew as well on Old Testament discourse. Booth quoted the prophet Isaiah in a rite of colonization and settlement that stretched deep into the biblical past. From the vantage of 1819, Booth's "Worshipers of Jehovah" were rewarded for embracing the "Religion of Jesus" with the settler-style improvement of the wilderness.[51]

For Booth and his readers, Methodist settlers participated in a conflict with Indigenous cultures and the spiritual and material land claims deriving from those cultures. While few Methodists directly participated in the expulsion of Native people, many Methodists found in words like Booth's the confirmation they wanted for their place in the continent's history. With Indigenous populations pressured or forced from fertile agricultural lands, white Methodist settlers stood ready to gain lands that would now "blossom as the rose," and their good fortune, they could believe, was both a part of a providential plan and a result of their own religious devotion. In this way, the ideology of settlement sanctioned and sacralized the dispossession of Native peoples and the ensuing possession of their lands by ordinary settlers.

Booth's text was not alone in carrying forward the discourse of colonization and applying it to western Methodism. Methodist settler histories extended that work through the middle of the nineteenth century. Probably the most read history was *The Autobiography of Peter Cartwright: The Backwoods Preacher* (1856). If anyone claimed to be the voice of western Methodism, it was circuit rider Peter Cartwright. In his autobiography, he placed Methodism in the settler colonial tradition. On the first page of the first chapter, he framed his life as a poor Virginia boy, son of a revolutionary veteran migrating west into a wilderness populated with dangerous so-called savages.[52] Cartwright recounted the racial violence that marked postrevolutionary settler expansion and combined it with the rapidly deployed organizing power of Methodism.[53] That combination—settlement discourse and Methodist organizing—gave the MEC its substantial influence in the trans-Appalachian West.

Cartwright told his family story in racialized language meant to clearly separate white Protestant settlement from the supposedly dark, demonic spirit-scape of Indigenous lands.⁵⁴ Cartwright's father symbolized the nervous masculinity of the pioneer as he protected his family and others. They traveled "an almost unbroken wilderness" in which they frequently saw "white persons, murdered and scalped" along the trail. "Many Indians were seen through the day skulking round by our guards," Cartwright wrote. "Every heart quaked with fear" as the migrants reached "'Camp Defeat,' where a number of emigrant families had been murdered by the savages a short time before." Tasked as a "sentinel," the senior Cartwright fired at a threatening presence "grunting like a swine" under cover of darkness. As the Gospel preacher proudly recalled the event, "My father's rifle-ball had struck the Indian nearly central in the head." The father secured the future of his party with one shot. The son grew into the most traveled and prolific of western Methodist circuit riders.⁵⁵

From that bloody and subsequently glorified moment, Cartwright's narrative quickly transitions from insecure frontier to developing frontier. Cartwright's family had been among the advance guard of settlers entering Kentucky. They brought the trappings of both war and home, the essential couplet of settlerism. The violence of Cartwright's father was what Cartwright called "a peaceable and quiet possession."⁵⁶

The "country," Cartwright wrote, "soon filled up and entered into the enjoyment of improved and civilized life." There Cartwright introduced Methodism explicitly, showing his awareness that Methodism's main role in settlement was after the initial violence. The preacher's link to the violence of settlement was his father, but his link to Methodism fittingly was his mother. According to Cartwright, she was a member of the MEC. She connected her family to two itinerants whom Cartwright celebrated "as men that are to be numbered as early pioneers in the West." The preachers were "build[ing] up the infant Methodist Church in the wilderness." Eventually a Methodist class meeting formed near the Cartwrights, and after a bout of revival the community "built a little church, and called it Ebenezer."⁵⁷ Those Methodists chose a symbolic name for their frontier context. "Ebenezer" came from 1 Samuel, in which a stone is laid to memorialize the Israelites' defeat of the Philistines. The symbolic parallel was the settlers' defeat of Indians. This Kentucky reenactment of the Old Testament story followed the Methodist model: initial settlement, formation of a class meeting, revival, growth of the class and building of a church.

As the building of Ebenezer—a stone of commemoration—illustrates, the relationship of religion and settlement was more than language. The church building was just the type of improvement to the land that, in the Anglo-American tradition, marked legitimate possession.[58]

Cartwright also placed Methodist social organizing squarely within the processes of settlement and illustrated how local Methodist leadership performed secular functions in the community. He recalled that not long after a Methodist class formed in their part of Kentucky, the class leader devised a scheme to link the settlers to a federal fort on the Ohio River. Saltpeter, a basic ingredient of gunpowder, had recently been found on the Cartwrights' property. The class leader built a boat to carry a cargo of saltpeter down the Red River to the Cumberland and up the Ohio to the fort. Before embarking, the class leader called for other settlers to submit orders for provisions that were scarce in the settlement. The saltpeter would be traded to the military for coffee, ribbon, cooking utensils, and other implements of settled life.[59]

The local Methodist leader was well-placed to organize such an expedition because of the MEC's synthesis of religious bureaucracy and social networks. This organizational grid held within it the promise of an institution adaptable to the mobility of American society unleashed from the American Revolution, especially in rural areas. Through ensuing decades, settlers found numerous uses for Methodist institutions. Those uses were not limited to the spiritual as often conceived, stretching to earthly concerns of land and wealth, yet many Methodists spiritualized even those earthly concerns. At the same time, the MEC's everyday institutional power must be understood as not only benefiting common white settlers; it also confirmed dispossession of Indigenous communities through the building of interconnected white settlements on their lands, securing those lands to the republic through everyday means that governments and the military could not deploy. As Methodism grew and spread geographically, its social significance was magnified. At the top of each Methodist region, that social significance was organized under an annual conference of traveling preachers.

The Western Annual Conference: Rationalizing Methodism and White Settlement in the Trans-Appalachian West

The associational culture of Methodism and its potential for social capital spread west with migration as Methodist itinerants followed in the footsteps of settlers. Many migrants, especially women such as Peter Cartwright's mother, carried their Methodist commitments to the West. Some worshipped as Methodists in their homes or with neighbors, but many had outrun organized religion. These dislocations resulted from the vast demographic changes of the postrevolutionary era. The goal of the itinerants was to organize disparate settlers into the Methodist circuit system. In 1796, the year after the closing of the Northwest Indian War, the Western Annual Conference formed to contain the western circuits and the growing settler population constituting them.

More than any other part of Methodism, the Western Conference indexed the expansion of the United States as a settler nation. By 1805, Francis Asbury mentally surveyed this administrative unit and could see the "magnitude of the Western Conference." It covered already perhaps 1,500 miles by his estimate, not including the potential vastness of "what will be explored." An estimated "13,000 members" and "half a million of hearers" were regularly in Methodist meetings or within earshot of Methodist preachers across the West. Subdivided into "5 grand districts" that stretched from north of the Ohio River and linking the rustic communities of eastern Tennessee to the frontier outposts surrounding Natchez on the Mississippi River, the Western Conference organized a grand territory.[60]

The formation of the annual conference brought Methodism's grid structure to the West. Horizontal social bonds existed anywhere Methodists associated. The conference system connected those local bonds to the layers of the grid. Whether energized from the top or bottom, local bonds in the rural West became tied to class meetings, circuits, districts of circuits, and finally to the annual conference of itinerants and the office of bishop. At each level were more horizontal relationships. Traveling preachers and exchanges of correspondence delivered by traveling Methodists connected otherwise separate locales.

When Asbury wrote in numbers, geography, and administrative units, he was only describing the bones of the great religious body that was Methodism's Western Conference. Because he had visited many of the homes and meetings constituting it, he knew that socially the conference was a vibrant network of social exchanges that shot the spectrum from sacred to secular. Various religious groups created meaningful bonds at the local level, but what separated Methodism from the many other religious bodies populating the early republic was the regional and national structure that enveloped those local bonds.

During the first decade of the nineteenth century, the Ohio River watershed flooded with European Americans. Likewise, Methodism surged in those years. Not only were US settlers filling lands that had been the sites of geopolitical rivalry and had been taken largely through violence and coercion; a substantial number of those middling settlers turned to Methodism—one of the few significant social institutions that had moved west—for the forms of community they deemed civilization.[61] The populations of the states forming the core of the Western Annual Conference of the MEC skyrocketed. Kentucky swelled from 220,955 in 1800 to 406,511 by the 1810 federal census (an 83.98% increase). Tennessee more than doubled from 105,602 to 261,727 (147.84% increase). Ohio's population surged from 42,159 to 230,760 (447.35% increase).[62] At the same time, the membership of Methodist societies in the Western Conference grew from 3,347 to 22,904 (584.31% increase).[63] In a decade of tremendous migration and settlement, when western states doubled or quadrupled in population, Methodism grew nearly 600 percent. No wonder one denominational historian declared that in the broader Mississippi Valley, Methodism "has performed her greatest achievements."[64]

More than a decade before the founding of the Western Conference, the MEC had begun its move into the West. Coinciding with the close of the Revolutionary War, the Methodist itinerancy followed migrants to the areas of early trans-Appalachian settlement: the upper drainage basin of the Tennessee River, which connected southwestern Virginia, western North Carolina, and eastern Tennessee, and the Redstone country of western Pennsylvania south of Pittsburgh. Settlers had arrived, but the Methodist organization had not. That came only with circuit preachers, who stitched together scattered communities of believers and tied them to a national organization. The first forays occurred in the 1780s, when confederated Native power retained a strong hold in parts of the greater Mississippi watershed. The revolutionary settlement in the West was still a decade in the future and highly uncertain. In 1782–83, the Methodist movement made its first official commitments to the trans-Appalachian West, dispatching circuit preachers to communities around the Holston River, a tributary of the Tennessee. The circuit that formed there reported sixty members for 1783. In 1785, the expansion was in the North, as three preachers took appointments over the Allegheny Mountains to form the Redstone Circuit. A Methodist local preacher had settled in the area, and itinerants had traveled there tangentially before the conference made official appointments. The Methodist minutes of 1786 tallied 523 members. The membership of each of these early circuits was recorded as entirely white. The same year, Presiding Elder James Haw and junior itinerant Benjamin Ogden formed the first circuit in Kentucky. The Kentucky Circuit had 90 members the following year, and by that time Holston's membership had increased by 390 members. Through the rest of the decade and the early 1790s, circuits formed in areas of new settlement: Cumberland in middle Tennessee, and Lexington, Danville, Salt River, and Limestone Circuits spanned the Bluegrass region of Kentucky, from Maysville along the Ohio River to east of Louisville.[65]

The early expansion of the itinerancy into these areas of Pennsylvania, Kentucky, and Tennessee drew on the resources of local Methodist clergy and laypeople. Women and men who were emigrants from the Upper South preceded them and sponsored their travels by providing a base of operations. Although the records only occasionally provide details on the gendered division of labor, the support on which Methodist itinerants depended came most immediately from the domestic work of women in patriarchal households, where scattered itinerants regularly lodged and held services. Methodist documents and histories tend to associate households with their male heads, carrying forward patriarchal presumptions and obscuring important logistics of itinerant preaching. Historically, evangelical women were more motivated than their husbands to open their homes to preachers, thereby tying their households to organized Christianity. We can safely assume that evangelical women were among the primary points of contact for Methodist preachers as the foundations for the Western Conference were laid.

By the mid-nineteenth century, Methodist historians were busy shaping these early itineraries into a golden age of primitive Christianity. Veteran itinerant and chronicler James B. Finley framed Methodist expansion in terms fitting a colonial project. Using Old Testament language favored by English colonizers since the sixteenth century, Finley gave the story a special spin toward itinerancy: "When all the western country was a waste, howling wilderness . . . the pioneer Methodist preacher might have been seen urging his way along the war-path of the Indian, the trail of the hunter, or the blazed track of the backwoodsman, seeking the lost sheep of the house of Israel in these far-off, distant wilds." Whereas, he continued, historians tended to "record the deeds and achievements of mighty warriors of olden time, effected by the sword," Methodist readers of his book would "follow the Christian pilgrim warrior over the fields of his labor, and toil, and sacrifice, and recount the victories achieved by the cross."[66]

Finley diverted his readers from the "mighty warriors" who achieved "by the sword" and focused instead on "the Christian pilgrim warrior" who "achieved by the cross." The earliest western preachers symbolized rugged individualism and providentialism for nineteenth-century readers. Finley cast the "pioneer Methodist preacher" as a type of heroic figure peopling the civilization narrative described by nineteenth-century settler historians, which culminated in the work of Frederick Jackson Turner.[67] Finley and other Methodist writers lifted the Methodist circuit preacher as a literary figure above the complexity of the past. The emphasis on rugged, nearly sacred individuals detached them from the worldly associational culture they helped create. And while Methodist histories did include violence against Native Americans, as seen in Peter Cartwright's story, that violence was itself abstracted from the state-based force that opened the West to settlement.

Even though Methodists often described their expansion in purely religious terms, the fundamental context was the transformation of the Ohio Valley from a contested borderland into a secure, commercializing region of primarily white settlement. That process involved migration and the expansion of Anglo-American military power for the purpose of security. During those years, settlers like the Cartwrights in Kentucky lived anxiously within fortifications. Walls marked the short reach of Anglo-American sovereignty. Faith surely figured largely in this climate, but organized religion did not. Religious institutions—like those of local governance and civil society—required security.

Methodism's development depended indirectly on military resources and was concomitant with state formation in the West.[68] The four years of 1794–1797 laid the groundwork for the organization of settler religion in the West. The era saw military pacification, Methodist institutional establishment, and sustained religious revivalism. By 1796, when the General Conference of the MEC created the Western Conference, more than thirty years of intercultural conflict marked the history of Tennessee, Ohio, and Kentucky. The empires of Europe had vied with each other, with their own subjects, and with Native American groups for control of the area's resources in the second half of the eighteenth century. Security was a primary concern for settlers and Native Americans alike. Natives relied on Kentucky for important elements in their economies, particularly large game. When settlers encountered Indians traveling in the area, violence ensued. Not until the end of the War of 1812 was Indian power fully broken in the Ohio Valley and the Upper Midwest, but beforehand a series of military conflicts with members of what became the powerful Northwest Confederation eventually brought enough security to the frontier for European Americans to establish settlements. Virginia victory at the Battle of Point Pleasant in 1774 in Lord Dunmore's War limited the ordinary mobility of the Shawnees to the north bank of the Ohio River, in exchange for the promise that Virginia settlers would remain south of the river. The result was a measure of security for the settling of Kentucky, though the threat of Native reprisals persisted.[69] Over the next thirteen years of militarized settler pressure from Kentucky and fallout from the Revolutionary War, residents of Lower Shawnee towns relocated farther north in the Ohio country or to the Illinois country, leaving most of southwest Ohio with no permanent Native communities by 1783.[70]

In those same years, hunters and settlers in Kentucky and Tennessee feared the military power of Ohio Natives from the north and Cherokees from the south. Raiding continued through the 1780s. Settlers and Native

Americans targeted one another's agriculture, aiming to destroy the other's sustenance.[71] From 1784 to 1794, the conflict between Natives cooperating with the British and European American settlers was "an equal contest." A critical loss by General Arthur St. Clair's federal troops and militia to a confederation of Northwest Indians in 1791 at the "Battle on the Wabash" embarrassed the Washington administration. George Washington and Secretary of War Henry Knox pressed Congress to strengthen military power in the Ohio Valley, resulting in the victory of General Anthony Wayne's forces at the Battle of Fallen Timbers. One year later, in August 1795, the Treaty of Greenville banished Natives from the southern half of Ohio and secured a path for further settlement of the Ohio Valley.[72] Thus the infusion of Federalist-backed military power solidified settler control over lands that Shawnees and their allies had been fighting to hold throughout the revolutionary era. Indigenous power remained in key areas of the Midwest through the War of 1812. Nevertheless, the lands of southwestern Ohio between the lower Scioto River and the lower Little Miami and Great Miami Rivers opened to white settlement. That securitization allowed the flourishing of social institutions, including the Methodist circuits of the Western Conference, which formed in the hinterlands of the emerging settler hub of Cincinnati.

For one early Methodist writer, the mid-1790s securing of the southern Ohio, Kentucky, and Tennessee portions of the Ohio River drainage marked a "new order of things."[73] The MEC was one of the first denominations to take advantage, but its growth nationally had made it unwieldy. The solution was a Madison-esque consolidation of the annual conference structure, streamlining what Francis Asbury called "the Federal Constitution of Methodism."[74] (It is worth noting that Asbury also claimed that the MEC's structure inspired the federal structure of the United States government.[75]) Therefore, as American military power finally subdued Native military power and began a "new order" in the area, the MEC began reordering itself and turned its focus toward rationalizing its expansion in the West.

From 1773 until 1780, one conference had convened each year. Methodist itinerants gathered with their superintendents, mainly Francis Asbury, to learn the coming year's preaching appointments and to address administrative issues. Not all preachers enjoyed traveling to an annual conference, but the system was efficient from the organization's perspective. However, for the next decade and a half, the preachers' conferences divided haphazardly. Starting in 1781, two conferences were held. More southerly preachers gathered in Virginia, while the main conference occurred in Baltimore later in the year. This began a sixteen-year trend wherein preachers gathered regionally rather than travel to one central conference several hundred miles from their homes and circuits. Three conferences met in 1785, in western North Carolina, the Southside of Virginia, and Baltimore. Three years later there were seven conferences; the following year, eleven; and the year after that, fourteen. By 1793, the number had risen to nineteen separate conferences for the year.

This was disorganization at its peak. The large number of conferences made it difficult to compile, print, and distribute the minutes of the conferences before the next round began. The conference minutes were an annual snapshot of a developing social network and should not be discounted in their importance as documents of settlement. Annually, the MEC's book concern published "the statistics of the church" for the closing year. In an era of growing interest in the data of civil and cultural institutions, readers of the *Minutes* (figs. 1 and 2) found the geographic assignments of all circuit preachers along with the number of members, demarcated by race, populating each circuit in the nation. Each year, a new set of minutes therefore displayed the extension of the Methodist circuit system across the land and the changing density of each circuit. Readers who reflected on the previous year's pamphlet or who surveyed the minutes in volumes combining multiple years saw the statistical development of a powerful cultural institution over time. The area of the nation that showed the starkest extension year over year was the West, as the *Minutes* chronicled the absorption of new settlement areas into the MEC. The *Minutes* were among the MEC's most popular and important publications. It is no surprise that preachers disliked finding themselves ignorant of their colleagues' whereabouts and their denomination's development because of the disorderly conference structures of the 1780s and early 1790s. They raised the call for reform.[76]

The General Conference of 1796 restructured the MEC, settling on six annual conferences: New England, Philadelphia, Baltimore, Virginia,

South Carolina, and the Western. The reorganization addressed issues of institutional knowledge, reputation, logistics, and the pressures of domestic masculinity, which were fundamental problems of the young early republican society. Fewer conferences meant that a higher proportion of attendees at any given meeting would be "senior preachers, whose years and experience had matured their judgments." Larger conferences would ensure "that dignity which every religious synod should possess, and which always accompanies a *large* assembly of gospel ministers." Coordinating the transferal of preachers from one area to another would be more efficient. Finally, limiting the number of conferences, and thus increasing the area of each conference, would help bishops take into account preachers' domestic circumstances when making appointments. A larger conference geography offered more flexibility. The single preachers could range widely within a conference's bounds while married preachers could travel closer to their families.[77]

The creation of the Western Conference in 1796 grouped western Methodist societies into one body. By the next decade, the Western administered circuits not only in Kentucky and the Ohio and Tennessee Valleys but also the lower Mississippi Valley and the Illinois country.[78] The Western Conference grew in part because its birth helped to create a surge in revivalism in the West. The year 1797 marked a turning point for Protestantism in the trans-Appalachian West when a "skilled phalanx of revivalistic Presbyterians" arrived in western Kentucky and began praying and watching for a work of God.[79] Late in the summer of the following year, revival broke out among a congregation at Gasper River in Logan County. Over the next four years, it spread through Kentucky and nearby parts of Tennessee. In late summer 1801, settlers gathered at Cane Ridge in the Bluegrass region of Kentucky for a meeting that made western revivalism famous. After Cane Ridge, the flames of revival burned through the Ohio Valley and extended to surrounding regions. Camp meetings occurred with greater frequency and thousands experienced religion. Originally interdenominational gatherings, by 1805 excesses in worship eroded the cooperative spirit of the camp meetings throughout the South and West, particularly among Presbyterians and Baptists. The extended, outdoor assemblies fell mainly to the use of the Methodists.

Minutes for 1807.

Quest. 14. What numbers are in Society?

WESTERN CONFERENCE.

Holston District.

	Whites.	Col.
Holston	600	52
Nollichuckie	576	22
French-Broad	554	16
New-River	380	36
Clinch	519	42
Powell's Valley	185	4
Carter's Valley	209	10
	3023	182

Cumberland District.

Nashville	677	118
Red River	456	28
Barren	328	12
Roaring River	386	24
Wayne	461	19
Livingston	334	13
Hartford	303	16
Illinois	110	—
	3055	230

Kentucky District.

Limestone	1186	20
Lexington	746	70
Hinkstone	603	19
Danville	652	36
Salt River and Shelby	895	40
Licking	194	7
	4276	192

Ohio District.

Miami	752	5
Mad River	332	1
Scioto	662	10
Hockhockin	671	2
Muskingum and Little Kanawha	270	4
Guyandott	121	5
White Water	67	—
	2875	27

Mississippi District.

Natchez	94	58
Wilkinson	70	1
Claiborne	102	33
Appalousas	17	—
	283	92

SOUTH CAROLINA CONFERENCE.

Oconee District.

Appalachee	745	58
Sparta	907	326
St. Mary's	102	14
Milledgeville	111	14
	1865	412

Ogeechee District.

Louisville	536	56
Augusta	62	13
Little River	906	129
Broad River	789	138
	2293	336

Seleuda District.

Reedy River	442	34
Enoree	904	87
Bush River	435	46
Keewee	440	18
Edisto	400	74
Cypress	600	100
Charleston	80	749
	3301	1108

VIRGINIA CONFERENCE.

Norfolk District.

Norfolk	281	152
Portsmouth	194	139
Camden	533	430
Suffolk	1065	366
Bertie	620	251
Greensville	746	418
Mecklenburg	280	50
Amelia	588	59
Brunswick	526	129
Sussex	646	100
Petersburg	67	18
	5546	2112

Camden District.

Columbia	137	114
Santee	360	517
Little Pee Dee	958	97
Rocky River	331	108
Montgomery	623	74
Great Pee Dee and Georgetown	835	745
Bladen	1222	375
Wilmington	34	356
	4500	2416

Swanino District.

Buncombe	227	13
Morganton	275	23
Union	348	9
Lincoln and Catawba	775	115
	1625	160

Richmond District.

Williamsburg	736	147
Hanover	500	130
Gloucester	1065	88
Orange	658	93
Amherst	777	158
Bedford	795	267
Cumberland	674	62
	5205	944

Salisbury District.

Caswell	534	58
Franklin	451	96
Yadkin	723	100

	Whites.	Col.
Salisbury	495	24
Guilford	702	36
Haw River	435	153
	3340	467

Newbern District.

Trent and Goshen	1216	738

BALTIMORE CONFERENCE.

Baltimore District.

Annapolis	107	201
Severn	663	612
Calvert	900	1644
Prince George's	266	1068
Washington city	70	32
Baltimore cir.	584	158
Fell's Point circuit	700	203
Harford	583	318
Fell's Point	277	138
Baltimore city	1068	640
	5218	5014

Alexandria District.

Winchester	509	192
Berkley	520	91
Fairfax	618	188
Stafford	300	43
Alexandria	170	198
Georgetown	151	81
Montgomery	613	534
Fredericktown	45	47
Frederick cir.	622	259
Lancaster	554	182
	4102	1815

Susquehannah District.

Wyoming	440	—
Tioga	276	1

PHILADELPHIA CONFERENCE.

Chesapeake District.

Philadelphia	1378	792
Bristol	244	29
Chester	524	65
Dauphin	374	53
Cecil	615	514
Kent	420	559
Queen Ann's	943	707
Talbot	1238	962
Wilmington	112	96
	5848	3777

Delaware District.

Smyrna	989	675
Dover	1133	730
Milford	1351	426
Lewistown	1122	475
St. Martin's	1064	708
Accomack	1238	672
Annamessex	768	572
Somerset	1129	538
Dorchester	1569	1304
Caroline	1491	604
	11853	6704

	Whites.	Col.
Pamlico	350	30
Roanoke	692	528
Tar River	973	316
Mattamuskeet and Banks	311	21
Newbern	102	512
	3644	2145

Canestio	139	—
Lycoming	522	8
Huntingdon	395	—
Bald Eagle	192	7
Lyttleton	392	3
Carlisle	575	60
Juniatta	123	4
Northumberland	342	1
	3396	84

Monongahela District.

Redstone	622	22
Monongahela	656	30
Greenfield	645	2
Pittsburg	379	2
Shenango	309	1
Erie	647	—
West Wheeling	857	8
Ohio	478	28
	4593	93

Greenbrier District.

Rockingham	616	103
Staunton	209	88
Bottetourt	376	89
Monroe	324	15
Greenbrier	511	37
Randolph	180	6
Pendleton	361	25
Alleghany	818	84
	3398	417

Jersey District.

Asbury	550	4
Freehold	308	27
Trenton	352	65
Elizabethtown	499	15
Burlington	823	48
Gloucester	930	75
Salem	1255	152
	4717	386

Genesee District.

Chenango	414	—
Westmoreland	520	2
Otsego	374	—
Pompey	490	—
Cayuga	350	6
Seneca	223	2
Lyons	228	3
Scipio	200	—
Ontario	343	16
	3142	32

Fig. 1. The *Minutes* allowed Methodists to track the geographical and numerical growth of their preaching circuits year to year. (*Minutes of the Annual Conferences of the Methodist Episcopal Church*, 1807)

Minutes for 1809.   171

Portland District.				Whites.	Col.
	Whites.	Col.	Hallowell	117	
Durham	327	1	Vasselbo-		
Portland	169	2	rough	100	
Scarborough	131		Bristol	203	
Falmouth	291		Union	227	
Conway	74		Union River	67	
Bethel	84		Orrington	200	
Livermore	288		Hamden	206	
Poland	183		Palmyra	39	1
			Georgetown	55	
	1547	3	Boothbay	12	
Kennebeck District.					
Readfield	221			1673	1
Norridgwock	226				

RECAPITULATION.

	Whites.	Col.
Western Conference	17931	1117
South Carolina Conference	16344	6284
Virginia Conference	18502	5739
Baltimore Conference	19272	7200
Philadelphia Conference	26365	10534
New-York Conference	22717	937
New-England Conference	10023	73
	131154	31884
	31884	
Total	163038	
Total last year	151995	
Increase this year	11043	
Preachers 597.		

Quest. 15 *Where are the preachers stationed this year?*

The elders' names are printed in Italic.

WESTERN CONFERENCE.

HOLSTON DIST. *Learner Blackman*, P. Elder.
Holston, *William Pattison*, Moses Ashworth.
Watauga, *Thomas Milligan*.
Nollichuckie, *Thomas Trower*, Horatio Barnes.
French-Broad, *Nathan Barnes*, Isaac Lindsey.
Clinch, *Isaac Quinn*, Lewis Anderson.
Powell's Valley, *James Axley*.
Carter's Valley, *Moses Black*.
Tennessee Valley, Milton Ladd.

CUMBERLAND DIST. *Miles Harper*, P. Elder.
Nashville, *Elisha W. Bowman*, William Virmillion.
Red River, *Frederick Stier*.
Barren, Joseph Bennett, John Lewis.
Roaring River, *Zadok B. Thackston*, John Travis.
Livingston, Thomas Kirkman.
Hartford, Samuel Sellers, Jacob Turman.
Duck River, John Cragg.
Elk, Thomas Stilwell.
Dixon, William Lewis.
James Gwinn, missionary.

KENTUCKY DIST. *James Ward*, P. Elder.
Limestone, James King, Wm. Winans.
Licking, John Clingan.
Lexington, *Caleb W. Cloud*, William B. Elgin.
Danville, David Hardesty, John Henninger.
Salt River, *Peter Cartwright*.
Shelby, *George Askin*, Henry Mallory.
Green River, John Watson, Richard Richards.
Wayne, Sela Paine.
Cumberland, *Richard Browning*.
Hinkstone, *William Burke*, Eli Truitt, J. Blair.
Fleming, *Joshua Oglesby*, Edmund Wilcox.

MISSISSIPPI DIST. *John M'Clure*, P. Elder.
Natchez, Thomas Hellums.
Wilkinson, Jedediah M'Minn.
Claiborne, *Anthony Houston*.
Appalousas, *Benjamin Edge*.
Washataw, Isaac M'Kowen.

INDIANA DIST. *Samuel Parker*, P. Elder.
Illinois, *Jesse Walker*.
Missouri, *Abraham Amos*.
Maramack, *Joseph Oglesby*.
Cold Water, John Crane.
White Water, Hector Sandford, Moses Crume.
Silver Creek, Josiah Crawford.

MIAMI DIST. *John Sale*, P. Elder.
Cincinnati, *Wm. Houston*, John Sinclair.
Mad River, Hezekiah Shaw, Wm. Young, S. Henkle.
Scioto, Abbott Goddard, Joseph Williams.
Deer Creek, *John Collins*, Wood Lloyd.
Hockhocking, *Benj. Lakin*, John Johnson.
White Oak, David Young.

MUSKINGUM DIST. *James Quinn*, P. Elder.
Fairfield, *Ralph Lotspeich*, John Bowman.
Wills Creek, *James Watts*; Wm. Young, last six months.
West Wheeling, *Jacob Young*, Thomas Church.
Marietta, *Solomon Langdon*.
Little Kanawha, William Mitchell.
Guyandott, John Holmes.
Leading Creek, *Thomas Lasley*.
Robert Cloud, missionary.

SOUTH CAROLINA CONFERENCE.

OCONEE DIST. *Lovick Pierce*, P. Elder.
Appalachee, *Hilliard Judge*, Wm. Redwine.
Milledgeville, *James Jennings*, Thomas Mason.

Fig. 2. The *Minutes* allowed Methodists to follow itinerants' circuit assignments each year. (*Minutes of the Annual Conferences of the Methodist Episcopal Church,* 1809)

Methodists persisted with camp meetings and put them to much use as spaces for conversions and social exchanges under the preaching of itinerant ministers.[80]

As migrants filled the West and some of them filled Methodist societies, they entered into the broader Methodist network by way of the annual conference. The conferences were the organizational structure through which local societies and circuits connected. Traveling preachers tied Methodists to other Methodists in their region and ultimately across the country. In 1800, the Western Conference covered parts of southwestern Virginia, Tennessee, Kentucky, and southern Ohio. Soon it stretched to Natchez in the lower Mississippi Valley. The Western begot individual conferences that organized Methodism across the continent as it came under US settlement. After 1812, it split into the Ohio and the Tennessee Conferences. By 1844, separate conferences existed for Missouri, Mississippi, Kentucky, Illinois, Alabama, and Memphis, and Holston in the southern Appalachians.

Over time, the Western Annual Conference and its successors encompassed a larger share of the nation's Methodists. In 1800, the Western's share was not quite 5 percent. By 1840, the annual conferences of the West were more than one-fifth of the national church, a body of 1.3 million people in a nation of 17 million.[81] More people were affected by Methodism than became official members, and religious adherence, which is distinct from belief or religious self-identification, was low in western areas.[82] These numbers, therefore, only begin to capture the true influence of Methodism over the American West.

The Western Conference was the kind of organization that eastern nationalists wanted for the West. It gathered migrants into religious societies that encouraged relationships beyond the family, it provided a narrative of pioneering hardship and righteous acquisition of Native lands from which settlers could draw common meaning and moral comfort in the ensuing decades, and it connected local communities to a national organization that supported the nation's Protestant consensus. This was not civilizing but it was a cultural institution contributing to the settler consolidation of the trans-Appalachian West.[83] The Western Conference was itself only a yearly meeting of preachers; the bulk of the settlement work that it organized occurred in the districts, circuits, and meetings wherein Methodists, lay and ordained, fellowshipped and exchanged news of the world and the world to come.

Districts and Presiding Elders: The Communication Hubs of Western Methodism

Beneath the annual conference were regional districts of circuits. Just as each local Methodist meeting was linked to others nearby as part of a circuit, each circuit was grouped with others nearby into a district. Districts were the level of the Methodist grid between the circuits and the region-wide annual conferences of preachers as well as bishops. Districts have rarely attracted much attention outside of denominational histories, but from an institutional standpoint they were crucial, being the administrative units closer to the lives of common Methodist settlers than the annual conference. Thousands of souls gathered to form Methodism in the West. Religious migrants joined local religious societies that started as nothing more than neighbors in a room. Yet every time a circuit preacher appeared, those cells of holiness joined with the national itinerancy. Methodism was a religion of the heart, but its public power grew through regular meetings. Some meetings were populated largely by laypeople, others solely by itinerants. Some were heavily administrative while others were worshipful. Some were small and local, others large and national. In all, a fundamental concern was for "solemn times of assembling."[84] Linked by preaching circuits, the meetings constituted the grid through which love flowed horizontally among peers and through which authority (ideally accompanied by love) coursed vertically between officeholders. The more rural a circuit, the longer and less populated it was, meaning a traveling preacher spent more time traveling than preaching. The more dispersed a circuit's population, the fewer opportunities the circuit preacher had for society meetings and visits with individuals. Most circuits became denser with time, creating thicker social networks.[85] In an expansive nation, distance threatened to erode connections needed for social harmony, economic development, and political unity. With circuits tying together meetings from a multitude of locales, the MEC combated on the religious landscape the same problem the new nation encountered on the civil plane: "tyranny of distance."[86] Districts were the primary administrative units for turning local circuits into parts of a national system,

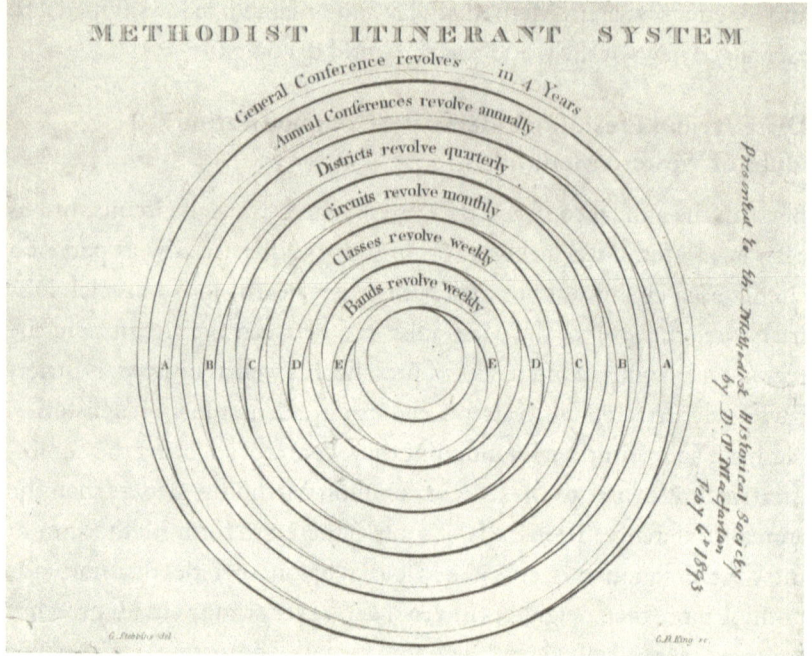

Fig. 3. Illustration of the "corporating genius of the Methodist Connexion." Whether as a grid or interconnected orbits, the Methodist Episcopal Church was understood as an efficient system of meetings. ("Methodist Itinerant System," John C. Totten, printer, 1810–1811; courtesy New York Public Library Digital Collections)

and through the elders who presided over them, they were vital hubs of communication touching topics of all kinds.

Groups of western circuits were organized into regional districts. In 1797, the first year districts were readily recognizable in the minutes, two districts constituted all of the Western Conference. They covered 10 circuits and 2,373 members. By 1812, the Western's 30,741 members and 69 circuits filled 8 districts. Each of those districts held on average 8 circuits. In size and density, districts reflected the areas they covered. That was true in 1797 and remained true in 1825 when, for example, the 7 circuits of western Kentucky's Green River District amounted to 3,308 Methodists and 1,000 miles that the presiding elder needed to travel to oversee his circuit preachers. The same year, the Kentucky District, centered on the populous Bluegrass region surrounding Lexington, also had 7 circuits, but they contained 4,136 members concentrated within about 200 miles of travel. The expansive Green River District might require ten weeks to travel, much longer than the geographically smaller but numerically larger Kentucky District. As settlement condensed, districts shrank in size and grew in population.[87]

A presiding elder traveled and administered each district. Like districts, the office of presiding elder has received little attention outside of denominational histories, but the men holding that office were among the most connected and powerful in the Methodist movement. A sign of the position's importance, the power and accountability of the presiding eldership in one way or another was at the root of the two most important disruptions in early American Methodism, the O'Kelly schism of 1792 and the Methodist Protestant schism of 1828, which were revolts against episcopal power. Presiding eldership was, in fact, a sustained tension through the first decades of the nineteenth century. Still, the issue simmered but rarely boiled. The institutional and social work of presiding eldership was much more impactful than the tensions reverberating around the office. A presiding elder was a veteran itinerant in charge of one district for a four-year term. Like regular Methodist elders, presiding elders conducted baptisms, communions, and marriages. Constitutionally and practically, their powers were greater. Unlike most offices in Methodism, presiding elders were appointed directly by a bishop. They were the "assistants," "agents," and "lieutenants" (or, according to a critic, "creatures and tools") of the bishops and exercised by proxy nearly all the authority of the bishop. They traveled the circuits of each district and oversaw all "spiritual and temporal business of the societies" therein. They ran the quarterly meetings of the circuits. They cared for the training, education, and discipline of each preacher and reassigned them when seeing fit. They gathered information about each circuit through observation and correspondence and reported conditions to the bishops.[88]

Given those crucial roles, Francis Asbury claimed that presiding elders could wield more influence in the Methodist network than bishops, especially with the rank and file.[89] Especially important for Methodism's role as an institution of settlement was the position of presiding elders in the information network that was the MEC. Presiding elders were information hubs connecting the local religious societies to the high ranks of the denomination. Bishops, especially Asbury, craved news and data about the Methodist movement, but its growth and expanse were impossible to monitor personally, despite Asbury's traveling about five thousand miles per year. Not only did presiding elders receive written reports regularly from circuit preachers but they had wide webs of personal relationships spun over many years of service. Because presiding elders were veteran itinerants, they had traveled many circuits in their careers. They knew Methodists on many circuits, sometimes in different states and sometimes in different regions of the nation. These experiences gave them a broader perspective on the religious and secular happenings within a specific region of an annual conference. This caused people, from common Methodists to bishops, to look to them for information and advice. A part of their qualifications for office was their experience "not only in the ways of God, but in men and manners." Their worldly experience increased their usefulness in both religious and secular business. Much of their job revolved around gathering and transmitting "information." As Asbury instructed one presiding elder, "you will collect all the information you can.... *Know men and things well.*"[90]

Along with the office's broader perspective, its holders were meant to "enter into small details" of each circuit. Asbury pressed on another presiding elder the necessity to "most carefully examine the characters and qualifications of our local preachers and exhorters, leaders and stewards."[91] The objective was to gain information that would help the church, but the asking and listening for details of character meant that presiding elders encountered information on the secular affairs of Methodists as much as the explicitly spiritual. The state of one's farm and finances, for example, impinged on the state of one's soul and usefulness to the church. The responsibility to know of problems arising on circuits and then to reassign (or rebuke) preachers meant they communicated closely not only with circuit preachers but with the laity of the local Methodist societies.

Additionally, far from being narrowly focused on spiritual affairs, presiding elders remained engaged with the world, sometimes too much so. Asbury once complained that some presiding elders spent only half the year on district business and the other half on their worldly concerns.[92] To Asbury, their absence depleted the church's resources, but their coming and going across the line between church and settlement meant that each departure and return, like a needle and thread, further stitched the network between Methodism and settler society. Across this level of the Methodist network, presiding elders harnessed their "thorough knowledge of the state of [each] district, and of its resources" and "preserve[d] in order and in motion the wheels of the vast machine" and kept "a constant and watchful eye upon the whole."[93] The resources they were charged to watch and manage were the affairs of the denomination, but their knowledge and influence extended beyond matters that were clearly church business. As they collected data on "congregations, meeting houses, numbers," they also compiled information on "the face of the country" and "eminent persons." The latter were key terms in the language of settlerism, surveying in the same phrase both geography and status.[94]

Worldly news and opportunities frequently came before elders' eyes and ears because of their duty to monitor the lives of Methodists. Presiding elders made information flow efficiently throughout the network. They made the MEC a distribution system that at times complemented and at times substituted the nation's postal system. For example, Asbury could advise a New York City colleague to send a letter to a "presiding elder [in South Carolina], and he will spread the news through the Carolinas and Georgia."[95] At another time, he wrote, "If a bishop, at any distance where a mail can go, has consequential business to the whole Conference, he has only to communicate to one man; he to write to the other presiding elders; they to communicate to the men who have charge of stations and circuits; the work is done."[96] The result was that Methodists up and down the organization looked to presiding elders not only for affairs of the spirit but also for the secular matters of settler society.

Asbury thought of presiding elders as the "eyes, ears, and mouth, and pens" linking together the episcopal structure from the bishops down to the itinerants and the people and back up again.[97] He knew well that they were the key nodes in a communication network. Preaching circuits fanned out across their districts, encircling cities and coursing up and down river valleys. These circuits, of course, were the sites of activity and information that presiding elders monitored. Asbury considered commissioning a history of American Methodism that would employ the ties between presiding elders and preachers to gather essential data about things spiritual and material that related to the MEC. Although he moved on from the project amid his manifold episcopal duties, he had no doubt that the project could be completed comprehensively and rapidly, and it demonstrates how much data about the settler environment existed in the itinerancy. Each preacher would supply a circuit history to his presiding elder. Asbury's desired information shows that not only did circuit preachers have data on numbers of chapels and souls converted but that they had a view inside the private homes of members on their circuits. They knew through their travels and conversations a great deal of physical and social geography, and they knew the "notable characters" of the communities they visited.[98] They knew no single tract of land as well as the farmer who worked it daily, but they knew the broad landscape better than any farmer probably could. Circuit preachers were, in short, daily surveying American settler society. They traveled as much as postriders but conversed more closely with the population. And while postmasters were known for the intelligence that flowed into their offices, they traveled less than circuit preachers and had access generally only to information brought to them.[99] Circuit riders, in contrast, moved systematically from one community to the next, presiding at religious meetings where middling settlers swapped stories and reports of their affairs in the interstices of prayer and hymn-singing. Much of that information they transmitted up the chain to their presiding elders, who were in a position to aggregate it. That was the root of the presiding elders' information and influence.

Circuits, Meetings, and the Methodist Network

Through each annual conference and district ran the preaching circuits. These were the conduits of Methodist experience. Itinerant preachers traveled the circuits on the mission of declaring saving grace and Christian love, which was to enliven Methodist meetings. Rural circuits especially constituted the MEC's "interesting and perilous field of toil," in words from a nineteenth-century historian evoking the settler sentiment that itinerants worked amid the wilderness.[100] Understanding the structure and function of circuits is essential to grasping how the MEC worked as a social and communications network.

Despite the focus in American culture on frontiers people living in spacious independence, the main trend of settling the West was congregation. Methodist expansion exhibited the process, but until settlement thickened in a region, some circuits covered three hundred to six hundred miles.[101] At the end of the 1780s, the Danville Circuit covered a third of Kentucky while the Lexington Circuit snaked through six other counties.[102] In 1814, one Virginia native found himself on a large circuit in eastern Ohio, "embracing all the country in Jefferson, part of Harrison, and Belmont Counties." It was a four-week itinerary that brought him to fifty classes and a membership of one thousand Methodists.[103] The Little Kanawha Circuit of western Virginia in 1817 was long and its membership scattered, covering five hundred miles. A preacher there had to keep appointments that were at times forty miles apart. Despite these long circuits, a "fairly typical example" of a circuit was the Vincennes Circuit of Indiana in the early 1820s, which comprised a round trip of about 175 miles and required 3 weeks of travel to complete.[104]

The itinerancy was the MEC's main way of countering the challenges of distance. As an itinerant traveled a circuit, he met with members both individually and in groups. The value of frequent contacts between the circuit preachers and the people did not escape the attention of the church's leaders. Usually, two itinerants (one senior, one junior) were assigned to a circuit; they traveled separately to increase contacts with Methodists. Itinerants also distributed printed tickets that granted Methodists entry to private meetings such as love feasts. Each quarter, new tickets were required. The policy's objective was more than simply regulating attendance at intimate religious gatherings; as the *Discipline* explained, it created for a preacher "an opportunity of speaking closely to every person under his care on the state of their souls."[105] In these ways and others, the circuits threaded together myriad points of contact between individuals as itinerants traveled from one settlement to the next.

Methodist men and women gathered in a hierarchy of meetings to practice the religion of the heart.[106] Good Methodists were to host regular prayer meetings with their families and neighbors.[107] These scheduled gatherings, intimately convened in private homes, were important occasions for building bonds of love among members of neighborhoods and between the generations. Additionally, the meeting hierarchy included bands, classes, quarterly meetings, annual conferences, and general (or quadrennial) conferences.

Among the smallest, most local meetings at the turn of the century were bands. "As soon as there are four men or women believers in any place," the circuit preacher was "to put them into a band."[108] The goal of band societies was to create small groups where trust ruled and spiritual edification flourished among likeminded individuals. Likeness of mind was more than a shared commitment to Methodism, for the church included individuals who "vary exceedingly in the state of their minds and the degrees of their experience." The heart, Francis Asbury and Thomas Coke wrote, was "such a cage of unclean birds" that no Methodists would "lay before their brethren all its secret movements" unless the conditions of fellowship were right. Hoping to nurture "these little families of love" and to support "social intercourse," all tensions were guarded against in bands. Thus, the sexes were separated. To the minds of Bishops Coke and Asbury, this almost went without saying: "The propriety of separating the men and women in these bands, must be evident to every one who considers the account here given of this means of grace." Gender was an important marker of one's capacity to interact with fellow Christians, and it combined with others. The *Discipline* also advised separating the married from the single, which "arises from the peculiar circumstances in which they are situated, and from the closer union which is likely to subsist between those who are circumstanced alike." While each "little family" had a leader to ensure order as the band society lifted its prayers and voices to God, the desire was to admit as much equality in worship as possible.[109]

Class meetings were designed for a membership of twelve, but sizes varied. Unlike band societies, class meetings were open to any who showed "a desire to flee from the wrath to come, and to be saved from their sins." That desire was the sole requirement for entering into society with the Methodists. (A higher barrier to entry would hamper evangelization.) Class meetings were private settings in which Methodists questioned the states of their souls. The class leader was obliged to "enquire how their souls prosper," "to advise, reprove, comfort, or exhort." For those joined in society, rules of behavior were prescribed. Seekers were to "continue to evidence their desire of salvation"; look after the physical well-being of their fellow men and women, especially the weak; and instruct, reprove, and exhort the souls of "all we have intercourse with." They were to place Christ before themselves in all ways as an example to those around them, and they were to worship in public, partake in the Lord's supper, be diligent in "family and private prayer" and "searching the scriptures," and practice fasting and abstinence as appropriate.[110] Those obligations bound leaders and members. The goals were accountability and edification, which were at the heart of the Methodist discipline.

Enforcement required watchfulness. Methodists could learn much about their class members and by extension the goings-on of their community as accountability ranged from carnal temptations to business practices, as sin might occur anywhere. Because class leaders bore responsibility for examining members, they especially gained information. They were, in turn, expected to pass on their knowledge to the circuit preachers. Class meetings, which outlived bands as an institution in the United States, were thus the footings of the Methodist structure of communication. The class leader of Peter Cartwright's recollection who organized a saltpeter trade with a military fort in Kentucky illustrates the spiritual and material advantages held within the class leader role.

Quarterly, a circuit's entire membership gathered in fellowship. At quarterly meetings, a circuit's senior itinerant oversaw affairs by meeting with the lay leadership. He consulted the steward regarding his care of the circuit's finances. He examined class leaders, local preachers (who were licensed to preach from scripture), and exhorters (also licensed but barred from preaching from a biblical text). Thereby the itinerant enforced orderly worship on the circuit. The quarterly meeting began in Britain for the purposes of circuit business but transformed into festivals for worship. Observers noted that American Methodists traveled twenty and sometimes forty miles to fellowship with circuit members they did not see during local meetings. By the 1780s, the typical quarterly meeting convened on Saturday and lasted through Sunday, when attendance was greatest due to the ability of enslaved and poor white people to leave their work. Numerous preachers and exhorters—all those living on the circuit and some from neighboring circuits—led Methodist services. Quarterly meetings hosted preaching, love feasts, watch nights, the Lord's supper, all the trappings of revivalism, and administrative sessions.[111]

Quarterly meetings were devout affairs, but they were also regional social occasions. Although less frequent than class meetings, quarterly meetings offered a more expansive religious society for the average Methodist. In this fact lay their significance for the creation and maintenance of regional networks. People broke from their local routines and ventured beyond the narrower orbit of the village. The settlers of the western states and territories enjoyed regular socializing in communal gatherings such as barn raising, and evangelicals added to this their own set of occasions. Camp meetings derived from a transatlantic Presbyterian tradition but over time were mostly absorbed into the Methodist schedule of meetings, often occurring in conjunction with quarterly meetings.[112] Representatives of each rank of the Methodist itinerancy attended quarterly meetings. Circuit preachers who regularly traveled well over a hundred miles a month, a presiding elder who visited settlements on an itinerary that might stretch to one thousand miles, and local preachers who traveled informally to minister to their neighbors all came for fellowship. Added to this were regular laypeople of varied stations and occupations. The result was fertile ground for exchanges of information and the building of relationships.[113]

Information of this world and the next circulated in small local meetings, flowed along circuits, and climbed above quarterly meetings in the MEC hierarchy to the annual and general conferences. Only circuit preachers held membership in the annual conferences, which often stretched across political borders, guided more by regional and physiographical considerations. In the highest tier of the system, itinerants from across the nation convened in a general conference every four years. It was the highest level of Methodist administration except the office of bishop. An important function of the itinerant system—especially of the high-level conferences—was to guard the church against the invidiousness of local interests. James Madison argued in Federalist 10 that extending the sphere would protect the republic from faction; Francis Asbury placed his faith for the MEC in centralized control in the annual and general conferences. Local interests, Asbury believed, were worldly interests; they had the potential to narrow the vision of the church. Asbury's frequent concerns about the distractions of local interests are testament to the power of local networking at the base of the MEC. In contrast,

Asbury valued the annual and general conferences that provided circuit preachers opportunities to socialize with their professional peers from across the young nation. Older preachers gathered with younger preachers. Annual conferences especially functioned as exclusive fraternities of preachers, but that did not stop the flow of information from the local meetings through preachers.[114] Itinerants assigned to distant mission circuits often arrived to trade news with brethren in more settled areas. Frequently an annual conference was the only opportunity for former traveling companions to reunite and restore the bonds of Methodist love. And at sessions of the General Conference, New Englanders mingled with Carolinians and so on. This encouraged Methodist itinerants, and observant non-Methodists, to think of the MEC as one of the great cords of national union.

Whether ecclesiastical conferences or gatherings of laypeople, Methodist meetings were spaces of social interaction. Linked by preaching circuits, they were the architecture of the rapidly growing denomination. The MEC was hierarchical and orderly but also contained a pietist energy. The current coursed through the grid of the MEC, quickening the hearts of members and hearers. Methodist social capital formed at the intersections of bureaucracy and emotion. Often enough, there met such networking elements as information and trust.

Thus, a movement rooted in the English Reformation and continental pietism crossed the Atlantic, passed through the American Revolution, and traversed the trans-Appalachian West, helping to create European American society in lands wrested from Indigenous control. Methodism emerged from the metropolitan, state-based religious culture that sought nothing less than to combat Catholicism and spread Protestantism across the globe. Along the way it achieved nothing less than to promote and reproduce Anglo-American settler society. The worldly power of Methodism was cultural and social. Methodism repeated and confirmed the Protestant colonizing discourses that had girded imperial expansion since the Elizabethan era. It also created networks of everyday exchange. Western Methodists were settlers, and though they gathered primarily for worship and accountability, once joined they were poised to discuss the affairs of the day, the conditions of crops, the prices of goods, and the availability of land. The regular meetings, fluid circuits, emotional ardor, and bureaucratic efficiency of the MEC made the culture of everyday exchange powerful. Methodism was by no means the only institution of settler colonialism but it was an especially fit one for the many who embraced it.

Francis Asbury and other Methodist leaders understood well the value of Methodism as a network, one that might unite believers across the continental American Empire. The itinerants were only a minority of the church, but their movements over the frontier of that burgeoning settler empire provided the social exchanges that created the value of Methodist connections for middling people. The history of those circuit riders of the West is covered by many coats of frontier myth. Stripping them off allows us to see anew the original textures of the itinerancy.

2

PILGRIMS AND SETTLERS

The Culture of Methodist Travel in the West

Peter Cartwright was an exceptional character by all accounts. He traveled widely in his ministerial labors. Near the end of his life and after a long career in the West, he tallied 10,000 souls that he had brought into the Methodist Episcopal Church (MEC), baptized 12,000, and preached 14,600 sermons.[1] He had all the marks of the frontier. He was large and rough-hewn, bold and vigorous. He took all comers. He was, some claimed, learned without seeming bookish, at once theological and plain-spoken.[2] At seventy-two years old, he wrote, "I certainly have toiled and suffered enough to kill a thousand men, but I do not complain."[3] His reputation was not confined to the American West. After an 1861 lecture at New York's Cooper Union, "thousands rushed forward to shake the hand of this old veteran christian warrior, as if he were a prince, or a president."[4] James D. McCabe Jr. in his *Great Fortunes, and How They Were Made; or, The Struggles and Triumphs of Our Self-Made Men* placed Cartwright among thirty-eight men—with the likes of John Jacob Astor, Benjamin Rush, Cornelius Vanderbilt, Samuel Colt, and Samuel F. B. Morse—whose stories illustrated that "the chief glory of America" was that it was "emphatically a nation of self-made men."[5] Like a Methodist Andrew Jackson, he symbolized a type of masculine presence that Americans admired. One British reviewer read his *Autobiography of Peter Cartwright, the Backwoods Preacher* and had "some difficulty in believing it to be a true narrative, and not a fiction." It was "the strangest, raciest, go-ahead picture of life and clerical duty the European world has ever seen." The reviewer had no difficulty identifying Cartwright's story as part of the long-term Anglo-American colonization of North America. "His discourses are composed amidst the primeval forests and vast solitudes of the backwoods of America, and are delivered to hearers who boast of being half horse and half alligator," he wrote.[6] These two fictions—the ancient, empty continent and the hybrid horse-alligator creatures—were, respectively, from the lexicon of colonization and from a song, "The Hunters of Kentucky; or, Half Horse and Half Alligator." The first was meant to clear away Native culture for the march of Christian settlement while the second celebrated the western common men who had brought the War of 1812 to a gloriously sanguine culmination in the Battle of New Orleans, unleashing the settler nation's self-appointed destiny.[7] Peter Cartwright was a man made for such folklore, a brawny symbol of toil, sacrifice, and frontier myth in the making, and he lives on in our textbooks.

Cartwright came to embody western Methodism, and the mythology of the masculine frontier cast his exceptionality as quintessentially American. His stories still are taken as representative. Able historians have focused on Methodism along the Atlantic seaboard, but the mythology of the frontier circuit rider (the use of the singular deserves note) endures. Western itinerants were not the raucous heroes of frontier myth that Cartwright seemed to exemplify. Rather, they were part of an emerging professional class in a settler population. They were agents of settlement, even as they thought of themselves as pilgrims set apart from the workaday distractions of the world. Closer attention to this traveling vocation allows the unpacking of the myth and ideal of the frontier circuit rider and the repacking of the parts of circuit riders' careers that solicited pilgrimage and settlerism.[8]

The experiences of circuit travel in the West were certainly formative. Incidents on the road influenced how preachers viewed themselves and their vocation. After all, itinerants spent more time traveling than preaching. Because they typically traveled alone, itinerants had ample time to think and read, to contemplate how they fit into the settler society they served and how they did not. Their experiences of travel gave itinerants a special cultural role. It even allowed them to develop cultural capital.[9] At times, they used that capital to admonish settler society, but they also employed it to promote settler society and advance within it—this was why itinerants acted as both pilgrims and settlers. The circuit rider was a name for a religious office, but Methodists never separated the sacred and the worldly in their everyday acts as settlers. They could not purify the social principle within Methodism. A missionary movement aimed primarily at the settler population could never insulate itself from the forces—corrupting forces in the eyes of some—of settler society. Itinerants spent much time contemplating their place in the world and their hoped-for transcendence of the world, but the basic facts of their traveling careers show that they were not merely embedded in settler society but instead members and efficient organizers of it.

Inventing the "Circuit Rider": An Ideal of Protestant Masculinity in Frontier Lore

"Biographical mania" swept the nineteenth-century United States, linking individual lives to national character. Writers used the genre to fashion ideal selves, to model bourgeois respectability, to give meaning to their institutions, and ultimately to tell stories about who constituted American culture.[10] This was the Age of Jackson, the age of the mythical common man, when life stories were cultivated for mass consumption.[11] It was the era of the formerly enslaved turning the power of their biographies to the work of destroying American slavery. The mania swept up Methodists as well. Veteran western preachers took up their pens and became memoirists and biographers. Peter Cartwright was the most famous, but he was part of a larger project. Over the next century, an ideal type of Methodist itinerant emerged from religious publishing. That creation, the circuit rider, was idealized, masculinized, and sanctified, and thus with ease entered the lore of the American frontier. The circuit rider was the pioneering character in Christianizing the westward expansion of the settler nation. The extension of the Protestant consensus infamously known as Manifest Destiny was, then, founded on the circuit rider.

The stakes were high for Methodists. They were well aware that critics had disparaged their faith since its beginnings in England. Like other groups with roots in the radical Reformation, Methodists found themselves pilloried with unflattering, often sexualized images of religious disorder.[12] They were chagrined that the English Romantic Robert Southey—certainly no Methodist—had penned the life of John Wesley. Western Methodists were committed to protecting their church's reputation. Cincinnati Methodists organized to support the work. Formed in

1839, the Western Methodist Historical Society in the Mississippi Valley called for preachers to write and for all western Methodists to contribute documents of church history. The project had several goals: to stave off external critics, to chronicle the growth of the church, and to edify Methodists. They guarded their legacy by publishing memoirs to ensure their history passed "complete" and "accurate" to posterity.[13] There was a broader goal as well. Through the pages of the *Western Christian Advocate*, the MEC's weekly newspaper for the western states, circuit rider memoirs by 1835 were meant to help sacralize a newspaper industry that had "some twenty years ago" been devoid of religious themes and to reach especially the poor, for whom "religious books were rare and costly."[14]

This print mission dovetailed with a broader chronicling of the Second Great Awakening. Congregationalist William Buell Sprague memorialized Protestant leaders in the nine volumes of his *Annals of the American Pulpit* (1857–1869). Sprague's biographical sketches emphasized piety and sacrifice. Such publications built pantheons of white, male, Christian respectability. Western Methodist memoirs did as well, and they added dashes of frontier life to claims that early Methodists had risked all for Christian settlement and civilization. The protagonists were overwhelmingly men, even as evangelical societies were mostly women. Readers found stories of men that included piety, sacrifice, and hard-won respectability. The western Methodist brand of "muscular Christianity" meant enduring Native violence, traversing countless miles of unimproved roads, and vying with uncouth hecklers at camp meetings. With such scenes, Methodists fashioned a masculine character for American folklore.[15]

The depiction of travel was also part of two contests among Methodists, one about the supposed transformation of American Methodism from a vital, primitive faith to a dull, respectable institution, and the other about the transformation of the American West in the transportation revolution. In 1866, after service as chaplain in the US Army, Reverend John F. Wright settled into his new assignment as a Methodist preacher at Milford in southwestern Ohio. Milford was in the orbit of Cincinnati and had been an early settlement on the Little Miami River. It was, in Wright's view, a location rooted more in the past than the future, having "not improved in proportion to its age." Wright described the geography of the surrounding region in expansive, modern terms. He referred more to railroads than rivers, sketching the recent history and physical layout of the area's tracks. He recalled how two decades earlier he had first traveled on "the Little Miami, Columbus, and Xenia railroad." The pace of technological change was clear: "I need hardly say, we had not the T rail then.... The speed was slow but very safe." Wright celebrated the "wonderful change" that had come in the intervening years. There were more lines in 1866, which stretched across the Northwest, stitching together the bounty of Ohio and the wider world. Steel arteries brought into one system Dayton, Cincinnati, Hamilton, Toledo, Sandusky, Chicago, Detroit, Cambridge City, Indianapolis, Richmond, and many points farther west and east. "We live in an age replete with incalculable advantages," Wright concluded.[16]

Wright noted that "our ancestors" had lacked these improvements as they filled the West in the late eighteenth century. Without technology, they had lived as "patient, heroic men and women." Chief among their early work was that "they brought with them God's revelation, and ministers of religion, that they maintained civilization, a pure Christianity, and perpetuated the worship of the true God in the wilderness. Such a courageous and faithful people, ought to rank next to our pilgrim fathers and 'be in everlasting remembrance.'" Wright took an optimistic view of the nation's future, and that future was indebted to the "hardy" spirit and spirituality of pioneer Methodists.[17]

Others took a dimmer view of the present and future. Former circuit rider Henry Smith, writing from Baltimore at the age of ninety-two, believed the passage of time had weakened itinerancy. In contrast to Wright's vision of a promising future founded on a strong pioneer past, Smith recalled a distant past, one that was fading from view. Rather than progress, Smith saw decline. As an example, he recalled associating in 1795 with "cross-bearing, self denying, enterprising men, such as the age and circumstances called for—men who could glory in privations, hardships, reproaches and sufferings in the cause of Christ. If they had an effeminate, complaining brother among them," Smith continued, "they laughed at him and encouraged him; but, if not cured, he soon left them."[18]

While Wright and Smith agreed that virtue defined the pioneer past, Smith held that contemporary society lacked the experience of hardship and sacrifice which had produced the virtue of the pioneer generation.

While Wright celebrated the connections of rail technology, Smith was part of a rising chorus of ministers from an older generation that had cut its teeth riding backcountry circuits. Smith held that not all improvements were an improvement, and that modernization enervated and feminized Methodism. The difficulty of circuit travel was supposed to have made a strong, sacrificial corps of ministers. As Smith and former colleagues who shared his view perceived a decline in the moral strength of the ministry, they increasingly chastised that ministry for becoming weak. Both Smith and Wright venerated the early history of Methodism and specifically Methodist travel in the West. Both preachers agreed that preindustrial travel had created the network of circuits that became one of the most important religious institutions of the communications revolution. On the other hand, their disagreement about improvement illustrates the larger contest within antebellum Methodism. That contest played out in conversations and Methodist publications through the middle of the nineteenth century, shaping the depiction of Methodist itinerancy. Muscularity and sacrifice became major attributes of the mythical circuit rider. What was forgotten was the variety of characteristics of actual circuit riders.

Twentieth-century writers further reduced Methodist itinerants to an abstraction. Historian William Warren Sweet knew a great deal about his subjects, but in his synthetic writings, he distilled them to the essence of evangelical missionary efficiency. Instead of individuals, readers found "the Methodist circuit rider." (They could also find "the Baptist farmer-preacher.") Creating an ideal type was useful for explaining large processes like the expansion of evangelical Protestantism across a continent. Strong precedent supported the practice. Frederick Jackson Turner had famously listed stages of settlement through "frontier types": the fur trader, then the cattle herder, the miner, the pioneer farmer, the equipped farmer, and finally the figures of village life that signaled urbanization. As Turner influenced Sweet, Sweet influenced later historians. Sydney E. Ahlstrom's prize-winning *A Religious History of the American People* of 1972 transmitted "the Methodist circuit rider" to an ever larger mid-twentieth-century reading public. The ideal type of the circuit rider—respectable, democratic, muscular, and efficient—helped to create the Protestant consensus in America and to integrate it into the nation's dominant frontier narrative.[19]

The Lived Experiences of Western Circuit Riders: Ages, Places, and Careers

The circuit rider ideal was a sociological abstraction and an important character of narrative history but not a lived reality. Instead, there were thousands of individual Methodist itinerants across the country. Older Methodist histories were so busy memorializing itinerants as pioneers, saints, and martyrs they omitted important information. Those histories, for example, glossed over the later lives of preachers, except to note that here and there one led a respectable family or died a good Methodist death.[20] What a man did after leaving the itinerancy was often ignored. A fuller accounting of itinerants' lives is essential for understanding the enduring social value that Methodism imparted to many settlers. That accounting begins with basic facts of place, age, and labor; as variables in the settler aspect of Methodist manhood, they were as fundamental as the exceptional ruggedness, toil, and sacrifice associated with Methodist pilgrimage. These professional attributes were key stabilizing factors for white, middling setters working to possess the early American West.

Former itinerants were not like modern employees who retire from a firm. They maintained connections and influence within the MEC, locally and sometimes nationally. Their connections to the MEC also allowed them to maintain influence in their communities. The basic facts of western itinerants' lives do not clearly support the ideal of a youthful "stern fraternity."[21] Nor were these men simply self-sacrificing frontier preachers as folklore cast them. Rather, itinerants pursued their work and fashioned their personalities within a hierarchy of age and experience. Especially important factors that formed their identities were travel and the variety of professional experiences that preachers encountered over their long careers and lives. Put another way, itinerants were not short-term figures worn down by the frontier. Their itinerant experiences equipped them with skills and social connections that established them in settler society.

Neither were western Methodist itinerants simply products of the frontier, as the folklore suggests. The nineteen full members of the Western

Conference in 1801 represented a variety of geographic origins.[22] Of those preachers whose origins can be determined, most came from southern states. Seven of the nineteen were natives of Virginia and four of Maryland, reflecting Methodism's early strength in the Upper South and Mid-Atlantic regions. North Carolina and South Carolina produced two each, and one itinerant was from Long Island, New York.[23] Their places of death suggest where the 1801 preachers went in the years after that annual conference. Virginia, Ohio, and Tennessee each claimed three of the preachers. Two died in Maryland and another two in Mississippi. The remaining four preachers whose final resting places can be identified passed away in Georgia, South Carolina, Kentucky, and Indiana.

By 1810, the Western Conference had grown. There were then sixty-seven itinerants who were full members of the conference. For more than half of these preachers, a place of birth can be determined with reasonable certainty. As in 1801, Virginia provided the bulk of the preachers, with seventeen, and the middle states contributed heavily. Four were from Maryland, four from New Jersey, and three each from Delaware and Pennsylvania. Seven more preachers were natives of South Carolina, North Carolina, and Tennessee. There was one New Englander, Solomon Langdon of Massachusetts. Of those preachers whose places of death have been identified, the majority passed away in the early frontier states of the Ohio River Valley: twelve in Ohio, eight in Kentucky, and four in Tennessee. Only two died in Virginia, which had produced so many preachers. Three had settled and passed away in Indiana and Illinois. Finally, four came to their end in the early southwestern states of Alabama, Mississippi, and Louisiana. As this small sample shows, Methodist preachers, like many American settlers, were scattering near and far in the wake of the American Revolution.[24]

Some evidence suggests that Methodist itinerants in revolutionary America served short terms in which they suffered greatly from the strains of travel and experienced high mortality.[25] Methodist church historians pointed to the rigors of travel as evidence that youthful itinerants sacrificed their bodies and secular opportunities in the cause of spreading salvation and Methodist teachings. The data of nineteenth-century Methodist preacher and historian Nathan Bangs seems to confirm that view, but his 1839 publication date prematurely caps several careers that stretched beyond that date. Based on Bangs's numbers, the average tenure of service of the 1810 membership of the Western Conference was about seventeen years. However, the famous Peter Cartwright, for example, served the MEC for more than a decade after 1839.[26]

Riding circuits for a living was at times hard, dangerous work. According to one estimate, more than 60 percent of itinerants who died before 1819 while in active service did not reach their fortieth birthday.[27] The percentage somewhat justifies the tones of martyrdom found in a number of nineteenth-century Methodist histories. It fits, for example, the story of Learner Blackman, who became a symbol of itinerant sacrifice on the frontier. Blackman was born in southern New Jersey in 1781. He volunteered for the western mission field at a meeting of the Philadelphia Annual Conference. For the next several years, he traveled circuits in the Holston region of eastern Tennessee and southwestern Virginia and around Lexington, Kentucky. He then spent four years in the distant Natchez District in the Mississippi Territory. He returned to Tennessee, eventually marrying and settling in Sumner County. He served as a chaplain in the Tennessee Volunteers during the War of 1812 and continued to itinerate until he drowned in the Ohio River near Cincinnati in 1815.[28] Blackman died young in a travel accident—a death of itinerancy. His memory was lifted up as an example of Methodist martyrdom: "The Church was deprived of one of its most gifted and [in] every way promising young ministers."[29] Blackman's untimely passing ensured his place in Methodist history but statistically he was exceptional.

Most of the preachers in the Western Conference in 1801 lived long lives. There were nineteen full-time itinerants, and age at death can be estimated for fifteen. All but three reached their seventy-fifth year. More of those preachers died in their eighties than their seventies, and two men reached the ripe age of ninety-three. Even with the three low ages of thirty-three, forty-seven, and fifty-eight, the average preacher lived just over seventy-five years. By the end of the decade, the average age at death had decreased. Three members of the 1810 Western Conference did not reach their thirtieth year. Yet the average age at death of the 1810 class of itinerants was over sixty-two years. More men died in their seventies than in their twenties, thirties, forties, fifties, or sixties. Keeping in mind that western circuits were often rural and difficult to travel, these facts make clear that the image of Methodist circuit riders as being worn down by their travels is not the entire picture. Rather than being debilitated and disoriented by frequent professional travel, many lived long lives, surviving their yearly itineraries in the West and succeeding as settlers.[30]

Preacher, Farmer, Doctor, Slaveholder: Composite Occupational Identities

Occupation is essential for grasping Methodists' engagement with settler society precisely because their language was so fixed on criticizing the world and ultimately transcending it. Like many nineteenth-century Americans, Methodists believed that life occurred in a sacred, providential context. The spirit of God pervaded the world. Confusingly, their language also assumed a sharp break between worldly and religious acts, between the flesh and spirit.[31] The ambiguity of the social principle within Methodism meant there was no clean division in Methodists' lives. Still, there was value for Methodists in reproducing a distinction between the affairs of this world and the next. They could stand on one side of the line as pilgrims set apart from material concerns and, when convenient, critique those concerns as distractions, knowing that fellow Methodists believed in the Wesleyan concept of perfection and yearned for ultimate transcendence. The fact remained, however, that their worldly and spiritual pursuits occurred within the same social context of settlement, and therefore those pursuits reinforced each other.

Methodist itinerants were paid travelers, but their pay could be irregular or insufficient. When collections fell short, frustration rose, and the complaints became tales of hardship endured by circuit riders. Problems of pay would have been a major problem if traveling preachers were in it for the salary, but that was not their main interest. Recruiting preachers was not a major problem for the MEC and never an impediment to its remarkable growth. Beyond faith and calling, itinerants desired the social resources of travel. Circuit preachers developed status, knowledge, and relationships that allowed them a variety of opportunities to work and earn. The variety within preachers' careers was lost in the emergence of the ideal type of the circuit rider. Preachers developed several roles precisely because preaching was not lucrative in the short term as a salaried position. Many preachers had many jobs throughout their lives and all the while maintained the important professional status of preacher of the Gospel.

Itinerants commonly remarked on their low pay, which was nominally sixty-four dollars per year before 1800 and eighty per year after that. This compared poorly to contemporary Congregationalist clergy, who received four hundred dollars per year.[32] Bishop Francis Asbury found with some regularity that collections were insufficient to pay preachers their full salaries.[33] Not until the year 1796 could Asbury record that "we had great love and great riches also: never before have we been able to pay the preachers their salaries; at this conference we have done it."[34] Although preachers emphasized low and irregular salaries, that lamentation has distracted historians from the significant point that occasional salary problems actually increased preachers' engagements with settler society. Because Methodist preachers could not always count on full salaries, they pursued other opportunities, leaving and sometimes reentering the itinerancy. Moreover, being an itinerant did not stop them from taking other work or resources. Itinerants knew how to use their social networks because they lived in a society where salaried positions were uncommon. Ample salaries could have allowed itinerants to cloister themselves, like some priests, but the reality was that insufficient salaries drove Methodist preachers to engage with settler society and build the forms of capital that created substance in early America.

Shortages of pay pressed some itinerants, especially those with families, to leave the traveling ministry. However, little barred those preachers from returning to the itinerancy, and they commonly did. Itinerants balanced their desire to preach with their desires for financial progress and family. Valuable opportunities resulted from preaching full time interspersed among periods of secular employment.

Many Methodist itinerants had what can be described as a composite occupational identity, akin to what has been called "the Baptist farmer-preacher." The Methodist model differed in a significant way. Methodist preachers shifted between the economic independence of the Baptist model and the travel-based social connections of the Methodist itinerant. When not traveling full time, Methodist preachers pursued such careers as farmers, teachers, and justices of the peace, fundamental positions in the reproduction and regulation of settler society. Secular employment increased these men's connections—for good or bad—to their fellow citizens and complemented their identities as religious leaders. The result was professional status combining religious and secular attributes. Far more than the rugged masculinity of frontier lore, this composite professional status defined Methodist manhood and fastened the MEC to the development of white settlerism in the trans-Appalachian West.

Several occupational arrangements can be seen over the course of the lives of the 1801 Western Conference preachers. John Sale's life illustrates the assumed course: he died in 1827 while traveling his circuit in southwestern Ohio. Benjamin Lakin traveled in the itinerancy for approximately two decades before retiring to a modest lifestyle, supported by the church's assistance for retired preachers. William McKendree became the MEC's hallowed third bishop—the first of American birth—and spent the rest of his life in that office, traveling until his death like his predecessor Francis Asbury. A number of their 1801 colleagues, however, did not spend their lives as full-time itinerants. A few examples show the variety of roles itinerants took. Lewis Garrett had a multifaceted career. He joined the itinerancy in 1794, traveling an array of circuits before settling around Nashville in 1824 after a year on that circuit. There, for roughly the next two decades, he preached, managed other itinerants, worked at the local book depository, edited a newspaper, and likely taught school. Between 1840 and 1850, he moved to Madison County, Mississippi, where he joined the Mississippi Annual Conference, and died there in 1857.[35] Samuel Douthit located (the Methodist term for resigning from the traveling ministry) in eastern Tennessee and spent the next decades of his life as a preacher, farmer, and physician. The author of one early twentieth-century local history remembered him as Reverend Samuel Douthit, M.D.; his occupational credentials were the bookends of his professional identity and his role in his community.[36] Others took public offices. Samuel's brother James worked as a tax collector in the South Carolina piedmont.[37] William Burke served from 1814 to 1841 as the postmaster of Cincinnati, although during part of that time he was expelled from the church. He never severed himself from the MEC socially and was later readmitted to the Ohio Conference.[38]

At least seven of the men from 1801 held the occupational status of preacher or Methodist clergyman on the 1850 and 1860 federal censuses, suggesting they presented that title throughout their lives. A few of these were also listed as farmers, indicating they drew a living from the land. Some preachers settled in southern states and owned slaves, ranging from one to as many as fifteen.[39] Although their primary income probably came from owning a farm cultivated by family and, in some cases, enslaved laborers, these circuit riders continued to assert their clerical status. Methodist preachers performed a complex professional identity based on landholding, agricultural labor that included slavery, at times a learned or bureaucratic office, and finally an obligation to a religious calling. Such an occupational composition provided preachers with multiple ways to contribute to their settler communities, but the clerical facet carried organizational and spiritual weight and remained primary in how they identified themselves. Preachers clung to their professional identity, even when it was not their main economic support because of its social value in the white, commercializing settlements of the trans-Appalachian West.

Travel as Occupation and Identity

Circuit travel was the distinguishing fact of Methodist itinerants. As professional travelers, the requirements of traveling a circuit affected all aspects of circuit riders' lives. Driving them were prearranged schedules and the expectations of Methodist laity. They slept in the homes of friends and strangers, in public houses, or under the stars. The comforts of their homes were rare. Itinerant preachers itinerated more than they preached, making travel fundamental to understanding their work and masculinity. To fulfill their mission to the white settler population, Methodist preachers needed to fit its culture enough to maintain access. Motivated too by the desire to advance in that population, many itinerants pursued its values. Traveling so often, they spent days and days in the saddle traversing dispossessed lands and the settler society they were stitching together and their futures within it. Their reflections, borne of travel, positioned them as professionals peculiarly constituting settler society, episodically considered set apart from terrestrial affairs and yet always existing within them, at once pilgrims and settlers.

As they rode, they wrote. Circuit riders kept diaries at the encouragement of the MEC leadership and knew their diaries might be shared with other Methodists or published.[40] Rather than pouring forth their thoughts, they crafted reflections on travel and vocation. Through travel we can better understand a group often caricatured as "ignorant" and anti-intellectual. Esteemed scholar of American religion Perry Miller judged of western revivalists "that, in relation to the accumulated wisdom of Protestant theology, they had few ideas and were little capable of cerebration."[41] It is true that the first generation of western Methodists and their counterparts were not systematic theologians, that they did not parse the thought of Jonathan Edwards and debate the niceties of the New Divinity as one might in a seminary, but they were curious about the world and the fate of humans within it and the world to come. Benjamin Lakin read mostly about Christianity but also about mathematics, history, nautical navigation, and the experiences of Africans, as his commonplace notebooks show. A. G. Thompson used his correspondence to play with language, writing poems to colleagues. They were bad poems, but few people write good ones. Seely Bunn also delighted in language. He peppered his letters with needless, rather pompous vocabulary like *contumacious, obtest, indagate, contumelious, thrasonical,* and *misogamist*. Yet he was self-aware, admitting that "I am no etymologist," forewarning his colleague to "look for more of my Jargon," confessing "my Dictionary is so little," and asking his correspondent to "excuse ... my prolixity, Rhapsody, & solecism, or barbarism." He had an appetite for words and even words about words. As with Thompson the point is that common itinerants were mentally adventurous. They were curious about the nature of the world and invested in questions current in the popular Enlightenment. Thomas Scott wondered about "animal electricity," paralleling Methodism's founder, the Oxonian John Wesley. Nearly all itinerants studied and disseminated medical knowledge through the popular Methodist manuals *Primitive Physic* and *The Family Adviser*. They did not claim to be scientists or theologians but neither were they pioneer dullards or anti-intellectual in any simple way.[42]

Methodist itinerants read and wrote a fair amount, but they traveled so much they often read and wrote in the saddle, and thus the metaphor of travel suffused Methodism. Preachers' itinerations were analogous to the spiritual quest of their souls in Methodist theology. That theology was itself an evolution from the English puritanism that gave the world the travel allegory John Bunyan's *Pilgrim's Progress*. The continual journey along "the path to holiness"—the process of sanctification following conversion—was one of Methodism's guiding theological principles. Like the traveler who might grow weary or stray from his path, Methodist doctrine held that Christian salvation was not permanent after conversion. Rather, salvation required constant attention and energy. This stance made Methodists unique from their Calvinist competitors and was the theological root of the tensions among those groups. Whereas true conversion in the eyes of Calvinists imparted to believers permanent justification of their faith in the eyes of God, the imperative for Methodists was constant renewal of one's faith along the path of life.

Theological travel converged with the movement and expansion of American settler society. As the opening of western lands in the early American republic triggered large-scale migration, ordained itinerants advanced across the expanding landscape in an inverted pilgrimage in which the priests came to the people. To Methodist leaders the itinerancy was the circulatory system of the MEC, pumping spiritual vitality to the farthest reaches of the American community. As Asbury put it, "We must draw resources from center to circumference."[43] What Asbury described in administrative language, itinerants carried out with their feet. Itinerants were motivated to document their travels because, for one, they participated in a movement that was sweeping the nation and, for another, their daily occupation of travel ritually aligned with the theological essence of their faith.

The middle of the nineteenth century witnessed the publication of many memoirs written by itinerant veterans that emphasized the pilgrim experiences of toil, sacrifice, and separation from society. Preachers' sacrifices admonished believers in an era when Methodism had grown into a larger, sedentary body. It has long been known that "the circuit rider dismount[ed]" over time, but the itinerancy's engagement with settler society long preceded the dismounting bemoaned by the early generation.[44] Asbury had long railed against a settled ministry precisely because settlement always threatened the itineration he idealized. Veteran itinerants' criticisms of settling give the impression that the itinerancy was set apart from settlement during its most mobile years. As veteran itinerant Henry Smith lamented, "O, how ought those to be esteemed, who have sacrificed their health, and almost their lives, in the cause of God."[45]

Indeed, abundant evidence confirms that circuit travel was often arduous and at times debilitating. Francis Asbury's biographer suggests that his travels led to two decades of congestive heart failure which eventually killed him. Exposure to the elements brought Asbury near-constant fever and strep throat, which "damaged his heart valves."[46] When Henry Smith's many historical reflections were offered to readers in a volume in 1848, the *Methodist Quarterly Review* pitched it as pilgrimage literature, "a means of keeping us in lively remembrance of 'the way the fathers trod,' and of preserving in healthful and vigorous action our excellent system."[47]

The focus on the struggle and sacrifice of pilgrimage also promoted a particularly able-bodied conception of preachers' masculinity that did not, in fact, represent most itinerants. In 1905, the *Methodist Review* noted in an article titled "Our Heroic Inheritance" that frontier circuit rider Learner Blackman, who drowned crossing the Ohio River, was numbered among many "of herculean frame [who] could stand the ordeals which in most cases the preachers of those days were expected to undergo."[48] The best example was the bombastic Peter Cartwright, who noted the intense physicality of the practice of preaching and related his long service to his bodily vigor. Later audiences looking for stories of frontier bravado latched onto Cartwright's exploits: how he once fought two men to a draw, how another time he intimidated a duelist by eschewing pistols for first cornstalks and then fists and offering him "the worst whipping you ever got in all your life." And yet, his *Autobiography* can be read as a catalog of the "feeble health and strength" of so many of his contemporaries and at times the western MEC itself. Cartwright himself admitted that he was unique, and that "thousands of the thrilling incidents . . . attributed to me" related to his being "constitutionally an eccentric minister."[49]

The *Methodist Quarterly Review* was correct when declaring there was value in remembering "the way the fathers trod," quoting a classic pilgrimage hymn, but the value was not the muscularity, hardship, and sacrifice emphasized through Smith, Blackman, and Cartwright.[50] Rather it was in seeing the Jeffersonian empire through the eyes of some of its greatest travelers. Those travelers trod back and forth between the separation of pilgrims and the engagement of settlers with the world.

Circuit Travel, the Western Environment, and the Itinerant Self

In the world of farmers characteristic of settler society, agricultural labor was the main way of interacting with the land. Itinerants, however, were distanced from the fixity of farming until they located from the traveling ministry. Instead, circuit riders in the West experienced the land as the wilderness of settler colonial ideology. This was especially true for itinerants traveling lands only recently taken from Native peoples. In their minds, those lands remained wild. The western environment included, in their minds, the land, their bodies, and peoples they believed characteristic of the West, especially Native Americans. Thinking as pilgrims and settlers in a centuries-old colonial tradition, itinerants were not discovering wilderness; they were discovering themselves in unfamiliar western lands. That self-discovery was an important intellectual step for claiming their place in the West.

The on-the-ground experience of circuit riders was deeply tactile, mixing emotion, intellect, and physiology. Surviving manuscript sources show that they mulled their environmental experiences as they rode their circuits. Travel offered Methodist men opportunities for expression and discovery. Although a routine complaint was the meager support on which they lived, their diaries are filled with a mixture of chronicled drudgery and fascination with the cultural and geographic diversity they experienced. When compared to their nonelite contemporaries, Methodist preachers were not as poor and uneducated as many scholars have described them, but they were not elite or wealthy either.[51] Methodist expansion to the West allowed men of an upwardly mobile cast sufficient resources to partake in travel as a cultural activity typically restricted to the wealthy. Methodist circuit riders enjoyed a career that brought them a rare opportunity before the rise of middle-class tourism.[52]

As circuit riders traveled in the West, they reflected on this changing context as they worked out their own identities as professional religious leaders. Several examples illustrate how traveling preachers engaged with the evolving western environment. Itinerant Learner Blackman's road to the West extended from New Jersey through Virginia and over the mountains. Blackman's recollections of his experiences of the road emphasized distance, which he used to quantify the practical and metaphorical facets of travel. Near the beginning of his career in the itinerancy, he had volunteered "my services for the Western Country" at an 1802 meeting of the Philadelphia Annual Conference. This commitment placed Blackman in a new landscape that encompassed longer roads than those with which he was familiar. While in the East, he was accustomed to "travelling more than 7 or 8 miles a day" but grew weary at any pace that exceeded "25 or 30 miles a day for 2 or 3 days." The road to the West represented a greater challenge. He recalled, "We hardly averaged 30 miles a day traveling out to the west that time. I have since traveled near 50 miles a day for a week together on the same road."[53] Blackman relied on descriptions of distance to relate his travel experience. Itinerants routinely logged their progress to the next preaching appointment and used the metaphor of distance to measure their experiences in the itinerancy.

In Blackman's case, the long roads of the West represented the many changes he had experienced traveling as a young man. He recalled his feelings of awe upon seeing mountains for the first time. Reaching his assignment on the New River Circuit in western Virginia, he compared the mountainous geography to a "bosterous ocean wrought up by a tempest." Blackman emphasized the challenges of the new landscape: "It was very steep. I attempted to walk up; I thought I would walk to the top before I stopped. I walked on until I was well-nigh fainting before I stopped. I could hardly stand or keep from slipping back in many places without taking hold of the bushes."[54] The new landscape, he imagined, must have been the "most mountainous country on the continent," noting how greatly it differed from the flat circuits between the Delaware and Chesapeake Bays.

Looking back on a decade of service in the Methodist itinerancy, Blackman assessed the travels that had taken him from the eastern states to the West. Blackman's perception of the western geography aged. As he struggled through his commitment to the itinerancy, he found consolation in patience and hope. Traveling brought Blackman, a man of ordinary means, intellectual stimulation and a feeling of personal expansion: "This disagreebale and mountainous country seemed as a plain when my soul was happy in the Lord." He believed travel formed his personality. "Many new scenes were almost daily unfolded and disclosed to my view after I left Baltimore," Blackman wrote in his memoir. "Mossy rocks broken in ten thousand diversified forms, lofty mountains, pearling streams, and flowing rivers. This to me was truly the sublime of nature; it expanded my mind by enlarging the field of meditation." Although he suffered occasionally, he believed his "coming to the west was directed by Providence & that it would most undoubtedly work for my good." Through the practice of travel, Blackman recalled, "I have learned some things since I have left the State where I was raised." "That I could live," he continued, "where I would have starved once."[55] "That I could live where"—this was a statement that fewer and fewer Indigenous people could make of the ancestral lands of the trans-Appalachian West. The road from New Jersey to Kentucky and later to Natchez represented the challenges he faced in a journey toward self-discovery and settler-colonial possession.[56]

As with Blackman, travel formed the intellectual and spiritual identity of Benjamin Lakin, a Maryland native. Lakin's diaries reveal an introspective person. He represented the pilgrim traits of circuit travel, and his reflections show how Methodists reproduced that metaphor in the trans-Appalachian West. Self-examination was a continual process for this disciplined itinerant, who frequently analyzed his thoughts and deeds. One evening he noted, "I began to examin if there was anything in me to move the love of God toward me, I found nothing but sin and misery by nature." Another day he recorded, "as I rode, examining myself."[57] Through an array of personal encounters and reflections on the mundane, Lakin fashioned his identity as a Methodist itinerant and devout evangelical as he struggled to comprehend his spiritual life and the environment in which he traveled to fulfill his calling. Along his circuit, he read books, cataloged the weather, and mused on the landscape—all while contemplating his spiritual commitments.

While Blackman's reflections, composed several years after his travels, recorded a longer-term progress into manhood in the West, Lakin's diaries come closer to his experiences on the ground. They reveal an interpretive process in which the body and the physical environment were important components of religious reflection. Memoirs recorded and published long after an author's itinerancy omitted these more complicated views of the body and the environment. Yet, such thinking was not uncommon in the early modern Atlantic world.[58] Circuit riders at times feared for their safety in the West, but their attentions more often focused on the interplay of the physical environment and the body. Turn-of-the-century travelers and settlers of the frontier believed the physical environment was an active agent in the construction of individual and social identity. This understanding had roots in ancient medicine and was common in the early modern Atlantic world. The theory of the four humors, the basis of older medical knowledge, held that fluids in the body responded to external stimuli, determining health. Regulation of the humors centered on ingesting and expelling elements. Enlightenment physicians added a mechanical model in which nerves and vessels underwent tension imposed by external forces.[59] This emphasized the body's interaction with its physical environment.

Eurocentric perceptions of strangeness in the Atlantic world amplified this body of knowledge in settlers' minds. The high degree of travel in the Atlantic world brought individuals into an intimate relationship with the physical environment. Whether extracting mineral resources or scraping a daily living from the land, individuals often believed the mundane—whether the air and soil, too-great exertion, or a sudden jolt—impacted one's constitution. Settlers feared disease in particular landscapes, and some colonial travelers worried that exposure to New World climes might change one's race or sex.[60] These ideas influenced travelers' understandings of the trans-Appalachian West.

In September 1809, Lakin attempted to cross the Scioto River in Ohio when his horse "plunged into deep water." Soaked, Lakin collected himself and struggled to gather the gear that had fallen from his horse during the plunge. "Just as I got my baggs and started," he recalled, "the Ague took me[.] I rode about three Miles [with] my wet clothes on, [shaking], and pukeing till I puked blood."[61] The rapid onset of sickness is striking, but more significant to Lakin was that it began a lingering illness.[62] On and off, the ague stayed with him for the remainder of September and into early October. The fever weakened him and interrupted his duties, confining him to bed at times. He traveled to the annual conference in Cincinnati with Francis Asbury and two other preachers and failed to keep pace with the group. Asbury "gave me a sweat with a solution [of] tarter in wine," Lakin recalled. The remedy brought temporary relief, but fever returned several days later as he rode under "an excessive hot sun." Lakin missed much of the annual conference in Cincinnati because of illness, and then regretfully received reappointment to Hockhocking Circuit. During the previous year on Hockhocking, Lakin had worried greatly that his wife would die, and the circuit year came to an end with debilitating sickness. Lakin reflected on his "afflictions and the cause of them." God, he reasoned, was humbling him, demonstrating his excessive "pride" and "formality," and Lakin found that he lacked faith and failed to fulfill the tenets of Methodist discipline. He took spiritual lessons from his afflictions. The rigors of travel made the itinerant body a central interpretive space as Lakin attempted to comprehend God's instructions.[63]

Lakin also believed that the health of the body and soul were linked. In the middle of December 1809, Lakin attended a preaching appointment that required him to ride seventeen miles in a falling snow. As he preached, "such a Stupor of Spirit and drowsyness came on me that I do not remember ever to have experienced the like. I could (either in prayer or preaching) scercely keep from falling asleep. And . . . sometimes spoke nonsense." Lakin suffered immense fatigue, and he experienced chills and fever that night. He noted a deeper significance than physical weariness, that the real danger was to his spirit. "Surely," he wrote, "the corruptible body presses down the Spirit." Here, Lakin recognized a relationship between body and soul that matched John Wesley's descriptions in *Primitive Physic; or, An Easy and Natural Method of Curing Most Diseases*.[64] For Lakin, the physicality of travel, which he considered an act of Christian duty, was an important component of his spiritual life. In fact, the hardship of travel was more than a duty and sacrifice for Lakin. He perceived it to be a real variable in the health of his spirit. Three categories of Lakin's traveling life were entangled: human sinfulness, lodged in the flesh; the preacher's experience with his environment, in the form of rigorous travel; and performance of clerical duties. Lakin's seventeen-mile winter ride mingled with original sin to form his identity and his spiritual state. The "body presses down the Spirit," Lakin wrote, and "we need support from heaven for both." In this way, he emphasized that helplessness was an important part of the Christian's life and, most likely in his view, an unavoidable part of human life in general.[65] This belief that weakness held spiritual value stands in contrast to later memoirs' assertions of a muscular, masculine faith. Whereas some later authors desired public recognition for their sacrifices, Lakin reasoned that physical weakness and therefore suffering were part of the road to spiritual perfection.

However, the significance of traveling went deeper for itinerants. Because citizens of the early modern world understood nature as fluid—that the land, atmosphere, and one's body constantly interacted—early traveling preachers faced more than fatigue on their errands. As Benjamin Lakin's experience indicates, itinerants were not quick to welcome physical struggles, but they did reflect on them when they came. This contrasted with Henry Smith's bold recollection of associating in 1795 with "men who could glory in privations, hardships, reproaches and sufferings in the cause of Christ."[66] Bodily challenges brought opportunities to contemplate human weakness and sinfulness. Circuit riders turned contemplation into an understanding that they followed a special profession. This mentality set them apart from their fellow citizens of the West even though most itinerants never truly eschewed the practices and values of settler society.

Travel and Methodist Notions of Respectable Settler Society

Traveling allowed circuit riders to turn their attention from their own lives to the character of western society. As men engaged in a spiritual occupation, they scrutinized the moral development of the West. These were the concerns of close observers rather than the detached judgments of the eastern moral reformers historians tend to cite. Itinerants adapted to their purpose the enduring Anglo-American discourse of settler colonization. They critiqued class distinctions and the dissipation of the elite. They indicted the settler population for the coolness of its piety, at times appropriating Indigenous culture as a foil. They also praised aspects of western social life. The combination offered western settlers a middling vision of upright social order as the West transitioned to Anglo-American possession.

Blackman's recollections in his travel memoir tied together his process of self-discovery and his discovery of western life. To a young man like Blackman from an eastern state the developing West appeared ripe for interpretation as a mission field. Nature, geography, and Providence converged in Blackman's mind. His language reads like a seventeenth-century colonization pamphlet. "How much like old Canaan," Blackman noted, "is the wilderness of America." The West was the "American Israel" and the land of "milk and honey." He explained that Native Americans had three names for Kentucky: the "middle," the "bloody," and the "dark" ground, each of which signified the fertility of the land through images of the seasonal confluence of peoples; the bloodshed of hunting and violent competition; and the shadows of dense, lofty forests. Much of Kentucky profoundly transitioned during Blackman's life into a commercial society. These changes brought moral advantages and disadvantages. Focusing on the area surrounding Lexington, Blackman reinterpreted the metaphor of the "dark" land. The Bluegrass was a landscape in which "the hand of industry [was] pulling down the forests" and erecting a new style of community, where "science and religion [were] exerting their mighty energies to enlighten the people and show them the high road to happiness." The land, however, remained "dark" as "infidelity hath prevailed among the higher ranks in society."[67] Blackman imagined Kentucky emerging from its dark past, but only partially. He espied enlightenment but believed it would remain incomplete as long as settlers' faith was incomplete. By singling out the elite, Blackman expressed misgivings about those at the top of the West's emerging commercial society, misgivings that were common to Francis Asbury and other Methodists in the West.

While it was common for eastern cosmopolitans to fret over the alleged savagery of white settlers in the West, Blackman expressed an on-the-ground view of settler society. A perspective such as Blackman's is rarer among American Protestant writings but more representative of local and regional ministerial views. Blackman described the relative sophistication of the West, contrasted to the East. Contrary to contemporary assumptions, westerners, he asserted, were more diverse and better informed than Americans in the eastern states. "A general spirit of enquiry and thirsting after knowledge is more manifest," Blackman judged, "among all grades in society in Kentucky than in any other State I have travelled thro." He judged that this was due in part to the process of travel. Migration specifically had "enlarged" the views of many. Blackman based his assessments on his own identity as a vocational traveler (a Methodist itinerant). Traveling under a spiritual calling imparted to Blackman a feeling of authority to judge settler life, as he had seen more of the country than many others and certainly more of the West. He assessed the spiritual consequences of the mobility, commerce, and "enquiry" that he witnessed. The "rich and the great," in particular, in Kentucky were "disappated in many respects."[68] By traveling, preachers like Blackman not only connected settler communities but developed a moral framework for settler colonialism that celebrated white, middling Protestantism.

Circuit riders occasionally met people of color in the West despite the MEC's focus on white settlers. Two facts stand out from the records. Itinerants often depended on nonwhite westerners when traveling outside the bounds of Anglo-American settlement. Second, itinerants extended the colonial gaze and adapted it to the purpose of the nation's largest Protestant group as it attempted to shape settler society.

In 1804, Learner Blackman embarked on a mission to Natchez, a journey considered long and perilous.[69] He volunteered reluctantly, fearing for his health in a malarial landscape "said to be one of the most sickly countries in America and 15 or 1600 miles from home." He knew the irony that persons of robust "constitution" tended to suffer in "sickly countries" more than weaker individuals. "But what is a constitution?" he asked. Surely any sacrifice would equal the worldly riches that others had sought along the Mississippi.[70]

Adding to landscape and disease, he considered the road to get there "a howling wilderness inhabited by wild beasts and savage Indians." Blackman's recollection of the road to Mississippi had more texture than later accounts of the hardy "pioneer preacher" of legend. On the way to Natchez, Blackman headed toward the nations of the "Chikasaws" and "Chaktaws." Among Blackman's traveling party was Lorenzo Dow, one of the more eccentric figures to have served in the Methodist itinerancy. Blackman appreciated his broad travel experience. Departing middle Tennessee for the wilderness, the travelers heard rumors of hostile "Indians" on the road. The party bedded down uneasily, and Dow later woke in alarm, believing he had seen a Native. Yet, Blackman recalled that "no Indians interrupted us that night or at any time on our journey." Significantly, the group relied on Natives for sustenance. Although at times they found provisions meager, these remained important contacts in a trip marked by short supply. They met mixed-race communities and relied on their hospitality too. Blackman still judged the earthly and spiritual conditions of his hosts. Regarding the physical, he was squeamish: "Those that got the first drink of the milk fared the best," Blackman recalled, noting that only near the brink of starvation would he have "drunk of it after I saw the dirt rising like a cloud from the bottom of the vessel as soon as it was stired."[71]

After restoring their energy, the travelers ministered in these communities, mostly to the white and Black people living there. In one community, Blackman detected "some veneration for the Sabbath," which he said was due to "several white men [being] married among the Indians," a colonial judgment. While Blackman expressed some distaste for the material life of these communities, his tone was not harsh. He reserved his main critiques for Anglo-American society. These multiracial communities, especially their Native American members, served Blackman like the Enlightenment stereotype of the noble savage. Just as Methodism was a missionary movement directed at white settlers more than Native Americans, so did Blackman concern himself with Native Americans to assess his own society. That the Gulf South's polyglot, cosmopolitan history conformed poorly to his presumptions did not stop this settler-colonial travel writer.[72] During his travels, he perceived stages of society from the "new part of Virginia" through Kentucky to "the new settled part of Mississippi" and the intervening Indigenous communities. The range of conditions, especially those of multirace settlements, confirmed for him "that one half of the world does not know how the other half is living." Blackman implied that traveling overturned his understanding of Natives. He found some devoted to their God and thankful for their material sustenance, an example that would shame many Christians.[73] Blackman felt the West might serve as a morality lesson for the young nation. As he saw it, his record of traveling that country provided the credentials necessary for making such a critique.[74]

Benjamin Lakin also encountered people of color living beyond the boundaries of white settlement and annexed them into his vision of respectable Protestant settlement. In September 1810, he traveled with a few other men to Native American and African American settlements in the vicinity of Upper Sandusky, Ohio. Their purpose was a missionary visit to African Americans living in the vicinity and the Wyandot living in the town. Lakin's wariness of the landscape reveals that he was leaving the security of settlement and entering a borderland yet to conform to Anglo-American norms: "This plain is an open Barrans consisting of some scattering trees in most parts of the plain, and groves of timber; with a thin soil generally inclineing to wet. In traveling about 27 miles through the plains we obtained water once for ourselves but none for our Horses." Sandusky Plains was likely a tallgrass prairie, but early settlers did not yet associate such areas with agricultural fertility. When accepting the task, he considered "that it would be at the risk of my helth, if not my life."[75]

The "Negro Town" he visited was a mixed-race community where "some Negroes and some Indians dwell" as well as "George Wright, a white man that has a wife half Negro and half Indian." "We found about 10 or 12 person[s] that could speak English; among whome are two White men and one Woman." Significantly, Lakin's group camped outside the town to care for their horses, though they had "kindly" been offered lodging in the settlement. In town they led residents in prayer and song and interviewed several. They visited an old Black man who was "confined with the Rhumatic Pains," and Lakin observed that he "can read a little and has several Books among them there is a Methodist Hymn Book." Not until six years later would there be an official Methodist missionary in the area, but the products of the Methodist printing presses had reached the settlement. Lakin also recorded the dreams and visions of residents as evidence of God's visitations to the community. One Black man, Thomas Peters, had escaped from Kentucky, and another, Cato, from Detroit. Both had been found and taken in by the Indians, and both described religious experiences that Lakin deemed Christian. According to Lakin, Cato, after a remarkable dream in which he traveled a "narrow blind path" to a church and preacher, upon waking "he went on praying," regardless that "he had never heard anybody pray in that place before."[76] The hymnal and visions were seeds that gave Lakin hope for the area but an obstacle remained.

Lakin's group arranged for residents of the town to interpret to the Wyandots. Lakin believed the Wyandots capable judges of their affairs. He "discovered that they are much prejudiced against the Christian name. And no wonder considering the Charractors they have been conversant with, and with them a white man and a Christian is the same." There was a problem then of racial perceptions, but Lakin described an alternative plan that abandoned the use of missionaries and would solve this problem of perception. Lakin placed his faith in what he perceived as the decency of regular preachers and the laity who, if allowed "to visit them, to preach to them and converse with them," would "let them see that there is a difference between a white man and Christian."[77]

Lakin concluded that the "Charractors," as he called the scoundrel settlers, endangered the credibility of the MEC. The church did not abandon missionary work to Upper Sandusky, but Lakin's thinking represents an important presumption among western Methodists. While many Methodists would oppose Jacksonian-style deportation of Indigenous people, they believed Natives must conform socially. Lakin's idea of increasing contact with laypeople and preachers was a kind of "civilization" policy by osmosis. Premised on Methodists' being a better sort of settler, this thinking extended the Protestant paternalism of settler colonialism through the following decades.

Vocational Travel, the Mission to Settlers, and the Path to Social Capital

Western preachers traveled primarily in a geography of white settlement. In rural areas of the West, circuits usually ran along river valleys, where access to hydraulic power, transportation, and fertile soils attracted settlers. Most Methodist circuits took the names of the inhabited streams coursing down to major rivers like the Ohio and the Mississippi. Methodism's western connection pursued a growing European American settlement geography in the West that was peopling the most important routes of communication and transportation. This fact highlights the settler and missionary nature of the itinerancy, as evangelical ministers fixed their attention on these growing river communities. It distinguishes them from many other religious travelers in world history who traveled as ascetics and pilgrims. Rather than seeking retreat, for example, in mountainous reaches, Methodist circuit riders engaged in a ministry to the developing lowlands.[78] After roughly 1790, rather than converting and ministering to a simple, isolated backcountry population, Methodist circuit riders were more often traveling to communities oriented to one of the continent's great waterways. Residents, many newly arrived to the West, were poised for the opening of commercial opportunity or were already busily engaged in it.[79] In this context, traveling allowed itinerants a range of social and economic experiences and brought opportunities for reflection on self and society. While these experiences might bring hardship at times, they were not simply the saintly drudgery that later memoirs described.

The vocational character of their travels was front and center in the minds of itinerants, and it was the primary justification for their career, regardless of what other benefits or challenges might come.[80] Henry Smith recalled announcing his calling to a group of worshipers in the Scioto country, exclaiming, "I Am, hath sent me unto you." He also echoed a typical claim: "My call was among the poor."[81] Smith's declaration of his calling was confident. He needed confidence to earn the attention of his audience, but it is also a recollection from many years hence. Many other accounts reveal the uncertainty involved in being called. One preacher's words are illustrative:

> I now relate to you the exercise of my mind: when I consider the worth of dear precious Souls, & how many there is exposed to everlasting fire, & without repentance must dwell in the gloomy vaults of Damnation. Oh! the thought pierces my inmost Soul: Something tells me to go & warn them to flee the wrath to come; something tells me not; & I hardly know which to obey: Sometimes I seem ready to give up all & go, & then considering my weakness, & present condition, it almost shocks me; and perhaps if you were to go, you would do more harm than good, stay till you have a plain signal call: and thus, I am exercised from day to day; something urgeing me to go, & something soliciting me to stay. In all I do I am determined to keep a single eye to GOD's Glory, and my prayer to GOD is, that I may like Samuel of old, be convinced & obey. I hope you are in health of body & soul, & rejoice to see the pleasure of the Lord prosper in your hands.[82]

As circuit riders reflected on and publicized their callings, they legitimized their travels to themselves and their hearers. They defined their moral value. A preacher's sense of being called, once approved by church leaders, launched itinerants into a career that included several regular travel practices: preaching, self-maintenance of health, devotional reading and prayer, and facing both rejection and acceptance from communities.

Unlike pure recreational travel, circuit life mixed official and personal facets. It was planned, disciplined, and scheduled. It was occupational too, as circuit riders sought to earn a living from their travels. Like recreational and occupational travel, the vocational travels of circuit riders brought a number of earthly rewards. Preachers gained the satisfaction of fulfilling their callings, and it stands to reason that for many preachers, the harder the conditions of travel, the greater the moral satisfaction. Preachers also gained respect as religious leaders. While they sometimes faced derision from competitors and the irreligious, those experiences strengthened bonds to the growing community of Methodist adherents and to the fraternity of current and former itinerant preachers. Finally, circuit travel provided a broad set of contacts in a variety of communities in the West. These networking opportunities were important for those preachers who exited the itinerancy for other professional pursuits. They were important for long-term itinerants as markers of their stature and influence in an emerging middle-class community in the West.

In areas of new settlement, where no circuit yet existed, circuit riders searched for Christian, and hopefully Methodist, families, which they formed into local societies.[83] They knitted together separate societies into a circuit, a process of social integration of the West. In 1840, Henry Smith recalled founding a new circuit in the Ohio country at the turn of the century. Although four decades removed from the events, his sketch demonstrates how preachers, as professional travelers, conducted their work in areas of new settlement. What emerges are patterns of sociability and communication. Circuit travel, especially among new settlements, required constant gathering of information about people and places. This was the case in autumn 1799 as Smith traveled east along the Ohio River and then up the valley of the Scioto River. His mission was to form a new circuit in the area. This was a journey of approximately three weeks. Perhaps because of the time that had passed, Smith did not comment at length about the physical conditions that he experienced, though he recalled one day when he "had a very intricate path, and indeed sometimes none at all."[84]

Smith's method for working the territory and locating settlers relied on conversation. His success—and the success of Methodist expansion—depended on his reception among the residents of the Scioto Valley. He asked for Methodists as he went and directed his course according to the intelligence he gathered. At times he received no information from people he encountered and simply moved on. Leads were often vague. He heard one day of "four or five Methodist families still higher up the creek, who had formed themselves into a society" and met regularly. Another time, he was "directed to a family where I could get some information." Yet, upon arrival he found a man who had no information for him even though his wife had once been a member of a Methodist society. After speaking with them and entering their home, Smith asked the man to call his family for prayer. He "gave them a short exhortation, and left them all in tears."[85] That moment of Christian society, a flash of fellowship in an isolated settlement, was apparently powerful, but its impact was limited to a small family and a short visit. Itinerants keenly remembered hearts tearfully melted in desolate settlements, and those scenes were used as evidence of the itinerancy's pioneering reach to the outermost homes. However, Smith's account also reveals how important a critical mass of settlers was for the planting of organized Methodism in an area.[86] The family's locale lacked the numbers to establish a class meeting, and the itinerant moved on, leaving the family behind. If the wife wanted to worship with other Methodists, she would have to travel to the closest group of believers, which meant negotiating the issues of gender and geography that bound travelers on the frontier.

Itinerants had greater success where a concentration of practicing Methodists preceded them. When Smith found Methodists, he made use of their networks of relatives and neighbors to announce his arrival. He scheduled and delivered sermons and made appointments for return visits. According to his memory, Smith's journey, which took him through a newly settled frontier area, revealed a remarkable degree of Christian sociability. The three-week journey added a new area to the Methodist circuit system, but Smith found it neither remote nor uncivilized—except for acquiring some vermin from sleeping on a host's bearskin. Along the way, he stayed with "a kind Presbyterian family" and was pleasantly surprised to reunite on three occasions with Maryland Methodists. On ten separate occasions, he encountered Methodists, and the number of Methodists in each group increased as his journey progressed. Smith met a family he had known from his travels in Kentucky and a retired itinerant who had once preached in his father's house.[87]

Smith's was a humble but respectable tour in a newly settled area. He was long-suffering and searching as he fulfilled his call to deliver the Gospel. Relations with those he encountered were cordial. The domestic circumstances he observed were meager but bore marks of middling civility. One poor couple brought out their fine white linens, and the wife received him with the same care she showed her husband. People generally welcomed Smith. He recalled no instances of rebuke or dismissal. He was a bearer of religion, but as he saw it, he also represented a form of respectable civilization. However, Smith's recollection came from the distance of four decades and was only one version of circuit travel.[88] Smith's account of founding the Scioto circuit was pulled from distant memory, a curated view of the past, but it provides a clear description of how itinerants worked a territory. It also suggests the aspirations of western Methodism as a mission of Christian civilization primarily to white settlers rather than a civilizing mission to Native Americans—and decades before the task was pursued by agents of northern benevolence such as Lyman Beecher and Horace Bushnell and the many institutions behind them.

Men like Smith, Blackman, Lakin, and even Cartwright were more complex than frontier myth allowed. They contemplated and fashioned their identities as religious men while traveling the West, drawing on an Anglo-American metaphor of holy pilgrimage. But itinerancy delivered worldly benefits. If itinerancy restricted preachers' options in the short term, it expanded them for their later careers. Itinerant travel, inside and outside the bounds of secure white settlement, brought a variety of experiences, which broadened itinerants as much as it constrained them. This provided a level of worldliness to religious leaders, and that helped them forge careers beyond preaching. If circuit riders' worldliness was in tension with their desire to be set apart from the world as pilgrims, it did not hinder their lives as settlers. Their travels allowed them to observe and critique settler society but also to understand and exploit it. Beyond a form of labor, itinerant travel brought contacts with others and allowed for the creation of bonds. These bonds amounted to a social network for middling folk with Methodist commitments. That social network remained active as Methodists from the Mid-Atlantic and South moved southwest or northwest, and it served as an avenue for both spiritual and material activities.

3

THE SOCIAL PRINCIPLE

Settlement Networks and Sacred Capital in the Trans-Appalachian West

Bishop Francis Asbury regularly passed through Chillicothe, Ohio. He was familiar with the surrounding area and praised its features. He admired its fertility. The Scioto River Valley was "generally rich," and Paint Creek surrounded by "fat lands." He wondered over the spirituality of the land. Quoting Joseph Addison's *Cato,* he judged that "shadows, clouds, and darkness rest" upon the nearby Native American earthworks. But Asbury also knew that Methodists and other Christians from the East flooded these river valleys, making southern Ohio a place of sacred change. Methodist erasure of Native possession was not simple forgetting; they interrogated, criticized, and condemned Native symbols.[1] Cultural destruction complemented the network construction that was the power of Methodist settlement. The sacred capital produced by the Methodist social principle helped white settlers in their quest to supplant Native sacralization of the land with their own vision and structure of Christian possession. Through their religious networks coursed news of land, work, and courtship, making them settlement networks.

Asbury thought much about the land, and in Jefferson's empire he was clearly not alone. When Asbury visited Chillicothe, he lodged with Edward Tiffin, variously a physician, Methodist local preacher, Ohio governor, and land official. There Asbury found accommodations far more comfortable than normal: "O what a charming view presents itself from Doctor Tiffin's house! But these long talks about land and politics suit me not; I take little interest in either subject: O Lord, give me souls, and keep me holy!"[2] "These long talks" were the social principle that Methodism sought to channel toward holiness but could not shield from worldly affairs. In Asbury's mind, perhaps no more powerful combination threatened to turn Christians away from God and toward local interests than that of land, employment, politics, and marriage. These were the root and stuff of Anglo-American settler society. Asbury's words summarized his persistent concern that worldliness and localism would corrupt orthodox Methodism's singular and phenomenally successful mission of saving souls. As his fears suggest, the Methodist system in the West did more than lift sinners to heaven. For many of its members and especially its leaders, it brought white settlers into a complex social network, a web of relationships that included other Methodist itinerants and local preachers, laity, and all the varied associates that active, public figures might encounter on a commercializing frontier. It provided social capital, whether Asbury liked it or not. This was the other side of the Methodist social principle.

The social principle was at the core of Methodism. The principle's worldly value for settlers was not Methodism's mission, but it was a prime result. The social principle worked through the itinerancy. Especially important was correspondence with presiding elders, the bishops' officers who presided over districts of circuits. Presiding elders had many contacts because of their years on preaching circuits and in denominational meetings. They regularly corresponded with the duos of preachers serving on circuits in their districts. If a district contained five circuits, then the presiding elder was to receive reports from ten preachers at various times throughout that year. Information flowed to and from elders because of their position in the Methodist network, and that information included secular news nearly as often as religious.

It is true that most settlers exchanged news about prospects for land, employment, and marriage—those were among the chief concerns in propagating settler society—but Methodists exchanged such missives within the nation's largest religious network, a network specifically designed to circulate news, albeit the Good News. The itinerancy—the nation's largest person-to-person religious institution—was an efficient medium of reportage in part because it overlay and amplified common social ties. Itinerant connections merged with family connections; not uncommonly, Christian brothers and sisters were also biological or legal brothers and sisters or nieces and nephews. The itinerancy and the social principles coursing through it were also highly adaptable to different regional contexts. For example, Methodists long held a range of opinions about slavery, and Methodist networks benefited affiliated settlers in similar ways no matter their individual stances on the evil of slavery. The itinerancy produced antislavery social capital in the Old Northwest just as it produced slavery social capital in the Old Southwest. The institution of slavery did push some Methodists to the Old Northwest and pulled others to the Old Southwest. On arrival, the standard functions of the Methodist network were adaptable to different regional contexts. In turn, the itinerancy itself gained footholds in areas because of preachers' connections with society and took advantage of existing settler networks.

Asbury wanted Methodism to save the West from the dark past he associated with Indigenous culture and replace it with Christian holiness. He accomplished neither. Just as Native Americans would not relinquish their cultural ties to the land, neither would white settlers sway from the spirit of settlement. The MEC brought to the trans-Appalachian West the kinds of connections that created the Empire of Liberty on the ground.

Communication Networks, Literacy, and Itinerants

Methodism appealed to a broad range of people for a diverse set of reasons, but when individuals joined Methodism all of them came to an evangelical movement bent on spreading information, both spiritual and material.[3] Circuit riders established networks, and through them flowed personal news and gossip, geographic intelligence, and the emotional bonds of spiritual brotherhood and sisterhood. The result was not entirely different from the European Republic of Letters, though the correspondence was not limited to science, the participants generally not elite, and the scope not transatlantic. As in the Republic of Letters, which was so valuable for many of its participants precisely because they lacked local scientific societies, Methodists built and relied on their own communications networks in the years before local institutions gained a broad foothold in the West.[4] More immediately, the networks of Methodism were among the earliest forms of voluntary associations in the rural West. They were the grounding of one of the largest institutions of the early republic. They were also precursors of the formal organizations that Alexis de Tocqueville so famously identified with America. Historians of early American civil society have worked to recover the finer threads of the early American social fabric, noting the unexpected social and political importance of churches, academies, colleges, fraternal organizations, fire companies, library societies, dancing schools, and more. Not enough has been said of Methodism given that its eventual size and importance made it, in John C. Calhoun's words, one of the "cords that bind the States together."[5]

Methodist associationalism—*connectionalism,* to use their term—impacted high politics, but it was deeply local in the West, and its social functions were often not tied tightly to formal or informal politics.[6] Correspondence networks were particularly important amid frequent migration and high mobility. Literacy was a possession that brought some people together while excluding others, making it ultimately a form of "invisible" power. Manuscript letter-writing was a technology itself, and like other technologies was subject to social divisions and problems of access.[7] Although distance was very real for people living amid frequent migration, religion and literacy were useful antidotes. As one Methodist put it, brothers and sisters in Christ "must submit & rejoice in a literary intercourse."[8]

Communication was crucial to the functions of the Methodist organization, and it was much more than the shouts and groans associated with revival meetings. Neither inarticulate nor overly emotional, Methodists were astute, busy communicators who used a number of forms, from intimate conversation, prayer, and public sermon to manuscript and print.[9] Methodist social networks that relied on manuscript letters were more sophisticated than often assumed.[10] Those networks were profoundly important to the work of evangelicalism and the formation of social capital.

Methodist connectionalism provided relationships that individuals valued in pursuit of both spiritual edification and worldly goals. At the same time, these relationships exposed individuals to social and organizational forms of discipline amid ecclesiastical and personal hierarchies. The key intersection of the ecclesiastical and the personal was in the role of presiding elder. All Methodist clergy communicated information through the network, but presiding elders especially combined the years of experience and relationship-building in a midlevel position that connected local societies to the top of the hierarchy. This communication structure made Methodism more than a theology or ideology, the two characteristics historians have often emphasized. Historians have explained that the achievement of the itinerant system was to spread Arminian theology, which emphasized individual choice and constituted a democratizing ideology unrivaled in the early republic.[11] They demonstrate that oral forms of communication, especially hymns, were central to this Methodist evangelical phenomenon, which ultimately influenced other popular denominations and recast the character of American Protestantism. This argument captures essential and powerful features of nineteenth-century evangelism. Yet, it deemphasizes the structural attributes that defined the MEC.[12] Most individuals experienced the disciplinary pressures of Methodism voluntarily, and because the Methodist system of social networks overlapped with other social networks, especially through the presiding elders, they found access to an array of opportunities.

Networks of Religion and Settlement in the Old Northwest and Old Southwest

Methodist networks expanded into the trans-Appalachian West as part of the settler colonization of the region. Indigenous groups challenged that movement, many confederating their power to stymie settler expansion and the genocidal potential undergirding it.[13] The trans-Appalachian West came under settler possession in a contest with Native power and resistance stretching into the antebellum years. Methodist settlers were not trailblazers; they inhabited pockets of the Mississippi watershed as they were taken from Indigenous nations. As Methodists moved into the West after its securitization, they formed networks that served religion and settlement.

The Ohio country beckoned migrants after the middle 1790s. To the minds of antislavery Methodists, the prohibition of slavery by the Northwest Ordinance of 1787 christened the region for settlement. From the beginning, plans for land development and settlement were not always stable, but Federalists determined to secure the Ohio country with military power. After two defeats of American armies by Native armies, the overwhelming campaign by General Anthony Wayne and the resulting Treaty of Greenville in 1795 incentivized migrants.[14] Five years later, there were 45,365 Americans in Ohio, and over the next decade that number increased more than 400 percent to 230,760.[15]

Upland southerners, some from Virginia, some Kentucky, constituted a large portion of that increase. Those migrants brought Methodism to southern Ohio, where it flourished. Methodist social relations connected individuals and created communities despite the disruptions of migration. Virginians especially headed to fertile valleys west of the Scioto River in the bounds of the Virginia Military District. Eight years after the area opened for settlement in 1790, Philip Gatch, the first in a group of Methodists from neighboring counties in southeastern Virginia and one of the revolutionary-era American Methodist itinerants, migrated to the Little Miami River in southwestern Ohio. Over the next decade, other Methodists from eastern Virginia made the same journey as Gatch. Taken together, they constituted a communal migration in which the bonds of Methodist identity linked individuals and families across the distance from Virginia to Ohio.[16]

In 1796, to accommodate Methodists migrating under the protection of the Greenville Treaty line, the MEC created a new annual conference of itinerant preachers dubbed the Western Conference. The Western Conference was vast, containing all the settled lands west of the Allegheny Mountains, including outposts in the Illinois and Mississippi countries. Much like the large early territories of the United States, the Western Conference subdivided as it filled with people. After 1811, the Ohio Conference comprised the northeastern portion of Kentucky and all circuits north of the Ohio River and west of the Alleghenies, including the headwaters of the Ohio in western Pennsylvania and circuits in the Indiana Territory along the Ohio River.[17] By 1820, Kentucky was organized into its own conference, thus shifting the lower boundary of the Ohio Conference north to the river. By 1821, the Ohio Conference added a circuit in Detroit, stretching its northern boundary. The membership of the Ohio Conference, comprising full-time itinerants who had served a trial and passed examination, constituted the leadership of the Methodist network in Ohio. In 1812, 44 traveling preachers served 23,284 members in society. In 1820, 61 preachers ministered to 34,178 members.[18]

Methodism also expanded to the lower Mississippi Valley. It was propelled by the wave of Anglo-American migration and settlement unleashed after the American Revolution. The United States acquired the Natchez country from Spain in 1798 (fulfilling the 1795 Treaty of San Lorenzo), and the following year the first Methodist itinerant arrived. Some in the Old Southwest had experienced Methodist preaching in their earlier eastern lives, but the MEC had no institutional presence. That presence came through the MEC's adaptation of family networks already existing along the Mississippi. The results—a denomination with an enduring presence in settlers' lives—constituted a form of social capital. In the Old Southwest, two particular social networks benefited Methodism as an institution and Methodists as middling settlers. The first network surrounded the early missionary and South Carolinian Tobias Gibson. To establish a Methodist foothold Gibson drew on family ties to early migrants who became prominent slaveholders around Natchez.[19] The second network reveals the workings of the Methodist itinerancy in the 1820s, when slavery and cotton production transformed a borderland peopled by Spanish, French, British, and southeastern Indians into a hierarchical Anglo-American settler society. This second case is seen through a correspondence network between itinerant William Winans and his Methodist associates. Both cases reveal the fundamental importance of social exchange to the fate of Methodism and more broadly to middling society in the developing Old Southwest.

Methodism entered the Old Southwest on the eve of the nineteenth century and increased in membership over the next three decades. As in other regions, the circuit system touched many areas of settlement but thrived numerically in pockets. The town of Natchez, for instance, was notoriously hard ground for growing the church. During the first years of MEC work in the Natchez District, membership was limited to scattered extended families and their acquaintances. Sixty white settlers in 1800 constituted the Natchez Circuit, the label affixed to the settlements from the 31st Parallel (the southern border of the Southwest Territory) north to the communities of the Walnut Hills (near the area later dubbed

Vicksburg) in which Methodism's first missionary formed societies.[20] Within ten years of entering the area, the MEC had organized the Mississippi District, which comprised 4 circuits of 360 people (263 white and 97 Black). By 1820, the Mississippi District, along with the Alabama and Louisiana Districts, fell under the umbrella of the Mississippi Annual Conference (organized in 1817 from the Tennessee Conference). The conference as a whole in 1820 served over 2,600 Methodists clustered across the lower drainage of the Gulf of Mexico. By 1830, the 5 regular districts of the conference had grown to 16,012 white (11,765) and Black (4,247) Methodists. In 1830, the MEC membership outranked other denominations in most counties in the states of Mississippi and Alabama and reflected the socioeconomic and racial diversity of the Old Southwest.[21]

The MEC saw the Mississippi Valley as one more field in a national missionary enterprise and thus supplied the structure, motivation, and personnel to gain a foothold in the region. Methodism's expansion benefited at first from previously established social networks. It then developed its own networks, which helped to facilitate the accumulation of social capital. Finally, the social networks that Methodism engendered were the source of the organization's enduring presence in the region. Methodist social networks were not strictly religious, and that explains their strength. They encompassed ties of shared theological and moral beliefs, blood relations, fictive kinship, and worldly connections such as business relationships.

Another way to put it is that Methodist networks were settlement networks, and the same was true in Ohio. The lay membership of Ohio's Methodist societies, much like those in the Southwest, was socially and economically diverse. At any time before 1830 some Methodists lived in frontier areas and others lived in settled villages or towns, including the burgeoning hub of Cincinnati. Ohio Methodism included figures who were notable in their local communities in southern Ohio or in state politics. Early Ohio governors Edward Tiffin, Thomas Worthington, and Allen Trimble were identified with the Methodists. Tiffin was a licensed local preacher and deacon. Former Virginia itinerants like Thomas Scott of Chillicothe and Phillip Gatch of Clermont County had served in Ohio's first state constitutional convention and continued in careers as judges. Other Methodists like Thomas Spotswood Hinde and Nathaniel Massie were active land speculators. Massie himself founded Chillicothe and organized much of the land in southwestern Ohio. In addition to their political lives, Worthington and Tiffin were deeply involved in the land affairs of the booming state. At various times, Methodists also ran printing presses and published newspapers in the towns of the Scioto and Miami River Valleys. Most notable among this group was John McLean, who published the *Western Star* before selling his press in Lebanon, Ohio, to his brother and a Methodist itinerant in order to embark on a career of law and public administration that took him to the US Supreme Court. Longtime circuit rider William Burke was Cincinnati's postmaster for more than a decade.

While this list is not exhaustive, it is also not meant to overstate the prestige of Methodism's membership. Thomas Worthington and John McLean were not successful simply because they were Methodists. Most Methodists, whether laypersons or itinerants, never attained wealth or office. The key fact is that Methodism in Ohio had a complex settler profile, one that included individuals of unremarkable means but also a number of notable professional and public figures. These latter figures too were scattered throughout the southwestern region of Ohio. Methodist membership did, however, bring individuals into networks that included prominent people and news of wide concern, such as politics or economic opportunities. For those who wanted it, Methodist associational life offered social capital, and information—whether of church administration or worldly opportunity—was a useful currency for gaining that social capital.

Throughout the West, itinerants and their peers benefited from the information that traveling preachers gathered along their circuits. The frequency of Methodist travel in the itinerant system systematized exchanges of information. Itinerants covered their circuits roughly once per month and kept prescheduled appointments. They also presided over quarterly meetings of each circuit, which gathered local Methodist leaders and other worshippers together in conversations and camp-meeting activities. In addition, itinerants congregated for meetings of the annual conference. Finally, they exchanged letters to address matters of circuit business that could not wait on a quarterly or annual meeting.

If circuit travel and preaching were the direct modes of evangelizing the unregenerate and ministering to the Methodist membership, epistolary networks were a crucial part of the structure that made that work possible. The logistics of organizing preachers and distributing resources throughout the year to cover the circuits of the Ohio and Mississippi Conferences occurred largely through handwritten letters. As itinerants traveled their circuits, they updated presiding elders about the status of those circuits. They communicated with other itinerant preachers and supportive laypeople about gathering resources for their preaching circuits. Presiding elders especially funneled and redistributed information through the itinerancy. Over the first three decades of the nineteenth century, the forms of communication did not change greatly. This is significant because the early nineteenth century, mainly after 1815, hosted a communications revolution built on internal improvements and communications technology.[22] Methodism certainly benefited from those developments, but the core of its primacy in religious expansion was the network organization and forms of manuscript and oral communication that extended from the eighteenth century.

Methodist Migration from the Southside of Virginia to Southern Ohio

By reconstructing two migrations from Virginia to Ohio, we can recover the subtle ways Methodists used communications to build social capital. It also allows us to contextualize certain Methodists' choice of Ohio as their destination. Because the Northwest Ordinance restricted slavery in Ohio, Methodist settlers found the area an ethical destination, and that stood in contrast to those Methodists who migrated southwest. In reality, some settlers found means to extend the bondage of slavery into the Northwest, but that did not stop these Methodists from considering Ohio an antislavery paradise, especially contrasted to Virginia, Kentucky, and the southwestern territories.[23] When they wrote of antislavery, the language of their correspondence approached eloquence. However, eloquent language can make too much about slavery as a factor in their migration and settlement. These Southside Virginia Methodists wrote more frequently about the mundane benefits pulling them north of the Ohio River than about the unfree institution pushing them. If they left Virginia in part to separate from slavery, they did not dissociate from Methodists who held slaves. By tracing the Methodist movement out of Virginia, we can understand the full range of their motivations.

Methodist networks began to develop in the Southside counties of Brunswick and Sussex in the early 1770s.[24] Between 1774 and 1777, the number of circuits in Southside rose from 2 to 6, and membership jumped from 291 to 4,049.[25] The key point is that the men and women behind these numbers were joined institutionally and regionally. Meeting frequently as classes in each other's homes, Methodists formed bonds based on affection and norms of discipline and respectability. The process continued at watch nights and love feasts. Local sociability carried over into the quarterly meetings that gathered members from a larger area. Thus, Methodists formed relationships beyond the local level and, importantly, pursued a range of interactions from collective worship to discussions of personal business. Some meetings were open to other Christians, but they generally regulated entrance by requiring tickets and holding to rigorous standards of personal morality. The result was bonding social capital—networks linking similar people and benefiting insiders.[26] Those bonds held as westward movement uprooted people.

The striking persistence of Methodist connections over distance is seen in a cache of letters to early Methodist itinerant and Virginia slaveholder Edward Dromgoole Sr., who remained in Virginia as many of his fellow Methodists moved west.[27] Generally, the Virginians migrated to Ohio in groups. Philip Gatch traveled with thirty-six people, white and Black.[28] Settling near the Little Miami River, they immediately joined a Methodist society, the first in Ohio, which had been recently established by migrants from Kentucky.[29] Within six years of Gatch's arrival, more than five families, including the Bonners and Sales, arrived from Dinwiddie County, Virginia, forming the Union settlement on the Mad River circuit, not far from Gatch.[30] Like Gatch, several of the men in this group were active Methodist preachers in southeastern Virginia and the broader Chesapeake and were friends of the Dromgooles of Brunswick County. When additional migrants such as Samuel Pelham and his family arrived in the spring of 1807, the area had a strong Methodist presence.[31]

Important pieces of the migrants' former lives remained in Virginia. The Dromgoole family stayed in Brunswick County, and most of what we know about this Methodist migration results from Edward Dromgoole Sr.'s decision to keep his family there. Over the years, the Bonners and Sales, Gatches and Pelhams all corresponded with the Dromgooles, fathers with fathers, mothers with mothers, and so on, attempting to close the distance among them, which they measured in emotion and mileage. The correspondence weaved together an extended set of relationships embracing friendship, partnerships in land development, and the knitting together of community locally and far away. They wrote to their friends and loved ones about relationships and building new lives. They discussed their emotions, maintaining the web of spiritual brotherhood and sisterhood, and they formed a network of information exchange that focused on the land.

Entreating Dromgoole to migrate, his Methodist brothers explained the benefits of Ohio. Philip Gatch related details of the land before many of the other migrants arrived. "The Countrey is Beautiful in its situation," wrote Gatch, "and promices every advantage I believe that any Country in this Wourld can do."[32] Streams and rivers were plentiful; he had seen at least a dozen mills on the Little Miami, and several of the other tributaries in the area hosted good mills and promised opportunities for trade. Gatch not only described his own observations of the abundant water resources but relayed to Virginia the intelligence he gathered from others in the area. Three years later, Gatch still provided Dromgoole information. Gatch explained that Ohio's lands were productive if people were willing to work them without slaves, which he preferred while some Virginia migrants did not.[33] When John Sale wrote in 1807, he described the Ohio River as the "American Nile," down which Dromgoole might sell the agricultural goods he could take in as a merchant in the area. Dromgoole operated a store on his plantation, and Sale sketched out the possibilities for transferring that livelihood to Ohio. Goods were receivable from suppliers in Baltimore and Philadelphia, and Dromgoole could rely on a cash business and exchanges with eastern merchants, or he could trade mercantile goods for produce with the region's agriculturalists and profit from downriver markets.[34]

When Edward Dromgoole Jr. visited Ohio in June 1807, he too leveraged Methodist connections and reported to his parents on the state of the land. In Chillicothe, he lodged with Edward Tiffin, a Methodist and

Ohio's first governor. Tiffin was not only an influential Methodist and political leader; he was a busy land developer. Droomgoole Jr. queried Tiffin on tracts of land and sought meetings with other important figures in land sales. As he passed through the new state from east to west, Dromgoole was surprised by the land's high quality. One old friend seemed content never to see the lands of Virginia again. The younger Dromgoole passed through the Quaker settlements in Highland County and considered the lands nearby, but he favored Greene County for its healthfulness, accessible water, and the ease with which he could live in the Methodist community already formed there. He planned to "close a bargain for land[.] the tract contains 450 acres has two log cabbins on it and about 16 acres clear. One of the houses is very good has two Rooms below stairs. It also has a good spring."[35] The capital of Methodist networks was on display here. Methodist bonds amplified the family bonds between parents and son in the work of land acquisition and settlement.

From Virginia, Edward Dromgoole Sr. maintained a strong interest in Ohio lands and queried Methodists he knew in the area. From Frederick Bonner he learned of the variations in Ohio's geography and the risks of purchasing from a distance. With such information Dromgoole could avoid the surprises early settlers encountered as they purchased lands from Virginia that disappointed on arrival. Bonner also noted that immigration was increasing. In his few years there, he had watched as the country around him increased from "30 or 40 families" to "3 or 400 now setled & yet there is room." Immigration was a boon for trade, but a buyer had to be careful of the market: "Lands are rising." Prospects were sufficiently good to make inexplicable to Bonner Dromgoole's hesitation to leave a land of slavery. If Dromgoole wanted a sign, Ohio was it, a place provided by God "for the Vertuous sons of the Eastern States." Dromgoole's Methodist friends occasionally disagreed with his remaining amid slavery, but that ethical issue did not significantly hinder their social networking.[36]

Dromgoole's land agent and fellow Methodist Peter Pelham exerted the greatest pull. Within days of settling in Greene County, Pelham consulted John Sale and Frederick Bonner about a list of tracts that had drawn Dromgoole's attention. They reviewed the list, advising on quality and against tracts lacking clear title or under claim. Sale would consult Nathaniel Massie, one of the area's original surveyors, during his upcoming trip to Chillicothe. Pelham planned to move quickly to purchase land for Dromgoole. He also intended to purchase for himself some available lots in Xenia, "a growing Town, about 2½ miles from me," and offered to conduct similar transactions for Dromgoole. Dromgoole might also prosper, as Pelham advised, by establishing a mercantile store outside of the town to serve the area's inhabitants and avoid competition with the store already operating there. Competition in business was present, and immigration was raising commodity prices, all of which Dromgoole learned through his Methodist network.[37]

The bonds of affection between these Methodists created the network through which Dromgoole received information regarding Ohio geography. On the same day that Peter Pelham sat to catalog and pass on his observations to Dromgoole, another of Dromgoole's correspondents drafted a reply to a list of twenty-six questions he had received from the Virginian. The writer addressed the items he felt qualified to answer and noted that some were not pertinent. "The tools of husbandry," he counseled, "differ considerably from those generally in the lower part of Virga," a difference that "arrises principally from climate & soil." Greater surpluses came from less labor, a familiar comment on slavery. Cereals grew better than "indian corn" compared to in Kentucky, but corn could be bought. The writer addressed more than the agricultural: "The manners of the citizens differ much," and the state, he felt, was a "compleat mongrel both in manners & religion." But he was pleased with Ohio, which was continually developing, both in agriculture and in small industry.[38]

The author understood Dromgoole's method for gaining intelligence. He had used it himself. Dromgoole inquired of the men he knew, as his correspondent put it, to "gather from several & from different parts of the State" a profile of the country. The travels of his informants—with several being Methodist itinerants, they traveled often—provided a supply of information covering a variety of the state's parts, but the correspondent noted that it might also present conflicting opinions. Ultimately, Dromgoole would have to sort the reports according to his own criteria.[39]

The Pelham family continued to form an important connection for the Dromgooles. Exchanges of credit and debt and the bonds of Methodist society intertwined their lives. They mingled family economies as they updated one another on their health and achievements. Before describing the new home he was building, Samuel Pelham instructed Edward Dromgoole Jr. to bring with him on an autumn visit the cash he had recently collected on a Virginia debt owed to Pelham. He also asked Dromgoole to pay a bond for Bennett Maxey, another Greene County resident and former Virginia Methodist, to a man in Richmond. Pelham then described a short chain of debts through which the debt created by the bond payment would pass in order to reach Edward Dromgoole Sr. In short, Samuel Pelham's Richmond bond would be paid by the head of the Dromgoole household to discharge debt he owed the head of the Pelham household for purchases of Ohio lands.[40] Methodism brought efficiency and trust to this financial network.

Edward Dromgoole Sr. received more than information and credit from Peter Pelham. Pelham oversaw the lands he purchased for Dromgoole. In November 1807, he reported that Dromgoole's tenant had left the property and that he could not collect the rent. The tenant had ventured out to prepare a permanent home eighty miles away. Because of the tenant's absence, squirrels had destroyed the corn he had left behind, so it could not be sold to cover the rent, and worse, the ground had not been prepared for the following season.[41] The following March, Pelham received "applications" but had trouble renting the land.[42] Problems were predictable, but Methodist connections allowed Dromgoole to hold productive property in one of the growing settler nation's most desirable areas.

Despite the benefits of the Ohio country and the voices that beckoned him there, Edward Dromgoole Sr. never left Virginia. He visited but never resided on the tracts he owned. Many factors likely influenced his decision: inertia; a sense of the difficulty of picking up and starting anew; the comforts of Virginia, where he was successful; a dependence on slaves; the lack of a clear sign from Providence, as he interpreted it. His friends did not understand why he stayed, but their help allowed him to gather the fruits of settlement in both states. George Washington had used military service and development companies; Dromgoole used Methodism.

For all his ties to Ohio, he felt pressure from other corners. James Keys, another Methodist, who lived in middle Tennessee, had thoughts of returning to Virginia or North Carolina near the Dromgooles. He expressed his hope that they would stay in Brunswick County, where he might enjoy their company after his move.[43] Philip Gatch had felt pressure from neighbors not to migrate, but he was undeterred. Dromgoole's decision makes clear that Methodists weighed migration differently. Nonetheless, connections between the families persisted. Peter Pelham, for example, continued to manage Dromgoole's lands, and they all hoped for reunion in this world or the next.[44]

The mechanics of religious social network formation helped individuals adjust to the migration experience. While in the Southeast, Methodist relationships gave itinerants some independence from local credit networks, which freed them to criticize their economic betters.[45] The correspondence of Edward Dromgoole shows how Methodist connections were important in settlement. They facilitated for settlers nonlocal credit networks and avenues of exchange over great distances. Even more, this was the case for one who never moved to Ohio. Without relocating, Dromgoole settled Ohio in terms of business, as a landowner and landlord. Virginia slavery connected to Methodist settlement in Ohio through Dromgoole. His productivity and financial capital in the Upper South, based on real property and slaves acquired through marriage and others purchased later, was the base from which his concerns extended north of the Ohio River, and Methodist ties made an excellent mode of exchange.

Settler Networks and the Missionary Enterprise of Tobias Gibson in the Old Southwest

Traditionally, Methodists began their Mississippi story with the "heroic" missionary Tobias Gibson.[46] Sickly and still shy of thirty years old on January 1, 1799, the preacher received instructions to travel from his native South Carolina to the settlements of the Natchez country. Methodist memorialists often cast Gibson's mission as a lonely errand to a wilderness that made him a martyr, but the preacher did not simply leave all and follow his savior. He "had one advantage over any other minister of the Methodist Episcopal Church ... an intelligent, wealthy, and influential family connection—who had preceded him many years before from South Carolina" and "by whom he was cordially received and most hospitably entertained."[47] This was likely the prominent settler Samuel Gibson from South Carolina. From the beginning, the expansion of Methodism in Mississippi was based on relationships within settlement networks.[48] Again one can see the overlapping of family and religious institution in settler networks, as Methodism amplified the processes of settlement.

Southern settler society was built on landholding and slaveholding, and that was also true of Methodism in the Southwest. Parts of the Gibson clan migrated to the Lower Mississippi Valley during its British possession in the late eighteenth century.[49] In the Natchez country, the Gibsons preceding Tobias were citizens of substance in multiple communities. In the year Tobias arrived, for example, Samuel Gibson was named among the "Justices of the Peace and of the Court of Common Pleas" for Pickering (later Jefferson) County. Three years later, he was named the first coroner of Claiborne County, after its division from Jefferson.[50] Gibson's offices were expected of a man of significant property. He received multiple land grants, beginning in the Spanish period, and was the namesake of Port Gibson, the seat of Claiborne County, due to his donating the land for the early thriving town. At the end of Samuel Gibson's life, on the eve of Mississippi statehood, he was among the largest slaveowners in Claiborne County. Beyond Samuel, across the surrounding counties lay an extended family of Gibsons. Most of them owned slaves, ranging from three to twenty-three enslaved people.

Methodism's pioneer network thus primarily encompassed settlers who, before Mississippi left its territorial phase, attained positions in the slaveholding class. Many were small slaveholders, and a few, including Samuel Gibson, already owned enough enslaved people to rank as a large slaveholder by the later standards of 1860.[51] Put another way, when Tobias Gibson arrived, the region around Natchez was transforming from a frontier exchange economy to a substantial plantation economy based on exploitation of enslaved labor to work the land. Settlers acquired slaves through forced migration from the East and through domestic and international trade. Many of these white settlers were middling and rising—just the type that Methodism had attracted in other parts of the country. At that early date, the slaveholding class of the region was on the way to impressive wealth, and that growing wealth created cultural influence over the region's settler population.[52]

Through Tobias Gibson, that influence converted into social capital for the MEC. That Methodism did not immediately make rapid gains in the area does not discount the importance of Gibson's network.[53] It was a collaboration among settler families and the religious institution, and the foundation of the MEC's rise to primacy among Christian denominations in the state in the early republican period.[54]

Included among the Gibsons was the Reverend Randall Gibson, a local Baptist preacher, "so long and so favorably known in the counties of Adams, Jefferson, Claiborne, and Warren." Cooperating with Randall, Tobias planted Methodism in Washington, the future territorial capital. Tobias drew his cousin from the Baptists. Randall was a man of local reputation and religious sensibilities. After he answered Tobias's call, others followed, including Tobias's wife, his sister, and a man from Pennsylvania who had heard Methodist preaching there. Two married couples joined in, one white (William Foster and his wife) and one Black (whose names were not recorded). Called the "original eight," this was one of the first Methodist societies formed in the Natchez country. A third cluster of Gibsons lived in southern Warren County, near Warrenton.[55] Parts of the Gibson family rose to prominence in antebellum southern society. When Tobias arrived they constituted a network of slaveholding, landowning kin. Their locations were beneficial. Approximately fifty miles separated Washington and the Walnut Hills settlements (near the future Vicksburg). Port Gibson lay between, near the halfway point. The itinerant had family in each location, and each area was important for settlers who increasingly filled the hinterlands of Natchez. It was just the context that benefited the establishment of Methodism, for Tobias had well-placed supporters, and in winning them over, he did not have to vie seriously against Protestant Episcopal or Presbyterian influences, which would have appealed to members of a wealthier, more urbane family. The Methodist itinerancy quickly gained a network of sponsors from an established settler family.

The function of kinship connections can be seen in the case of Gibson's presiding at the wedding of Jonathan Jones and Phebe Griffing, the daughter of John Griffing, in October 1799. This case also displays the crucial role of gender and women's contributions—often erased in sources—in Methodist networking. John Griffing was the head of a family of New Jersey migrants who settled along the Natchez Trace in a settlement called Selsertown, near the site of the Mississippian-era Emerald Mound. His grandson (also a Methodist preacher) described him as a man of "considerable property." The bride's family was a boon to Gibson and Methodism. The men and women of the Griffing family had hosted Gibson and supported his preaching at their home. In officiating the marriage of a daughter, Gibson received Griffing's stamp of approval, and the Griffing family became an influential hub in the early Methodist network.[56]

At least as important, he gained the backing of Penelope Griffing, John's wife. Methodist expansion depended on both sides of the patriarchal household. Penelope "had much to do in securing the services of Mr. Gibson as the pastor of her family . . . forming the first Methodist Church in the community where she lived." If the husband's interest in Methodist spirituality was lukewarm, Penelope's was hot—and influential within their family. (Other female relatives were apparently in line with Penelope.) Six of the nine Griffing children became Methodists. One of those who did not was Phebe. She identified formally as a Baptist, likely because she married one in Jonathan Jones, but she held to Arminian beliefs and welcomed Methodist preachers in her own home. Four of her own children became Methodists. Two of them were itinerants.[57]

Women's contributions to Methodist networks were erased by many sources. That, in turn, misrepresented the role of gender in forging ties between Methodism and settlement. Phebe Griffing's marriage reveals those dynamics. As preacher, Gibson sanctified the linkage of two settler networks through marriage, fastening together the wealth and social capital symbolized by heads of household like John Griffing. The marriage confirmed the patriarchal social structure. However, Penelope Griffing held significant sway within her family, and here Methodism's success depended on winning her support. Penelope supplied the MEC with the bridge to a new generation, who in turn supported Methodism logistically.

Penelope also supplied the bridge to another settlement network in a different part of Mississippi. The Griffing family reached beyond the bounds of Selsertown, and therefore so did the success of Tobias Gibson.

Penelope Griffing, like her husband, was a native of Morris County, New Jersey. She was the granddaughter of the Reverend Samuel Swayze, a Congregationalist minister who in 1772, along with his brother Richard, acquired and settled nearly twenty thousand acres near the Homochitto River to the southeast of Natchez. Samuel was a leader of the Mississippi community known as the Jersey Settlement or Kingston. Gibson's reception among a traditionally Congregationalist family was credited to his "elevated talents, genial manners, and overflowing Christian love and zeal," which appealed to people "accustomed to an educated and refined ministry."[58] Methodist memoirs routinely explained Methodist successes through the personal charisma of preachers. However, from a social network perspective, the connection through an influential kinswoman was at least as important and surely provided the impetus.

The Jersey Settlement in the following years was a steady base for Methodism, and as elsewhere it was founded on the devotion, "mostly of the leading ladies," of several of the original New Jersey settler families.[59] This connected Methodism to the sort of middling settlement that nineteenth-century observers praised for bringing a refined Protestant version of settler colonialism to the Southwest. In the words of J. F. H. Claiborne, the Jersey Settlement was settled "by men of intelligence, energy and high moral character" and "became prosperous and rich; densely populated; highly cultivated; distinguished for its churches and schools; its hospitality and refinement. And, in the course of years, it sent its thrifty colonies into many counties, carrying with them the characteristics of the parent hive."[60] "Thrifty colonies"—an apt phrase for the bourgeois Protestant settler colonialism that Methodism helped build and expand through the West.

The Griffing clan occupied a third area where Gibson promoted Methodism. John Griffing's brother Gabriel had settled in St. Albans along Big Black River, between Port Gibson and Vicksburg. Not only were John and Gabriel brothers but their wives, Penelope and Hannah, were sisters. Gibson's "success" among the Selsertown Griffings gave entrance to the Griffings of St. Albans. As had been the case with Penelope, Gibson found a partner in Hannah, another granddaughter of Samuel Swayze. She supplied the local pious energy and domestic logistical support on which Methodist itinerants depended.[61]

Tobias Gibson established Methodism's foundation in 1799 and 1800 by engaging resources from a broad network of Gibsons and Griffings. Race was bound to respectability in this burgeoning slave society. In the late eighteenth century, the Gulf South contained much racial diversity. A confluence of Atlantic and continental worlds, the region hosted enslaved Africans and Atlantic creoles; Native Americans of southern tribes and communities across the Mississippi watershed; and Europeans from the British, French, and Spanish Empires. By the time of Gibson's arrival, American settler society was beginning its attempt to subordinate that diversity under the rule of plantation hierarchy and whiteness. Methodism was a force of Anglo-American Protestantism in this context. There is suggestive evidence that Tobias Gibson was himself multiracial. Genealogists trace his family line through a Gideon Gibson of the lower Pee Dee region of South Carolina and further to Virginia. Some other accounts trace the lineage to England.[62] Several historians have been persuaded that Tobias's ancestors—some white, some Black, and some perhaps Native American—acquired Virginia land, relocated to South Carolina, and passed from Black to white in the middle eighteenth century.[63] The Gibson family generally passed as white, but suspicions occasionally emerged. Probably the most egregious was a later nineteenth-century political episode involving Randall Lee Gibson, a planter, Confederate general, and US senator from Louisiana.[64] But the question also concerned John Griffing Jones as he wrote the history of Mississippi Methodism. His terms resembled those traditionally used to describe the mixed-race Mulungeon peoples of the Southeast, who supposedly descended from Blacks, whites, and Indians; directly from ancient Phoenicians; or from Spanish and Portuguese refugees. While one historian has found little evidence that the Gibsons of Mississippi and Louisiana were aware of a mixed racial heritage, Jones felt the need in the nineteenth century to address the question.[65] "From their religious principles and tendencies," he wrote, "as well as physical characteristics, they are thought to be the lineal descendants of some of those noble Spanish and Portuguese families who preferred banishment from their country to a renunciation of their Protestant faith, and sought an asylum from persecution in the Carolinas at an early period of their colonial settlement. Be this plausible surmise as it may, many of the Gibsons, both men and women, including many of their descendants of other names, have been, and still are, among the most firm and devoted members of our Communion."[66] Gibson, therefore, was possibly a multiracial missionary leading the work of transforming the "mongrel" (to quote Jones) and Catholic-tinged Old Southwest into a white settler society supported by the Protestant consensus in the new United States. The settler population would embrace the view that respectability and multiracial heritage were in opposition. In that context, association with family members who owned land and slaves, held respected religious and civil offices, and were accepted as members of white settler society and the slaveholding class was important for Gibson's missionary work.

Gibson's travels conformed to and reinforced whiteness and settler respectability and weaved a thread through much of the settled area of the Natchez country. Another set of converts likely welcomed him into the area around Fort Adams, one of the southernmost regions of settlement before reaching the border with Louisiana.[67] His successes were examples of social capital at work. Connections among families, friends, and acquaintances not only wrapped Gibson in relationships; they were the fabric from which Methodism was sown in the Old Southwest. Methodism depended on preexisting social networks for its establishment in this new territory. Family relationships constituted many of the important ties in Gibson's network. Much as many frontier histories have celebrated an American spirit of individualism, so too did some versions of the missionary story of Tobias Gibson, who was said to face isolation and danger to advance Christian civilization. Yet without the reception of an existing social network, Gibson would have faced true isolation, and Methodism would have failed in Mississippi.

Correspondence, Aspiration, and Respectability in Early Republic Mississippi

Methodism thrived in Mississippi during the early republic. Mississippi was becoming a slaveholding settler society that produced extreme exploitive wealth and a white social hierarchy that accepted, if not the example of Christ, an emerging, normative Protestant consensus. A close look at the correspondence to circuit preacher William Winans from his colleague John Seaton shows how Methodists used their networks in that context. Winans was born in Pennsylvania and entered the ministry in Ohio. In Mississippi, he preached, married, acquired slaves, taught school, and over time participated in voluntary associations and Whig politics. His itinerant profession was the basis for all of that. Specifically, his itinerant network—constructed from personal visits and manuscript letter exchanges with a variety of men and women—undergirded his involvement in formal politics, educational institutions, and reform societies. He developed a network of correspondents who engaged him as a mentor on matters spiritual and temporal well before he achieved the presiding elder rank in 1822. This was an important way for experienced preachers to disseminate their influence among fellow Christians, both other preachers and laypeople. One of these was John Seaton. Winans was an important contact in Seaton's quest for respectability and rise into the slaveholding class. While camp-meeting sermons and exhortations were perfect tools for mass appeal, letters like those exchanged by Winans and Seaton formed and nurtured deeper, enduring bonds. Moreover, they allowed communication about sensitive matters of the world that were essential to settler business and common among Methodists. The Methodist itinerancy was a hierarchy. Preachers of short tenure served under men of experience. A portion of their communications comprised reports on circuit conditions, required by the itinerant system. As will later be seen in the example of James B. Finley of Ohio, a presiding elder received reports from preachers riding the circuits in his district. The itinerancy was also a social structure, providing opportunities to correspond beyond submitting official reports. Secular information was valuable, and therefore the quid pro quo of itinerant communications was valuable. For an aspiring, middling, but unsettled itinerant and for a senior and settled itinerant, news of the world in a thriving slave society brought opportunity, even entry or advancement in the slaveholding class. Detailed reconstruction of the Winans-Seaton relationship shows how day-to-day exchanges—coated with anxieties of aspiration and respectable masculine reputation—within the Methodist structure built social capital and advancement for settlers.

Valuing the "best of bonds" (love and mutual devotion to grace), Methodists could not compartmentalize the personal and the professional. Winans and Seaton were both colleagues and intimate acquaintances.

Their personal relationships included their wives and children, for where there were "brothers" in Methodism there were "sisters" and "fathers" and "mothers." Seaton's feelings for Winans and his family were anchored to their infrequent but cherished personal visits. A telling example was that Seaton occasionally battled illness in Winans's home under the "kind treatment" of Martha Winans.[68] Here again we see Methodist women maintaining an itinerancy that was self-styled a fraternity. Seaton was indebted to Winans for his family's hospitality, but he also honored his stature in the itinerancy. Winans never attained the rank of bishop but he was the sort of man who might. Thus, Seaton cultivated their friendship even while distance separated them. Of their correspondence Seaton wrote, "I can assure you, I do and ever shall esteem it one among the many sweets (which kind Heaven suffers to intermingle [with] the bitters of life)."[69] Aware they were not equals, he was self-conscious of his letters. Seaton, for example, felt restricted when he took up the pen, unable to convey "the thousand things and more which I would tell you if I could see you or had time to write and room to write."[70] He criticized his abilities but made clear he understood the requirements of good epistolary style. After closing one letter, he reviewed his work with apparent dissatisfaction: "I find it to be a droll performance."[71] Seaton not only expressed the anxieties of the correspondent; he signaled his appreciation for the norms of respectable communication.

Middling settlers commonly performed this dance, but Methodists felt they practiced an exceptional religion of the heart and it quickened their language. Although insecure in his contribution, Seaton expected Winans to uphold his side of the exchange. When Winans lagged, Seaton deployed the sentimental language that struck at the loving heart of Methodist connectionalism: "I believe yea am sure that it is not for the want of affection toward me altho I know my merit never deserved you[r] affection yet I believe you have graciously bestowed it on me[.] And my dear Bro. I do know that many waters cannot quench my love which I have for you neither can the floods drown it."[72] Resorting to the language of affection was a powerful tactic. Love was the language of Methodism's social contracts, and it remained so long after Methodism achieved success within the culture of southern masculinity. Importantly, Seaton's personal complaint was tied to official work. Immediately after chastising

Winans, he invited him to attend the next quarterly meeting of his circuit. As the assigned circuit preacher, Seaton oversaw all facets of those gatherings, which combined worship and church business. Securing the popular Winans would contribute to the success of the meeting and to the reputation of its organizer.

Seaton's aspiration was also a product of their ongoing conversation about self-improvement. Reading was the mode of choice, though Methodism did not require a formal education. Unlike Presbyterians, Methodists removed that institution-based barrier to entry for their clergy. They valued in their preachers intelligence, education, and a measure of refinement—as long as those characteristics remained tethered to a middling style of comportment and did not steal the life from one's sermons.[73] Done correctly, self-improvement promised upward mobility and social capital.

Winans motivated and directed Seaton in his learning. Balancing self-improvement (one important reason men became itinerants) with the demands of the lay audience was a constant task. Seaton reported, "I have been endevering to pursue the plan which you recommend. I find it to be a most excellent one to gain knowledge." He understood audience demands: "I find after all our reading and study if their is not much prayer and faithfulness in all our performances[,] our Sermons will be cold and dead altogether contrary to the general characteristic of a Methodist Preacher." After nearly a decade of preaching, Seaton did not underestimate the task: "The more I study the duties of a preacher the greater the work appears."[74] He pressed on under Winans's mentoring. Winans assigned the exercise of writing six sermons. Accustomed to the usual extemporaneous method, Seaton found the task challenging and worried that any "person of common reading" would recognize that he was like Aesop's jackdaw, trying to be an eagle but meeting shame by taking the ideas of other writers.[75] But Seaton also understood that members of his audience were educated. Reaching them was one of his mentor's objectives. Seaton's pursuit of improvement, and his concerns about authenticity and respectability, was inherently social, as he considered the views of fellow Methodists and those outside the church. Knowledge of his mentor's connections in the Methodist hierarchy and respectable reputation magnified his concerns.

The rewards of study transferred to many professional pursuits in settler society, not only preaching. Seaton reported, "I have latly been reading Lock on the human understanding and think it to be well calculated to discover the necesety of a close application in order to make any proficiency in any calling what ever and perticularly that of a preacher, lawyer, &c."[76] Such thoughts were common among itinerants, and Seaton clearly understood that education was a marker of professional (not only pastoral) status.

The Methodist grid enhanced these exchanges. Valuable intelligence flowed up and down its connections. Seaton and Winans passed reports on circuit conditions and exchanged news of conversations they had with others about worldly affairs. Methodism was hierarchical, but reciprocity remained within the unequal relationships. Both men stood to gain from their exchanges. This was true in their capacities as representatives of the MEC and as private citizens. Because Winans had a mind to advance in the ranks of episcopal administration, information about preachers he might one day lead (or who might influence his advancement) was useful. Correspondents like Seaton were invaluable for such intelligence. Seaton described a disagreement between two circuit preachers about traveling the long distance to the quadrennial General Conference. One preacher's long absence increased the burden of the preachers remaining behind. Disagreements injured collegiality and morale and primed future conflict.[77] Winans was not yet a presiding elder but soon would be, at which point information would become valuable. The year after Winans became a presiding elder, Seaton reported on a preacher named Williamson, suspended from conference. He "continues to preach," Seaton wrote, "and it would seem his suspension has stired him up."[78] Nearly two months later the problem remained. "I learn Williamson has become much more industrious since he was ordered to be silent."[79] Senior itinerants had significant influence over junior itinerants, but they depended on them for valuable details from the ground, like a disgruntled rouser, which helped more senior officials perform their managerial duties and advance through church offices.

Seaton and Winans discussed a number of topics, but among the most pressing was courtship and the creation of patriarchal households. Regularly, single itinerants used their positions for this most basic type of social reproduction of settler society. Francis Asbury had long opposed the marrying of preachers, but he might have had more luck pushing the boulder up the hill than stopping this part of Anglo-American expansion. Seaton was in his late twenties and had marriage on the mind. Winans had married several years earlier, a decision that made him, in addition to a husband, a slaveholder and the patriarch of a small plantation. (The land and slaves apparently came through the generosity of his new mother-in-law.)[80] Already a professional mentor to Seaton, Winans was now a social model. Seaton appraised the women in his Methodist sphere. "I have seen Brother Lanes companion," he wrote, "and am of the opinion she is a most excellent woman, and indeed it would take such an one to be worthy so excellent a Man as Brother Lane."[81] Winans requested such intelligence, and Seaton supplied it. He wrote, "You wish to know who Miss M. V. was going to Marry[;] she is married to a Merchant of Natchez by the name of Henderson."[82] Perhaps she was a former love interest, but information on who was courting whom and which connections were formalized in marriage had value for social capital. As a church official and man of public affairs, Winans needed to monitor the evolving connections and resources in a dynamic Methodist network.

Beyond the irony that women could not enter itinerancy despite buttressing it, itinerants used their networks to become husbands in a patriarchal society. Seaton wrote, "Perhaps by this time you have learned that the Natchez [circuit] is famous for having the preachers Married." Seaton's interest in marriage was plain. He evaluated women for wifely qualities, and he did so urgently. He knew he should wait until he was "ready." "However," he wrote, "delays may be dangerous," as the conditions and availability of potential spouses were unstable. One woman "will soon be married." Another "has the consumption (in my opinion)." A third was "too old," though the real strike against her was being "so politic."[83]

This measuring of women extended to their bodies and finances, reducing them to resources of social aspiration. An Indiana man queried his itinerant brother about prospects in his New Orleans Methodist network. Marriage meant "advancing my present prospects in life." With cold transactionalism he continued, "I am therefore disposed to put up with even a fair prospect, and the girl which you describe to be about

25 years of age not exquisitely beautiful, but a fine portly girl, worth from 5 to 10,000$ would suit me very well and I should not hesitate confirming a marriage contract with her, without the least assistance of *Cupid*." If this commodification was not clear enough, he turned the next sentence to arbitraging Midwest corn in the Lower South market. He surmised from newspapers that high cotton prices might lead planters to buy rather than grow corn, but he depended on the itinerant contact for local intelligence on whether "the prospects of the market there will justify the adventure."[84] Methodists found their network adaptable and full of resources—as long as they were not overly concerned with the treatment of other humans.

Just as itinerants critiqued women as candidates for marriage, so too were their actions critiqued by the community. Talk about John Seaton's intentions with certain women imperiled his reputation. In March 1822, he summarized an accusation that he had promised to marry "Miss Sarah," later reneged, and then married another.[85] He relied on Winans, his presiding elder, to defend his reputation. Their discussion highlights the complex relationship between individuals and the MEC. Seaton's interactions with women were personal, but a preacher always, in the community's eyes, represented his church.

Problems of individual reputation implicated the MEC, one fact of many that troubles any depiction of circuit riders as simple pioneer preachers. As mentor, Winans had to advise a junior colleague while protecting the reputation of the MEC (and Methodism had long faced trenchant attacks from outsiders, especially with regard to gender relations).[86] Winans had experience with the thorns of the subject; as a younger preacher he faced rumors of leading women on to thoughts of marriage.[87] "I know I enjoy a blessing," Seaton wrote to Winans, "which the King upon the throne does not enjoy[,] a friend that will reprove my faults and foibles and indeed go a little farther. You have told me what you believed to be wrong in me and have given me an excellent charge with holsom advice, O! that I maybe enabled to attend to it fully." Criticism of the flesh was common among Methodists. "Brother," Seaton continued, "I have long since learned that there was in my 'nature' but very little real goodness, but had concluded that it was so far subdued by divine grace as not to break out in such a lawless manner as to 'Alienate the affections of some,

Slay the confidence of many, lessen me in the esteem of the judicious, and wound the cause of Christ in a lamentable manner.'"[88]

Seaton knew that damage to his reputation threatened severing him from his network. He claimed to have resigned himself to social isolation, leaving him God and the "only earthly society with which I can take delight, my companion," his new wife, Alice. He asked Winans to show mercy on his wife as he himself "wander[ed] alone in this world of affliction and sorrow." Despite expressing humility and guilt, he had no intention of wandering alone. He intended to repair his reputation and retain the benefits of his Methodist associations. Knowing Winans had better information on his situation, Seaton asked for names of "the many whose confidence I have slain."[89]

Winans, who maintained a good reputation, could mediate between Seaton and those holding him in low opinion. As long as Seaton kept Winans, he maintained his link to the Methodist network. Successfully mounting a defense to Winans secured that relationship and gave Seaton a means of communication to others. His pitch was partly admission of error, partly self-defense, and partly an accusation of his Methodist brethren. "I am truly sorry from my very Soul," he confessed, "that I should in anywise injure the cause of God," for which, he emphasized, he had been "laboring or suffering" for nearly a decade. He invoked the pilgrimage theme of sacrifice:

> It was not for gain, ease, honour, pleasure, nor health, that I have been doing this—Was it for gain I have never received it, ease I have never enjoyed it, honour I have not obtained, as for pleasure I have had but very little more than what arose from a good conscience; and ocassionally seeing souls converted to the living God. And if health has been my object I have as completely missed the mark, as when I set out for the purpose of contributing my feble might to the promotion of the cause of God. I have lamentably injured both.[90]

Methodist preachers routinely protested too much with claims of self-abnegation. There is rarely reason to doubt preachers' sincerity to God, but there is also rarely reason to believe they cared little for "gain, ease, honour, pleasure, [and] health." Methodists aspired as pilgrims *and* settlers.

Seaton recognized that Methodism's reputation was tied to his own. The Methodist social principle meant that his transgressions were not solely his responsibility. Seaton was explicit: "It may be my brethren who have watched over me (perhaps) better than I have over myselfe, may have discovered this tendency in my nature, But if they have watched over me, it has not been in love as they would have shown me this weakness, if they discovered such in me; it must therefor have been for some other purpose they have been watching over my words and actions." Seaton claimed to care much less for the opinions of non-Methodists, writing, "As it respects the world I have never expected it to speak well of me, for it did not of the holy Jesus, In this I am only partaken of his sufferings in which I very greatly rejoice."[91] But in calling the institution to account, he called it to his defense.

John Seaton was not as ready to deny himself and "the world" as his words suggested. His reputation among "earthly society" remained valuable to him. Within two years of this controversy, he located from the itinerancy, common for aspiring itinerants.[92] Within six years of that, the US Census listed him in Madison County, Mississippi, head of a household of twenty-two people, fifteen enslaved.[93] He accumulated property in enslaved people, and his wife, Alice, whom he married during his crisis of reputation, was from a substantial family. She was an Irwin, and one relative, Colonel John Lawson Irwin, had married into the Vick family of Warren County. Both the Vicks and John Irwin were prominent Methodists.[94] By seeing after his reputation through private letters, Seaton likely kept himself in good standing among that network of kin. Wives, slaves, crops, reputation, holiness—all parts of the sacred capital of Methodist networks that benefited settlers, especially men, in the trans-Appalachian West.

Presiding Elder Correspondence, Money, and Land in Ohio Methodism

Distance and frequent travel separated families—which grieved many—but Methodist connectionalism persisted in other ways. The experiences of presiding elder James B. Finley's family reveal how Methodist families maintained connections through exchanges of letters. Those connections had emotional value to Methodist men and women but also concerned questions of church logistics and money and land for its members and their associates. The history of popular religious communications has often focused on evangelical print culture and the songs and sermons of camp meetings, but manuscript correspondence built the Methodist movement and created much of its social capital. Christian expressions of relationship redoubled existing family bonds, as when one brother wrote to Finley that he was "with every sentiment of love and affection Your Brother by Nature & Grace."[95] In Mississippi and Ohio, the Methodist social principle functioned similarly, bonding settlers, amplifying family ties, and enabling exchanges regarding souls, land, money, crops, jobs, marriage, even slaves—establishing Anglo-American society in lands wrested from Native control.

The Finleys came west from New Jersey, where the father, Robert Finley, received the education of a Presbyterian minister. Settling in Kentucky, the family embraced Methodism, and several of the men entered the itinerancy. The Finleys drifted north and settled in southwestern Ohio. By 1812, James B. Finley's relatives were in Greene and Highland Counties, but James's circuit assignments required travel northeast in the counties of Knox, Licking, and Fairfield around the northern drainage of the Muskingum River. Separation weighed heavily. William P. Finley and his wife, Jenny, wrote James and his wife, "Thy great Distance which we are from each other renders our personal intercourse altogether out of the question—But Glory be to the God whom we Serve that we are not so far separate but we can have intercourse otherwise. I must here stop and shed a tear of biblical affection for an absent brother and sister with whom I once could converse with but now are gone."[96] These relatives lamented their separation but did not take for granted their contact through epistolary exchange, what they called an "intercourse otherwise."

James B. Finley is significant because he was a presiding elder, the administrator of a district of circuits through which flowed information of many kinds, accumulating as social capital. First an itinerant in the Western Annual Conference and, after the Western was divided in 1811, in the Ohio Conference, Finley served with the leaders of Ohio Methodism. In the Ohio Conference, Finley became presiding elder and superintendent of the mission to the Wyandots at Upper Sandusky. These positions brought him influence as itinerants reported to him from throughout the conference's jurisdiction.

An 1830 letter from an itinerant and relative illustrates how preachers exchanged information to optimize success on their circuits. The writer was James W. Finley, a nephew. The letter touched on family affairs but more significantly the uncle was influential within the conference and served that year in Cincinnati, the communication and commercial hub of the Ohio Valley.

That year the nephew, James W., was traveling a circuit in southern Michigan Territory, the northern periphery of the Ohio Conference.[97] A destination for New England migrants, the area contained few Methodists but was a field for growth. James W. reported on a camp meeting that had planted promising seeds. He also conveyed important information about local personnel. On his circuit were three local preachers and three exhorters. He communicated the health and morale of the itinerants serving that part of the district. The rapid filling of Michigan presented challenges and opportunities for the Methodists.[98] The challenge that James W. noted was the prevalence of backsliders. He was addressing the situation with sermons chosen to convict individuals who had professed faith but become lax after separating from eastern churches. Rapid settlement also provided opportunity for the Methodists. Many of the migrants were likely Congregationalists and Presbyterians, but the newcomers looked increasingly to Methodist itinerants. One Presbyterian deacon requested a Methodist preacher; James W. "told the old gentleman it was our business to hunt up the *reprobate*" but promised to see what he could do. To address the backsliders and demand for preachers, James W. wrote his uncle, "If you have any of the [competent] ministry who have no employment send them this way for I am supplying three of their Congregations, in the bounds of my circuit." He included a substantial order of books, in demand among Michigan migrants, and described the optimal transport route from Cincinnati to the territory. Finally, he noted, "many are anxious that you should come to the Territory, it appears to me that you might be more useful here than in any part of the Conference."[99]

James W.'s letter was unexceptional. Countless similar missives built the MEC into a vast institution. But the information sent to the logistical hub of the Ohio Conference was indispensable. On-the-ground data regarding local preachers and exhorters and even health updates for specific itinerants were essential for managing distant locales and high turnover. The status of competing organizations allowed conference leaders to allocate resources. When James W. pressed his uncle to visit the territory, he repeated a request common among itinerants who judged their circuits primed for revival if proper preaching talent were deployed. Methodists knew that laypeople, regardless of denomination, were discriminating consumers and that the itinerancy contained certain "sons of thunder" who might be brought in to achieve full evangelical effect.[100] Because the itinerancy did not have unlimited human resources, such reports to presiding elders were fundamentally important to MEC expansion in the trans-Appalachian West.

The itinerancy was not always efficient. Disagreements were common in the fraternity.[101] In fact, they could signal the secondary functions of the network in transmitting social capital. This was the distraction of settlement that Francis Asbury long foretold. An 1823 dispute between itinerants Samuel Baker and Alfred Brunson demonstrates this, and a question of money factored in unexpectedly. Presiding Elder James B. Finley received reports of the situation.[102] Baker and Brunson were assigned to the large Detroit circuit that year. Baker complained that Brunson was so settled in at Detroit that he was reneging on his agreement to travel to the remote parts of the circuit and assist Baker. Brunson's excuses—sickness, his wife's needing help, his poor finances, his having a boarder and servant—were to Baker's mind clear indications of Brunson's distractions from itinerant priorities. Baker emphasized that while Brunson sat in Detroit, he himself struggled with Presbyterian competitors and unreceptive congregations. Brunson also reported to their presiding elder, perhaps suspecting Baker's complaints. He warned Finley of Baker's trouble on the circuit. But the problem was entirely about Baker's capacities as a preacher. Allegedly, Baker's preaching was poor and disliked by eastern migrants with high standards for singing and sermonizing. Brunson disputed Baker's claim that "Yankee" audiences discriminated against his southern origins. As proof, he flattered Finley that he was a southerner (thinking of his Kentucky past) and remained popular in Michigan. He regretted speaking ill of his colleague but did so anyway. He did not address his own service, and it was widely known that authorities frowned on mixed priorities.

Brunson personally required Finley's good graces. Brunson, whose finances were tight, hoped to secure Finley's assistance regarding fifty dollars owed to him by another Methodist brother. Unsurprisingly, Brunson closed deferentially: "I mention these things not to dictate but to give you all the information I can."[103] An exchange that appeared to be about preachers' performance also reflected the social capital of the itinerancy. The worldly affairs of settler society crept into the itinerancy.

Personal and official matters regularly overlapped, a result of Methodism's grid-like structure as a social network. Communication channels allowing episcopal administration were turned to the needs of personal business and vice-versa. As seen from Francis Asbury's visit in the home of Ohio governor Edward Tiffin, he feared the creeping distractions of worldly affairs, echoing the tone set by John Wesley. Asbury knew that such snares lay particularly in the many rewards of Ohio, a state where acquiring land was for many nearly an obsession.[104] Asbury was right to fear its corrupting power. The value of the Ohio country had brought wars of conquest against Native Americans and legions of settlers. But Asbury's Methodism was part of that campaign because of the itinerancy's adaptability.

On the settler side, the massive land transfer of the trans-Appalachian West was riven with speculation and currency troubles. Such problems were exacerbated by the tendency of many westerners to pursue opportunities in distant locales. Trust, therefore, was extremely valuable for land business. In March 1831, itinerant George W. Maley took advantage of his "old Friend & Brother" James B. Finley's placement in Cincinnati. From fifty miles away in Wilmington, Ohio, he requested Finley's help with a land deal arranged with a doctor in Indiana. A Brother Reeves carried "$300 Mortgage, Notes &c" that he would pass to Finley. The Indiana doctor or his representative would contact Finley to receive the deposit and exchange the deed for the land. At that point, Maley cautioned, the transaction would become more complicated. An attorney in Indiana had drafted the deed, but the laws of Indiana and Ohio were not the same on all land matters; therefore, Finley must engage a local attorney and determine "whether it [the deed] is executed correctly." If it were not,

Finley must decide to cancel the transaction. If all went smoothly, Finley would hold the deed until Maley visited Cincinnati the following month. "Attend this concern for Me Bro. Finley, as it is important & I will repay thee," closed Maley.[105] A week later, Maley sent another letter to Finley by the hand of a Methodist brother. He was anxious for news on the deal because he was "in a strait."[106]

Valuable information and money commonly changed hands through Methodist communications. Methodist institutions such as the Wyandot Mission in Ohio, the book trade, and conference collections depended on currency transfers and goods collected by preachers and laity. These transactions relied on Methodists willing to hold items of value until they could be carried to their destinations and hinged on the knowledge that members were trustworthy.[107] When George Maley placed his affairs in the hands of Finley, these practices of exchange and trust had been tested over more than a decade. Maley could trust this well-placed friend during his time of need not just because he was personally trustworthy but because Methodism had developed a structure of trust and exchange—and settlers adapted it to their desires. And because of the frequency of Methodist itinerant travel, allowing letters to be conveyed by colleagues, Maley seems to have engaged his "Old Friend & Brother" without even paying for postage. Years earlier, Francis Asbury compared the itinerancy with the postal service, but this was not what he had in mind. It was the antithesis—an efficient and common conversion of a religious institution to worldly purposes. Maley used the preachers' network for land acquisition, turning the power of religious communication to the fundamental work of settlement. After the mid-1830s, Methodists used the church's influential newspapers to post classified ads regarding land and business and even to publish notices of lands for sale aimed at attracting Methodists to opportunities near and far. That print-based social capital resulted in part from innovation in print technology, but it was in fact merely an acceleration of social capital developed in the manuscript exchanges of James Finley and, earlier, Edward Dromgoole and his Ohio associates.[108]

This sacred capital was not reserved to seasonal itinerants. Young, aspiring settlers seized opportunity in Methodist circles. Significantly, even occasional connections to the itinerancy could provide ambitious settlers with prized information. In spring 1818, schoolteacher and sometime preacher Henry Matthews wrote from his new home in Adams County, southern Ohio, to Nathaniel Little, a friend and Methodist "brother" in his old home to the north in Worthington. A hundred miles separated the two young men but Methodist correspondence maintained their relationship. The news they exchanged was religious and sentimental. Matthews remarked on Christian society in West Union and requested word of the recent quarterly meeting in Worthington. Fulfilling an imperative in Methodist social life, he exhorted his friend in his spiritual journey. Matthews also included practical news, relaying that a nearby school needed a teacher; a mutual friend in Worthington, eager for employment, would find that information valuable.[109]

Matthews's richly textured letter was valuable to other young Methodists looking for opportunities in the southern part of the state. He reported on the nature of society and economy in Adams County and described how well Christians there received him and pursued their spiritual commitments. His teaching position gave him joy and fulfillment, allowing him to feel true to his spiritual calling to do God's work. Matthews benefited himself in conveying this information, for his descriptions suggest that by writing of his new home he better placed himself within it emotionally.

Letter-writing connected him to distant friends and relatives. Thus, his information came at a price to his friend needing work. This friend, Noah Tinkham, had to write Matthews personally to receive details of the teaching position. As Matthews said to Little, "Tell Br Noah Tinkham I am looking for a letter daily from him according to agreement & then I will inform him if there is a school made up for him."[110] Matthews expected friends to reciprocate his communications. This code of reciprocity was profoundly important for middling settlers in motion who were, as in the case of Matthews, living away from friends and family because of a job. They dealt with separation through letters, and a break in this relationship was painful, even as Matthews enjoyed the Methodist community of West Union.[111]

Matthews's ambition and resourcefulness is clear. He searched his surroundings for opportunities for himself and friends and did not need the itinerancy as a full-time career to gain its resources. He was admitted to the conference on trial in 1818, traveled on probation in 1819 and

1820, and then left the itinerancy voluntarily. That did not end his role as a preacher; in 1822, he applied to the conference as a local preacher and was ordained a deacon.[112] He prized his itinerant experiences. Traveling brought more excitement than the sedentary employment of teaching. In 1818, he had traveled temporarily in the Scioto District in southern Ohio. This allowed him to know senior itinerants to whose example he aspired. To his brother in Worthington, Henry wrote of his travels with "the preacher who is a linguist & an excellent & orthodox Minister."[113] He boasted to his friend Nathaniel Little: "I rode two weeks with a Minister on Chillicothe Circuit who enjoyed a classical education & found that I gained considerable information with regard to religious tenets & practice though the time I enjoyed the privilege of his company was short."[114] (This was likely either James B. Finley or his father, Robert W. Finley, both products of Presbyterian academies.) Methodist itinerancy offered Matthews entrance to a network of piety, education, and cultural respectability.

As he wrote enthusiastically of meeting respectable preachers, Matthews attended Methodist meetings and learned about land opportunities. Quarterly meetings were solemn occasions for collective worship, circuit business, and discipline. In 1818, Matthews used one near Xenia, Ohio, to gather information about prospects for western settlement and then passed the news to an older Methodist who, crucially, had unmarried daughters Matthews's age. The young minister had enjoyed "a precious time" where "the work revived, sinners trembled, saints rejoiced," and had spoken with Thomas Spotswood Hinde. Hinde was a Methodist, printer and publisher, and land speculator. Matthews knew him as the man responsible for establishing the town of Mt. Carmel on the Wabash River. As Matthews understood it, a number of Methodists had set their sights on the lands of the Wabash, and he learned from Hinde that that country "was healthy & handsomely situated every way." He passed this information to Russell Bigelow, along with well wishes from a mutual friend who also was thinking of moving west and hoped Bigelow would settle near him. Matthews attended the quarterly meeting because of his commitment to the MEC, but he did so with a settler's mindset. He thought his future lay west, where he would acquire land near likeminded people and marry, fulfilling the destiny manifestly apparent to

American Christians. For this there were few opportunities better than a Methodist meeting.[115]

Methodist Discipline and the Regulation and Costs of the Social Principle

As the MEC's *Doctrines and Discipline* explained, Methodists were "to spiritualize" the social principle and create "heavenly felicity."[116] As we have seen, they used the church to create worldly felicity as well. Methodism's ethic of discipline was meant to regulate the social principle and encourage holiness. Senior itinerants held junior itinerants accountable. Itinerants disciplined laypeople. Lay leaders examined the transgressions of people in their Methodist societies. Disciplinary cases show that Methodism was not all beneficent social capital and that there were costs to connectionalism. Under patriarchal control, white men could bear those costs, but women and people of color were most vulnerable. Often concern for church reputation overawed care for individuals.

In May 1823, James B. Finley heard about the expulsion of William Blair from itinerant John C. Brooke and from Blair himself. Finley was Brooke's father-in-law but also his presiding elder that year. Brooke explained that Blair and two other men were "all Expelled for getting drunk at the Election." They had "acted Most rediculous." And a judge—perhaps later postmaster general and Supreme Court justice John McLean—had distributed whiskey at what was probably a land sale. The consequence of these events was that they had "made considerable Noise in the country in general[.] Much is said and much more than what is true."[117] Gossip threatened the reputation of the Methodist societies.

Blair, a Methodist layman, wrote to Finley in self-defense. His expulsion severed his relationship to the MEC and to the social network of its members. Blair thus began his letter with formal distance: "Dear Sir, You will see by the head of my letter that I no longer address you by the endearing appilation of Brother—under my present Circumstances I dare not claim the privilege." He then described his hearing. He had admitted "imprudent conduct in being at the tavern and drinking too much Cider" and expressed "all the marks of humiliation I was capable of without acting the hypocrite." Blair related that three-quarters of the society felt "satisfied" at his confession, and the class leader confirmed that support. Yet,

Blair was still expelled, and he blamed Brooke, Finley's son-in-law. Rather than letting the affair rest, Brooke had gathered a committee, which "construed the discipline" to expel him. Blair understood the value of reputation within respectable Christian society and went on the attack. "I do not wish to hurt your feelings," he told Finley, "but I must say that I believe Mr *Brook* to be my violent enemy[,] for what cause I know not unless it be for my kindness in trying [to] oblige him and you"—a subtle reference to favors granted. Highly agitated, he lobbed an accusation among the worst possible in American settler society, claiming Brooke was in cahoots with a horse thief. Such histrionics aside, one might assume that Finley would trust his son-in-law and fellow itinerant, but the situation was muddled by Blair's helping Finley with a financial matter. A man to whom Finley owed a debt was near to Blair, who explained, "he wants some cash from you." Finley was one hundred miles distant, and as Blair pled his discipline case, he served as a medium for Finley with regard to this debt, including passing information from the local attorney involved in the matter.[118]

If William Blair grasped the fact that the same man who might redeem his reputation was also in his debt for information, he left it implicit in his letters to Finley. Rather than pointing it out, he loyally supplied Finley with news of his creditor, even communicating month's later the man's passing away. And he continued to express his fealty to Finley, while declaring himself answerable for his deeds to no judge but God, "judge of all the earth."[119] Blair continued to value the social relationships he had formed with other Methodists even as he eventually celebrated his severance from an organization he found arbitrary in its exercise of authority. Blair was fortunate because his value to men like Finley was social capital that protected his reputation.

Not all weathered Methodist discipline as well as Blair. Oriented to white settlers in a patriarchal institution, Methodist connectionalism benefited women and people of color less directly. At times it caused great harm to the vulnerable. An example comes from a disciplinary trial of itinerant Charles Waddell. Meant as "moral courts," Methodist trials often prioritized the reputation of the church to support evangelical success.[120] Relying on access to settlers' hearts and homes, the MEC's reputation was invaluable. Waddell called on people in their homes and fields around

Lebanon, Ohio, pausing at gates to discuss the path to holiness and to the next town over. According to three women in 1826, these errands led to sexual misconduct. The formal charges accused him of "conduct" that was "immoral," "immodest," "unchristian," "indecent," and "ungentlemanly." A "committee of investigation" lodged four complaints, the most serious being "Seduction and Adultery or an attempt to commit adultery."[121] The annual conference voted unanimously to expel him. The trial proceedings show how trust and reputation were wrapped in facets of power such as gender, age, and even rural space, as well as how the Methodist network exposed the vulnerable.

According to the record, Waddell manipulated women, claiming of sexual intercourse that "it would be wrong for wicked people to do so, but there is no harm in good people doing so." The preacher was allowed to cross-examine his accusers, opening them to criticism from conference leaders. They doubted a young woman's decisions and motives. Why had she walked with him rather than give directions to his next appointment? What did her dark dreams suggest about her state of mind? Was she exacting vengeance for his refusal to baptize her? One preacher judged her "non compus mentis . . . half way between common understanding, and Idiotism. And further that he believed she was under the influence of her parents in giving her testimony." Another stated, "She is what we would call rather an ignorant country girl, but not an Idiot."[122]

Top of mind for Lebanon's Methodist leaders was the church's reputation. When the allegations became public, they beseeched their itinerant, writing, "We therefore wish you to . . . take such Measures as will be best calculated to bring the thing to a Speedy [close] as in a few days it will be in the mouths of hundreds and we fear the cause of God will suffer more from the circumstances than from any other that has ever transpired in the M Church in Lebanon."[123] Certainly "the cause of God" needed care by the church, but the vulnerable did too, especially when the issue was so clear. Preachers were to be "blameless in life and conversation." They were to "converse sparingly and cautiously with women." Annually the preachers underwent examination of their character, and Waddell was likely in his fourteenth year with the Ohio Annual Conference. In fact, examination of character was meant to be much more frequent. Preachers were to "frequently ask" each other about their commitment to God, and preachers, really all Christians, were to examine themselves continually according to the questions laid out by the church: "Do you steadily watch against the world? Your self? Your besetting sin? . . . Do you deny yourself every useless pleasure of sense?" The list went on and on; indeed, the ideal, disciplined Methodist life was daily completing a mental questionnaire designed to pierce a corrupt, sinful heart that craved the captivating, blinding, dulling stimuli of worldly concerns and to refocus the mind, body, and soul on holiness.[124] Compared to the standard of the *Discipline*, which bore the stamp of Francis Asbury, the paragon of self-denial, Waddell had failed miserably. Nevertheless, the young woman, her family, and other women were scathed by an institution through which information flowed efficiently, and resultingly reputation mattered greatly. The church's reputation mattered not only to protect "the cause of God" but because so much touching on settlers' worldly affairs was also tied to the institution.

In the slave states, thousands of African Americans were connected officially to the MEC, often through slaveowners. As many historians have shown, however, enslaved and free Black Americans devoted themselves to their own religious institutions, the "invisible institution" of the slave-quarter churches or free denominations like the African Methodist Episcopal Church and African Methodist Episcopal Zion Church.[125] Black Americans preferred these institutions (along with autonomous Baptist congregations) because they knew the white settler MEC did not prioritize their visions of holiness. Still, Black Americans also knew that association with the MEC offered worldly benefits. Such was the case for Siney Bonner of Alabama, who sought to earn money by selling puppies to white townspeople. To entice one shopper, she denominated them "Methodist pups," but when that failed, she declared them Baptists.[126]

Failure to engage the benefits of Methodist institutions could easily have less benign results, especially when the church's concern for normative moral order was piqued. Two Black members of a New Orleans Methodist society learned this on bringing a relationship dispute before the itinerant. The two had lived together several weeks, with the man promising "to marry her, if on proper *trial* he like'd her," but he left and pursued another. The woman complained to the preacher because "she had done her part, and that if he was not satisfied, it was his own fault."

Being members of the church, they expected just arbitration, but they received the preacher's preoccupation with respectable Anglo-American Protestantism. Having judged all the members of color "pious, but all out of order," the preacher campaigned against "the old customs of concubinage, and adultery." Thus, he made an example of these two disputants and rather than counseling them, took them by surprise, "neither dreaming that any thought of charging them with the sin of adultery." Both were found guilty.[127] Critics of Methodism found the church "tyranical" and its discipline arbitrary.[128] These Black Methodists learned firsthand that the church's discipline was unpredictable and that not conforming to its mainstream Protestant values carried risks. They were quickly made outsiders.

Perhaps the least surprising groups to suffer from connection to the MEC in the trans-Appalachian West were Native Americans. Many historians have shown how Christian missionaries tried to subordinate Indigenous cultures to Protestant norms. In this regard, missions were essentially disciplinary sites. The same was true of the Wyandot Mission at Upper Sandusky, Ohio. However, the most important point for understanding the MEC as a settler institution is how unconcerned white Methodists were with Native American life. The MEC granted little priority and few resources to missions to Native Americans. Common Methodists and most preachers showed little interest or concern for Natives' physical or spiritual well-being. Methodism fell in line with what scholars of settler colonialism have found, that white Americans rarely showed concern for Natives except to relieve their own feelings of guilt or to convince themselves that they lived in a moral republic.[129] Occasionally Methodists donated their mites or gathered bushels of potatoes for support of the Wyandot, but the reality is that scant evidence survives of Methodists thinking about Native Americans as real people rather than characters of frontier imagination. Those donations carried costs, as children's donations through the Juvenile Finleyan Missionary Mite Society were tied to replacing Wyandot youths' names with Anglo-American names.[130] More common were statements that reinforced the feelings of distance and alienation that settlers often associated with Indigenous people. When James B. Finley served as missionary to the Wyandot, Methodists marveled at his life beyond the pale. One correspondent exemplified the detachment common among Methodists, imagining the preacher "in some smoky wigwam on the shore of Lake Huron" or "holding a prayer meeting with the natives of the forest," battling "idolitry." No matter that Lake Huron was nowhere near the Wyandot Mission; to Methodist settlers, their church's few missionaries and Native Americans were "in the wilderness." That wilderness was mostly a figment of settler imagination, something they remembered or read about only rarely and relevant mainly as confirmation of settler lives. That the Wyandot, like Native Americans at missions through the centuries and across the continent, "hybridized" religion, resisted missionary assimilation, and asserted agency against settler encroachment mattered little to mainstream Methodists. Their church was a mission to white settlers, focused by its evangelical, pietistic, Arminian theology on spreading the Gospel to those most likely to convert and maintaining holiness among its main membership. Methodist settlers could take this insouciant position because their duly elected governments had insulated them via military might, treaty lines, and civilization and removal policies, and because somewhere out there (a handful of) missionaries were doing the Lord's work.[131] Methodists could rest easy amid the fruits of the social principle.

Methodists embraced the evangelical discourse that they were set apart from the world and eschewed worldly things. The two faces of the social principle show that reality was different. If Methodists were set apart, it was because they enjoyed the privileges of membership in the nation's largest religious network, which facilitated the transfer of news, instructions, and gossip. All of this occurred because the personal bonds of itinerancy, affiliation, family, spiritual brotherhood and sisterhood, and Christian love knitted people together into a sprawling and fluid community. Membership in this community, Methodists believed, helped them get to heaven. Because their theological commitments included the belief that one could fall away from God's saving grace, frequent encouragement by loved ones to travel toward Zion was of real benefit to Methodists. The same channels that facilitated these spiritual benefits also helped the Pelhams and the Dromgooles find farms and employment in their settlement in Ohio. So too did men like Henry Matthews and William Blair learn of new opportunities and extend that information to their associates. Similarly, in Mississippi Methodists found worldly opportunity through their religious institutions. If Methodism helped Ohio settlers gather information regarding land, money, and marriage without compromising with or competing against a slaveholders' economy, it helped Mississippi settlers secure intelligence about the same matters and also, through marriage especially, enter the slaveholders' class.

These exchanges were social—from one peer to another—and organized through the itinerancy. The primary concern of the MEC was to give the Gospel to those destitute of the knowledge of God. That was a powerful organizing impulse requiring great coordination among itinerants and the many local preachers, exhorters, and class leaders constituting the church. The imperative to communicate knitted people together in many locales by combining personal and ecclesiastical interests. The connections created by Methodism's organizational requirements provided networks for individuals to pursue opportunities: Methodism produced social capital through its unique combination of vertical and horizontal relationships. Additionally, itinerant relations often overlay ties of family or neighbors. Methodism, therefore, extended and amplified the preexisting relationships that constituted the social structure of settler society. The flow of resources did not always proceed from Methodism to settlers. As the MEC's founding in Mississippi shows, the itinerancy benefited in turn by connecting to local settler networks. Tobias Gibson's work is one example demonstrating that process.

The creation of advantages, however, led inevitably to feelings of inequality. Criticism of Methodism's imperious character was common, as were complaints against the ruling hand of episcopal government. Some individuals determined that the benefits of association were not worth the costs. William Blair took such umbrage at the handling of his indiscretion that he gave up worrying about his standing with the MEC, but he knew that his expulsion did not entirely sever his social bonds to other Methodists. Many who were already vulnerable in Anglo-American settler society, people of color and some white women, found little refuge in the MEC and at times were sacrificed to the cause of church reputation. Those the MEC benefited turned their social capital to ventures ranging from politics to land or simply to establishing their reputations in the eyes of peers. Moreover, Methodist social capital was enduring for those it helped. Methodist history has mostly focused on itinerants, but the church had many other preachers and members. The itinerancy certainly provided exceptional access to the elements of social capital, but as the example of John Littlejohn shows, Methodists outside the itinerancy enjoyed its benefits as well.

4

THE TRAVELING LIFE OF JOHN LITTLEJOHN

Mobility, Exchange, and Settling in the Empire of Liberty

Word of the preacher's arrival in Louisville preceded him. To his surprise as he stepped onto the city's riverside docks, he was greeted by an enslaved woman, who beseeched him to visit her ailing mistress. John Littlejohn was a longtime Methodist preacher, but not in Kentucky. He had lived the last four decades in Virginia, but now in the autumn of 1818 he was migrating with his family to Kentucky. While sojourning in Louisville, waiting to take up a farm in the country, Littlejohn found his talents as a preacher quickly put to use in the local Methodist society. He presided at sickbeds, funerals, prayer gatherings, and class meetings on top of preaching several times per week. In turn, he benefited from the favors of friends in town. A former Virginia houseguest would take no payment for stabling the horses the preacher had sent ahead. Others bestowed gifts of firewood to warm his family against the chill October nights. Rather than relying on kinship, wealth, or elite status, Littlejohn exploited "social exchanges" to ease his migration.[1] He accessed a network of resources to acquire housing, employment, and property—the critical dimensions of settlement in the trans-Appalachian West. The westward movement uprooted people from the communities where they had passed most of their lives. Many never saw loved ones again after crossing the Appalachians. But there was also an "alternative migration story," describing connection as much as separation. The case of John Littlejohn allows us to detail that narrative's social mechanisms, which he developed in the revolutionary Chesapeake and carried to early republican Kentucky. At the center was Methodist sacred capital.[2]

The mechanisms were Methodist, and the frame was settler colonial. White settlers like Littlejohn experienced disruption but more easily found stability than others. As Littlejohn traveled voluntarily, many enslaved and Indigenous people migrated involuntarily, forced west by masters or expelled from lands by soldiers, settlers, and agents targeting bodies, crops, and cultures. Those coercions aided Littlejohn's successful settling. Not only was he greeted and guided at Louisville's docks by an enslaved woman obeying her master's dictates; he entered a land largely secured from Indigenous contest decades earlier. For example, the Shawnee had been pushed from the lower Ohio Valley in the 1770s, and the 1795 Treaty of Greenville line had opened southern Ohio and northern Kentucky to peaceful white settlement.[3] Maintaining unfreedom and pursuing expulsion, the American Revolution set favorable conditions for settlers like Littlejohn. The MEC then provided the network to capitalize on those conditions.

The American Revolution profoundly influenced Americans' mobility and their religious lives. Littlejohn experienced these changes intimately through the full course of his years.[4] He was one of thousands of migrants who traveled the Ohio River to Louisville in the late eighteenth and early nineteenth centuries.[5] Not all white westward settlers achieved prosperity, but those who did relied on social resources. Through religious associations, evangelicals maintained old bonds while creating new ones with strangers in western communities. Littlejohn's social network was Methodist, and it was founded on his work as a circuit rider. Despite the Methodist itinerancy's importance as a religious institution in early America, historians have only occasionally recognized the significant resources it provided individuals.[6] Instead, scholars describe Methodist itinerancy as a brief but disorienting experience for young men during the years of the early American republic. As the story goes, older preachers recruited poor and middling young men into an ecclesiastical system that demanded much personal sacrifice. The rigors of constant travel wore on circuit riders' minds and bodies, resulting in fatigue, emotional stress, and frequent early "location" (that is, retirement from the itinerancy). The worst cases ended in debility, insanity, or death.[7] This depiction, however, ignores important evidence. The Methodist itinerancy indeed presented individual and social challenges, especially when coupled with the disruptions of migration and warfare during the era, but Methodist sources amplify those challenges to the point of distortion. When historians have credited the benefits of itinerancy, it has been in the context of the formal bureaucratic development of the MEC in the middle and late nineteenth century.[8] However, the social benefits of itinerancy originated in the personal relationships of evangelical social networks, an organizational development that was far older than the popular evangelical churches that thrived in America during the First and Second Great Awakenings.[9]

John Littlejohn's journal allows us to construct a different model of the worldly significance of itinerancy.[10] Several fine works consider Littlejohn's life but within the confines of the late eighteenth century.[11] Unlike many other Methodist preachers' diaries, Littlejohn's includes material both from his two years as an itinerant and from later periods when he was a local preacher, his status on leaving the itinerancy. The entries range from his early manhood to his old age. The result is an excellent source for understanding how the Methodist itinerancy continued to impact preachers' lives long after they retired from official membership. As Littlejohn's example suggests, a relatively short period of itinerancy provided access to the long-term benefits of social networks and social exchanges. Littlejohn's story also reminds us that local preachers outnumbered circuit riders, though historians have said little about the former. Bishop Francis Asbury estimated in 1807, for example, that there were 1,400 local preachers, over two and a half times the number of itinerants.[12] Local preachers principally spent their time in nonreligious employment, receiving no salary from the MEC and only small fees from their communities, but they were influential in their locales. Many, like Littlejohn, actively engaged in the spiritual life and business affairs of their communities while maintaining religious and economic ties to broader networks of evangelicals. Such men's economic lives were a composite: Littlejohn was a farmer, saddler's apprentice, tenant, tax collector, landowner, land agent, preacher, assistant shopkeeper, and slaveowner. He was none of these for the whole of his adult life, with the exception of preacher. Due to frequent travel, Littlejohn reflected the fluidity of his time, but amid the economic and social disruptions of the early republic that brought ruin to many, he managed to steadily improve his lot. Networks of religion and business linked him to a multitude of people and places with varying degrees of emotional and geographic closeness. As a young man, his itinerant affiliations helped him find his place in the world. As he aged, his social ties gained economic value.[13]

This composite economic profile reflects the experiences not only of the bulk of white Methodist leaders but also of the Baptists, the early republic's other major popular denomination. Social networks were important to both groups. As recent historians of Upper South Baptists have shown, networks were the means for attracting and keeping converts, disseminating the Gospel, developing leadership, and ordering and disciplining the lives of laypeople.[14] These functions primarily served the goals of the churches and denominational bodies, but many individuals turned the networks to personal economic advantage. The MEC encouraged the practice with somewhat loftier intentions. John Littlejohn's story illustrates that transformation, one that evangelicals rarely acknowledged in their writings but that helped establish them among the middling ranks of commercial society in the West.[15]

Mundane episodes in Littlejohn's journal gain significance when our perspective combines exchange relations with social science scholarship on religion and migration. First, Littlejohn would not have found odd the theory that religious organizations can be bridges for the integration of migrants into new communities. That theory suggests that religious associations are valuable where extended families are inaccessible, that religious organizations function as "information-sharing communities," and that churches can serve as "means of collective and individual socioeconomic mobility."[16] Each of these facets of religious experience was important in Littlejohn's life. At the most basic level his access to these benefits occurred through a transaction, specifically a social exchange, and such exchanges were countless in Littlejohn's life. To understand them, we need only build on a simple definition of social exchange that includes any transaction of value between at least two people. The bulk of Littlejohn's exchanges happened in personal, often informal relationships. They lacked the detachment of a distant financial market and the efficiency and finality of a cash deal. Their terms were not clearly stated and agreed to in written contracts. That they were social rather than simply economic made them complex. They were also commonplace. A bundle of wood or a simple kind word from a host could be repaid by leading a prayer or a hymn in one's home. Of seemingly small significance, these were "valued goods," at times material and at times not. The framework of social exchange resembles the approaches of ethnohistory and directs our attention to specific transactions between individuals, highlighting the elements that underpinned categories of sociability such as friendship, kinship, fictive kinship, and patronage.[17] In practice, each of those categories formed and dissolved through a history of exchanges. None of them alone describes Littlejohn's varied relations, but their common denominator is exchange.[18] A transactional focus also invites us to consider the points at which the religious, the social, and the economic converged in evangelicals' daily lives, providing windows into lived experience, and it emphasizes interdependency, countering the practice of describing evangelicals within a simple dichotomy of independence and dependence.[19]

Social exchanges often held fleeting value as individual transactions but in the aggregate formed sacred capital for Methodists. They accumulated and drew on that capital, a means for individual and collective gain distinct, for example, from the culture of honor. The terms of social interaction (namely, exchange, resources, reciprocity, and reputation) reveal the subtle but profound significance of the Methodist itinerancy for those within the web, even as the itinerancy's gendered, racial, and behavioral boundaries restricted who could benefit from the social exchanges it offered. For his own part, Littlejohn discovered that opportunity. He made contacts, cultivated relationships, and ultimately built from his social exchanges a business as a land agent.

Pilgrim to Settler: Learning the Rules of the Methodist Itinerancy

Itinerancy exposed John Littlejohn to the elements of social exchange in the Methodist circuit system. While he suffered the typical pressures and sacrifices of the traveling life, he also gained a valuable social network. Perhaps one reason he profited from travel was that Littlejohn was accustomed to mobility from his youth. His first journey was as a boy from the town of Penrith, Cumberland County, near England's northern border with Scotland. He entered an apprenticeship in London but soon abandoned it and walked the 284 miles home. His longest trip occurred before his thirteenth year. While his family eventually followed him to America, Littlejohn traversed the Atlantic without them around 1767.[20] Although Littlejohn crossed the Appalachians in 1818 as part of "one of the great immigrations in the history of the western world," Littlejohn's earlier migration was part of another world historical movement. For more than a century and a half before his Atlantic crossing, tens of thousands of English people like Littlejohn migrated from the countryside to London and smaller cities to pursue work. Many then embarked to England's overseas colonies. While the rewards were not always great, the push of hard times at home and the pull of opportunity in distant places led many to travel.[21]

In America, Littlejohn joined another transformative movement—Methodism, which was itself a British migrant. A decade after his arrival in the colonies, Littlejohn had become a full-time Methodist itinerant. His two years of itinerancy gave a new pattern to his travels. Previously, his life had exhibited the instability often associated with migration. As with many colonial youths, economics drove his mobility. First in England, then throughout the Chesapeake, he labored as an apprentice. Those movements separated him from his family for varying periods, especially since his father died soon after arriving in America. Joining the itinerancy regularized Littlejohn's movements and framed his economic life—of no little significance at a time and in a region where mobility was just as often characterized by a downward economic trajectory. He ceased drifting from town to town for sundry employment. Ironically, travel grounded him, tying him to many places that he could call home and enveloping him in networks of intimate friends, business associates, and religious brethren who provided a sense of belonging and opportunities for spiritual and material improvement. From itinerancy Littlejohn learned important lessons about the social exchanges that constituted networks, and these defined much of the rest of his life.[22]

Accessing the social knowledge held within itinerant service required first gaining entry into its ranks. That process involved self-reflection and recruitment by other preachers. Like most Methodist memoirists, Littlejohn recounted his conversion in terms that emphasized his individual experience. He described feelings of anguish as he wrestled with the pleasures of the flesh and his fear for the condition of his soul.

When Littlejohn first heard Methodist preaching in Norfolk, Virginia, he yearned for spiritual direction and read *The Pilgrim's Progress,* the steady-selling allegory of individual struggle. But his struggle was as much social. Employment took him to Alexandria, Virginia, where he again encountered Methodist preachers. He tried, with limited success, to become close to them. He vacillated between devotion to God and worldly pleasures (gaming was his vice of choice). A series of dreams broke the pattern. Dreams are often considered internal to the self, but they attain social significance when communicated to others. By reporting his dreams, Littlejohn gained the attention of the preachers. In his sleep, he imagined a crowd chasing him through the streets, hurling mud and stones. He believed the dream was a portent of future persecution and a sign that he was called to preach, though he still struggled with doubt. Two months later, during his slumber he heard a voice announcing his salvation from sin. He was joyful but cautious. A week passed in that feeling before he felt assurance and cried in jubilation. The key to a closer relationship with the preachers was sincerity in one's testimony, for mentoring another young Christian required itinerants to invest time and energy, scarce resources for most traveling preachers. Littlejohn's dreams so troubled him that his sincerity appeared beyond doubt. After hearing Littlejohn's account of his recent torment, the itinerant John Sigman showed greater interest, and the two built a relationship. Littlejohn wrote, "Hence I got better acquainted with the principles & economy of the Methodists & desired to be joined with them."[23] Those principles and economy were the formal rules of behavior that the church printed in its annual minutes and then in *The Doctrines and Discipline.* Yet as these examples make clear, Littlejohn first had to gain the attention and trust of the Methodists in his vicinity. He did this by observing other, informal rules—that is, the preachers' expectations—which guided his experience and testimony of conviction and conversion. By fulfilling those requirements, Littlejohn won entrance to the social network of preachers.[24]

From that point his progression to the itinerancy followed the common stages of Methodist recruitment, during which he endured the social tensions that accompanied his new affiliation. Late in 1774, he joined a class meeting in Alexandria. Soon after, he and other young men organized "prayer meetings near the Falls Church." His next step was exhorting.

Those activities led to conflict with political and religious authorities, both the "Magisterates & the Minister." He entered a dark time in his life. Assurance of his soul's redemption did not guarantee a peaceful transition in his social relationships. Especially grieving, Littlejohn visited his mother in Baltimore and found her displeased with his new religious choice. In despair he contemplated suicide, another common feature of early American conversion narratives. Later, he feared that his exhorting disgraced the Gospel, and he considered drowning himself. Ultimately the darkness passed, and he embraced his new Methodist association and continued through the stages of recruitment. He became a class leader in Fairfax County, in a meeting sponsored by a man named Daniel Talbott. Soon after, in 1776, he took his first steps as a traveling preacher on the Berkeley circuit as an unofficial charge of senior itinerant William Watters.[25] Joining the Methodists could strain relationships, especially within one's family, but Littlejohn's preaching career brought new opportunities just as it threatened existing ones.[26]

Littlejohn's record of his first months of itinerancy provides a view of his travel routine.[27] The plan of the circuit system determined Littlejohn's schedule. Ideally, a Methodist circuit strung together enough settlements for a preacher to make his round in four weeks. Distances varied in practice.[28] As his new apprenticeship required daily travel from town to town, Littlejohn lodged with Methodist supporters or, less agreeably, in taverns.[29] Because many itinerants' journals catalog the full drudgery of circuit travel, one is tempted to focus on the most dramatic events—for example, a preacher's besting of a heckler or being tarred and feathered, evidence of Methodism's unsettling influence on revolutionary society. Equally significant, however, were the mundane aspects of the circuit's regimen: travel, scheduling, lodging, and sociability. On these details social networks were built.

Littlejohn's first itinerant errands were close to Fairfax County, where he formed comfortable relationships and worked amid a revival begun the previous year.[30] Littlejohn enjoyed this situation, but soon he was assigned to a new area. From the northern counties of the Potomac watershed, Littlejohn traveled south by way of Fredericksburg, through Hanover County, past Richmond, and into the vicinity of Petersburg. He was now two hundred miles from Daniel Talbott's class meeting and all the people and events surrounding his erstwhile home base. But the relocation also introduced him to a new part of the Methodist network in Virginia.[31]

Itinerating and Locating: Stability through Mobility in Virginia

In following their prearranged schedules, itinerants met a range of obstacles, which they negotiated with the help of social connections. A young preacher like Littlejohn had to develop relationships as he went, but he did not travel in a social void. Rather, he drew on the resources of the many individuals who populated the religious landscape. The support of women was fundamental, for they constituted the majority of membership in the evangelical churches. Female patrons ranged from "Mothers in Israel"—the devout Methodist sisters on whom preachers relied as they visited and lodged in homes on their preaching circuits—to sympathetic individuals from other churches. Because preachers executed much of their work inside residences, they came under the care of the women who ran those homes. Women's influence did not stop at the doorstep, however, as they helped preachers venture out into communities.[32] Littlejohn learned this lesson early. On his way to Winchester, Virginia, in September 1776, he was initially rebuffed by a group of Quakers. The next day, one of them came around, a Mrs. Bruce. She described waking from a dream that made her reconsider Methodism, though doing so might bring censure from other Quakers, and she resolved to help the young preacher. "I am going with thee," she said, "as thou art young & a stranger in Winchester, to get the people out to hear thee." With Mrs. Bruce's support, Littlejohn preached well. Thinking of his performance in spiritual terms, he recorded in his journal, "God gave me Liberty & Power," but in fact that liberty and power were equally founded on the social sponsorship of Bruce. Despite the MEC's devaluing of women, the itinerancy could not function without them. Like Penelope Griffing, who sponsored Tobias Gibson in Mississippi, Bruce provided Littlejohn with access to the valuable resources of local knowledge and reputation.[33]

Of course, supporters were not found in all places. At those times, young itinerants were apt to fill their diaries with plaintive cries for fellowship, with regrets about a woman or domestic scene left behind, and with doubts about their calling. These tales of sacrifice and suffering, which fill preachers' published recollections and color historians' descriptions of itinerancy, also exaggerate preachers' social isolation. Littlejohn's trek south toward Petersburg illustrates the interplay of social isolation and connection.

As he continued his journey, the assistance he had enjoyed around Winchester became only a memory. Reaching Fredericksburg, Littlejohn "found no room for Christ at the Inn nor in all the Town." Yet, as Littlejohn understood, an itinerant who skillfully absorbed information about his route might avoid such setbacks and periods of loneliness. From Fredericksburg he rode thirty miles more before locating a resting place in Hanover County. At Brown's Inn a Christian proprietor welcomed the weary traveler and invited him to preach the following day. This example illustrates that Littlejohn was part of a communication network and knew how to benefit from it, for he came upon Brown's Inn not by luck but by information. As he described it, "I had heard he loved my Master." The next day, Littlejohn repaid his host by preaching from the Gospel of Luke. A mainstay of a circuit preacher's routine was to deliver a sermon in the company of his hosts. The performance completed the social exchange as part of a system of lay sponsorship, based on reciprocal transactions, that allowed travelers to fulfill their circuit duties. There were also personal benefits, for in this case Littlejohn expanded his social network. He met another Christian, repaid a kindness, and would likely be welcome to return in the future. He might also send other itinerants Brown's way—much as Littlejohn had learned of the inn and its proprietor from a contact. By relaying word of his host to others, he established social credits with travelers eager for a warm reception in the area.[34]

The value Littlejohn placed on the exchanges at Brown's Inn is evident in the preacher's journal. He had been swinging between joy and doubt and pining for the affections of Sister Monica Talbott of Fairfax, but on arrival he enjoyed Christian fellowship. Beforehand he had wondered, "What can so ignorant a young Man do in a strange Land among a strange people," but now he preached to new friends from verses from Luke that captured his renewed confidence: "The Spirit of the Lord is upon me, because he hath anointed me to preach the gospel to the poor; he hath sent me to heal the brokenhearted, to preach deliverance to the captives, and recovering of sight to the blind, to set at liberty them that are bruised." At a low point of his journey, Littlejohn felt he was "without a known friend to councel with," but his time at Brown's Inn shows that the feeling was not constant.[35]

Pushing on from Brown's Inn, Littlejohn's good fortune continued, but only temporarily. His next host, a Brother Patrick, offered accommodations so edifying that Littlejohn wrote, "I could stay here all my life." Yet he knew his duty was to travel, and when he left this "land where the Christians live," his doubts returned. Two days after his departure, Littlejohn confessed his misgivings to fellow itinerant William Duke: "Yet I fear God never sent me." Littlejohn had wrestled with confidence about his conversion; he now struggled with his calling to preach. Seeking confirmation, he turned again and again to relationships. Not only did he understand reciprocity (though he did not use the term) but he speculated that God employed it to support him in his ministerial work. He wrote, "I think if God had [not] sent me[,] the people w[oul]d not take so great care of me as they do." Favors from other Christians were signs that he was fulfilling his calling.[36]

Ultimately, like most Methodist itinerants, Littlejohn chose to locate from the traveling ministry.[37] The choice between itinerating and settling down was difficult precisely because each had social advantages. He enjoyed forming relationships during his travels, but he also felt the pull of marriage and domestic life, in addition to facing the occasional challenges of traveling during a time of war. Rather than cloistering young men, the itinerancy thrust them into communities. Itinerants commonly met future wives on their circuits. Littlejohn encountered Monica Talbott during his recruitment to the traveling ministry while participating in her father's class meeting in Fairfax. He continued to travel and in May 1778 advanced from probationary to full membership in the annual conference. By the fall, he had resolved to marry Monica and cease traveling. They married in December 1778 and settled at Leesburg, Virginia, where Littlejohn built on his social status as a Methodist preacher. He practiced a trade and provided for his family without difficulty.[38] As a local preacher, he had a flexible situation. He worked in and around his community, unconfined to a pulpit and traveling as needed. He ministered to people at important times in their lives, including marriages and funerals. This was the typical lot of a Methodist local preacher (and resembled the experience of many Baptist preachers as well).

Historians of Methodism have too often passed along the biases of itinerants who saw the local office as a demotion from the traveling ministry. Local preaching had its own rhythms and significance. Taking a location, to use the preachers' phrase, altered the shape of one's social network but did not represent a stark change to one's vocational identity. Littlejohn's transition illustrates this continuity well. Because he traveled less widely, the active part of his network shrank in geographic scope and became denser through greater local attachments. He maintained the gravitas of being a veteran of the itinerancy but shed some of its burdens. Circuit riders sacrificed secular opportunities while traveling, but in locating, Littlejohn retained his status as a preacher along with its worldly benefits.

Journal evidence is scanty for the years after circuit preachers ceased traveling, and this is true of Littlejohn, who wrote of the signal events of life—his marriage, births, deaths, revivals—and allowed everyday facts to pass unrecorded. Yet he provided enough evidence from this period of his life that we might glimpse, if not reconstruct, the continued importance that social ties and his status as a preacher held for him. Littlejohn's life in Leesburg combined a good measure of domestic comfort and sociability, a pairing he rarely found while traveling circuits. "At Leesburg I had many friends," he wrote. He knew a number of them from his time in Norfolk. Under wartime conditions they migrated more than two hundred miles to Loudoun County, where they reestablished friendships with Littlejohn. His family consisted of Monica and her two sisters. According to Littlejohn, the three were united spiritually: "We all walked by the same rule & minded the same things, having the Glory of God & our own Salvation in view." "And, blessed be the Lord," he wrote, "our time glided sweetly on."[39]

Although life was not without problems, serious economic concern does not appear to have been among them. Recounting the eleven years since leaving the itinerancy, the located preacher felt blessed in his finances. He "made, by the blessing of God, a plenty to support us." His financial situation was based on work but was also social in nature. When Monica gave birth to twins in September 1789, he did not worry about how to provide. Yet when a Methodist sister visited the new parents, she grew concerned about Littlejohn's demeanor. Expecting more excitement from a new father, she concluded there must be money troubles. Littlejohn protested, "I have no fear on that ground," but the news spread anyway, from one friend to another, until reaching the future "Lord Fairfax' ears." (This was Bryan Fairfax, heir of Thomas, the sixth Lord Fairfax and a British peer and proprietor of the Northern Neck grant, who had died in 1781. Bryan became the eighth Lord Fairfax in 1800.) He visited Littlejohn with an offer. Two local parishes lay vacant. Littlejohn might take them up and benefit from the glebe support. Fairfax promised to use his influence to guarantee Littlejohn's ordination in the Church of England. As Littlejohn explained, the position "would place me beyond the necessity of following a trade, which [Fairfax] thot rather beneath the character of a preecher of the Gospel." But Littlejohn declined the offer, confident that God would provide.[40]

Whether God provided is not a question for historians, but Littlejohn's religious affiliation was a support. The patronage of British nobles was atypical in Littlejohn's life, but it makes clear that Littlejohn was enmeshed in a religious social network during his settled years. The story also reveals something of the network's shape. Littlejohn had a direct relationship with Fairfax but that was not the path the news traveled. We do not know the exact course of the information but not long had passed before "the rumer spread abroad." The links in the chain leading from the Methodist woman to Bryan Fairfax were Littlejohn's friends and friends of friends.[41]

The story also highlights that local conditions structured social exchanges. Littlejohn's Methodism did not hinder his relationship with the Anglican Bryan Fairfax. Indeed, cooperation between Anglican clergy and evangelical preachers, as in the well-known example of the Anglican minister Devereux Jarratt, spread revivalism in Virginia in the late eighteenth century.[42] After American Methodists broke with the Church of England and formed an independent church in December 1784, a range of sentiments existed between Methodists and Anglicans.[43] Fairfax was an ordained Anglican minister. Moreover, "Parson Fairfaxe" was cordial with Methodists, representing an important resource for circuit preachers who relied on Anglicans for lodging as they made their rounds. Such fellow feeling, however, was not ubiquitous in this part of Virginia. Some Methodists were hostile to Anglicanism and to those who socialized with Anglicans.[44] We can discern pockets of cooperation and competition within the social world of northern Virginia. Significantly, Methodists need not have been cut off from Anglicans, a number of whom were early settlers and large landholders. Although Littlejohn left little direct evidence about this period of his life, we can speculate that he was one who kept an open door to the broader community. His nonsectarian sociability, combined with the respectable status he garnered from being a preacher, brought the potential of financial support and perhaps actual benefits. The offer of support from Bryan Fairfax had the markings of a traditional patronage relationship. The value of Littlejohn's social network was that he could decline it.

Social Exchange and Land Settlement in Kentucky

Social ties and professional reputation were important facets of Littlejohn's life, but they did not trump the economics of land in turn-of-the-nineteenth-century Virginia. Although it grieved the Littlejohns to leave Leesburg, they felt they could better the family's situation by selling their small Virginia holdings and using the difference in land prices to acquire larger acreage in Kentucky. That decision took them to Louisville, where Littlejohn entered the town's social life from the moment he stepped off the riverboat. Despite a quick and friendly reception, Littlejohn and his family still needed to make a home in Kentucky, a task complicated by the state's history of disorderly and unequal land distribution. Migrants to Kentucky looked to relatives, friends, and acquaintances as they negotiated the inequalities inherent in settlement. Those with fewer social resources were at a disadvantage. Methodists relied on their ties to a community of believers. With this move, Littlejohn's journal returns to the details of daily life. The entries reveal the many exchange relationships that the preacher and his family developed in Kentucky. Those relationships were based on the practices Littlejohn had learned years earlier as an itinerant. In Kentucky those same practices brought economic opportunities.[45]

Of course, relationships with other Methodists, though formed amid shared beliefs, remained subject to tension. The first farm Littlejohn rented was owned by a Brother William Harrison. Rather than inspecting the site himself, Littlejohn took Harrison's word regarding the quality of the house and the fertility of the land. He had reason to trust Harrison, for Littlejohn's use of *brother* to describe him suggests Harrison was a Methodist. However, in this case the bonds of Methodism did not prevent an unhappy arrangement. The house on the property disappointed Littlejohn, and he felt Harrison had deceived him. Littlejohn could have sought retribution. When friends advised him to report Harrison to the class meeting, Littlejohn declined, even though marring Harrison's integrity in the Methodist community would have been effective retaliation. In his journal Littlejohn wrote the incident off as a loss and admonished himself for forgetting the prophet Jeremiah's warning to "Trust ye not in any brother." Seen from another angle, the episode may have been a gain. Evidence from the sociology of migration and religion suggests that members of religious groups often engage in social exchanges without demanding "immediate reciprocity." They value the "idea of community" more than immediate gains or losses. Littlejohn had the right to bring Harrison before a Methodist disciplinary committee, but such actions sowed discord among Christians, which Littlejohn knew all too well as a pastor. He may have decided to preserve peace rather than gain an advantage in a single transaction. Thus, Littlejohn moved his family to another county. Harrison's reputation was damaged among those who sympathized with Littlejohn, and by letting the matter drop Littlejohn could please those loath to see dissension in the local church body—good reputation was a valuable resource.[46]

Gains from social exchanges contributed to the broader composite of Littlejohn's economic life in Kentucky. The Methodists of Louisville recognized his energetic leadership and value when he arrived from Virginia. They offered him a salary to be their stationed preacher. Much as in Leesburg when offered an Anglican parish, Littlejohn demurred. He remained committed to the itinerancy's ethic that preachers should be unbound by a congregation and its local interests. He chose to earn a living in other ways. Like most Kentuckians of the time, he cultivated the land. When the harvest was plentiful, he rejoiced, "so good is the Lord to give us seed time & harvest." But his livelihood depended on earthly factors too. Important among them was the labor within his household. John enjoyed relatively good health, but Monica's struggles with disabilities limited her contribution to the household economy. Otherwise, the relative youth of the household's members suggests they were a productive set of hands for agricultural work. One member of the family was described in the 1820 census as employed in manufactures.[47] By 1830, Littlejohn had added enslaved labor to his household, becoming a small slaveholder but a significant one by the standards of Logan County, where the family now lived.[48]

Littlejohn moved his family to Kentucky for economic reasons, but accumulating wealth was not high among his values. He deplored how Kentucky capitalism affected Christians. Of his wife's cousin he wrote, "The cares of the world & deceitfulness of riches seemed to have had a banefull influence upon his mind." In Frankfort he found a similar case. The "overgrown wealth" of Colonel George Thompson had "blasted every spark of pious zeal," leaving the old Methodist "wicked & profane." As Littlejohn's use of "over-grown" indicates, his scruples were not with wealth per se but with its growing out of proportion to one's pursuit of holiness.[49]

Littlejohn was no lover of money, but he was no hater either.[50] He embraced material improvement so long as it served spiritual improvement, and he valued a basic social aspect of economic gain. Notes from one of Littlejohn's sermons, on the parable of the talents, show his thinking. On one level, his interpretation was about individual human nature. Littlejohn wrote that God gave humans "a soul poss[essed] of various powers [and] affections as reason, under[standing], will, memory, [and the] various affections." Humans also received "a body closely connected w[ith the] soul." These faculties of soul and body engaged "the distinctions and enjoyments of this world," of which five of the six he listed were decidedly social in character: "riches, power, perferment, intrust, connections, or respect." They were also endowments from God—and every bit as much as the soul and body. "We improve them," he continued, "when we render them conducive to the good of soul, [etc.] When so used we shall have more."[51]

In Kentucky, Littlejohn's economic life remained a mixture of travel and social connections. Although many of his resources were tied to the land and agricultural labor, he himself was not. His ministry and his business mingled in his travels—his preaching and the relationships it engendered supported and extended his secular business. In this regard, life within Methodism had any number of advantages, and they might take any number of forms. Littlejohn's horse illustrates this quality quite well. The preacher knew well the value of a horse: he had learned in his itinerant days the danger of an open corral and a footloose animal to a traveler's schedule. A horse thief was a bigger problem, but not one too big to best a well-connected Methodist. When Littlejohn's finest bay horse disappeared on a June night in 1821, the preacher and his son traipsed across the region in pursuit. Littlejohn found the thief in a Harrodsburg jail. The man protested innocence but offered a tip: seek the animal across the river from Louisville near Jeffersonville, Indiana. Littlejohn followed the lead but to little avail. The horse had been purchased and put in transit to Pennsylvania.[52]

Littlejohn estimated that he and his son had logged nine hundred miles tracking across the state, but the effort that mattered most was a letter sent to Thornton Fleming. Fleming had served in Virginia in the late 1780s, where he likely knew Littlejohn. He was now the presiding elder of the Pittsburgh District of the MEC and supervised its seven circuits, which encompassed the stolen horse's reported destination. In a matter of days, Fleming ascertained the location of the bay horse, enabling Littlejohn to recover it from a justice of the peace in Lawrenceburg, Indiana, thirty miles along the Ohio River west of Cincinnati. While the animal was "very much reduced," Littlejohn had recovered his property by making use of a Methodist network that spanned three states and much of the Ohio River Valley.[53]

At other times Littlejohn used his network to earn extra income by performing marriages as he traveled. For example, he received a twenty-dollar fee for uniting a Mr. Barker and Miss Wheeler in marital bliss. Although not a princely sum, the money was more than twice the wages an agricultural laborer could expect in a month. References to marriages he performed are scattered through Littlejohn's journal, with fees ranging from three to twenty dollars. Here too travel was important. It allowed Littlejohn access to a larger market of couples than if he had remained in his home community. The work was efficient. As long as he was licensed, the only investment required for each new service was time, for he had long since been ordained. Further, he drew on the pastoral reputation he had already cultivated and could officiate marriages while traveling for other business.[54]

Performing marriages and recovering stolen property were among the small economic benefits of Littlejohn's social network. Neither was sufficient for a living. Yet their accumulation was significant for Littlejohn. In the case of the horse, he held a form of insurance, the premium for which was paid through social relations. Presiding over marriages was a sideline, and the fees he received were a cushion to his income.

Social Exchanges and Land Agency

But social exchanges and travel were also the foundation of a larger venture for Littlejohn. He began a business as a land agent in which he tapped the value of his Kentucky and Virginia relationships. In 1819 and 1820, he took two trips, one to Virginia and one through the counties of the Bluegrass region. The first excursion returned him to his old home of Leesburg. There he immersed himself once again in a part of his social network that had become distant but not detached. He nourished old relationships. The benefits of friendship were manifest on arrival, and he even had to turn down favors: "My friend Charles Binns [a Methodist and the clerk of the Loudoun County court] kindly furnished a room for my accomodation, others were offered. With this kind and agreeable family I chose to stay, occasionaly visiting the rest." He returned not only as a friend and former neighbor but also as a minister. "I once more assended my old Pulpit," Littlejohn recorded, "& preached with comfort to a large audience." "After meeting broke up," he continued, "I had the pleasure of speaking to many." As these last words suggest, Littlejohn's stay provided ample opportunities to rejoin the social life of his old community, not only at Methodist gatherings but also at typical sites of civic interaction. For instance, being in the seat of Loudoun County, Littlejohn attended court day, where, he noted, "I saw a number of my old Friends and acquaintances." He also conducted marriages, six in less than two months, though he recorded no fees as he had in Kentucky. Having hosts in Leesburg allowed Littlejohn to make short trips to Washington, DC, and Georgetown for personal business. As he visited with friends, he likely relayed news of Kentucky. Travel between the two states was by this time more common than in the eighteenth century; therefore, the main value of news from Littlejohn was its trustworthiness. Although the preacher made no notes of conversations with his host, Charles Binns, they likely spoke of real estate, for Littlejohn returned west to work as a land agent for his Virginia contacts.[55]

Back in Kentucky, Littlejohn moved his family from Warren County to land near Russellville in Logan County in December 1819. He did not travel outside southwestern Kentucky but preached in a number of places while working as a land agent. In early February 1820, he embarked on his second trip, resuming the land agency work arranged in Leesburg, which kept him from home until April. His route to the Bluegrass counties took him once again through Louisville, where he relied on his social network for lodging in that important locale of trade and information.[56]

There he ministered and socialized among the Methodists of the city. From Louisville, he journeyed northeast into the "upper Counties," heading as far as Flemingsburg and returning along a loop south of Lexington. His itinerary included the commercial and civic hubs of the Bluegrass region: Frankfort (the state capital), Lexington, Flemingsburg, Paris, Winchester, Lancaster, Danville, Versailles, and Nicholasville. His purpose was to inspect lands for clients, including Charles Binns and members of the Lee family of Virginia. Littlejohn's business depended on amiable hosts for lodging: his wife's cousin John Talbott, a Mr. Hughes, a Captain Hunter, and his "old Friend Colonel Respess." They were friends, family, and, as the military honorifics suggest, members of postrevolutionary respectable society. Some are identifiable among the elite of their communities. Travel and sociability had been linked during Littlejohn's Virginia itinerant days. Now his social networks were the accumulation of years of relationships. This was social capital, which Littlejohn understood well. As he explained in his sermon on the talents, economy was not only providential; it was social, for "riches, power, perferment, intrust, connections, [and] respect" all fell under the same category.[57]

As Littlejohn entered new homes and returned to familiar ones, he built and strengthened ties. Colonel Respess and his family, fellow migrants from Loudoun County, Virginia, were Littlejohn's frequent hosts in Bourbon County, Kentucky. The value of this relationship is illustrated by the fact that Littlejohn's wife had stayed with the Respesses for nearly two months while John was arranging business in Leesburg the previous year. Littlejohn also lodged with Captain Hunter (likely the James Hunter residing in Franklin County in 1820 and 1830) on several occasions. While some of Littlejohn's hosts may have been mere acquaintances, these two relationships in particular were strong, and Littlejohn described them in endearing terms. Another example of their strength occurred several years later, in August 1828, at the death of Littlejohn's son Lewis. Passing away just shy of his thirty-third birthday, he left behind a young daughter. To ease the family's strain, the Hunters took in Littlejohn's granddaughter, at Monica's request.[58] Although the favor was exceptional, it was one of many exchanges that bound Littlejohn to others. He never arrived empty-handed; his contribution was pastoral. When staying with friends, he led their families in devotion. Sometimes friends of the families joined in to receive the preacher's ministry. If a larger audience gathered from the community, Littlejohn offered a public sermon. In this way, he satisfied his calling, returned value to his hosts, and extended his reputation as a religious leader. It was a pattern held over from his time as a circuit preacher.[59]

These were social exchanges, but Littlejohn converted their value to economic capital. As a land agent, Littlejohn was frequently in the saddle and calling on his contacts. As he noted in April 1820, "During this Journey, preeched occasionally, met with several persons whom I had known in Virginia & Maryland, and had a specimen of the difficulty I might expect in doing the business of my Land agency—Principle is lost sight of, where Interest is the stake." Dealing in land speculation did not wholly comport with Littlejohn's values, but he continued the work through the 1820s. Still, the land agency never displaced his preaching. In fact, several months after his Bluegrass tour, he agreed to preside for one year over the Methodist society in Louisville, a body torn with dissension from debt disputes among the brethren. The preachers of the annual conference had urged him to the task likely because of his experience and reputation for building relationships. The work filled most of his time, but he continued the land agency. The various parts of his occupational life remained entwined.[60]

For the remainder of the 1820s, Littlejohn, who turned seventy in 1825, traveled through Kentucky, preaching and viewing land. These efforts required physical and mental exertion. For example, in 1820 he had to attend auctions, "procession" the boundaries of tracts, and travel to the "Sales at Frankford." At times, he dealt with disagreements in business, as in 1822 when he "obtained an Act to secure Mr. Binn's Land, after having great trouble with Burtis Ringo, esq.," a dispute that exercised the state and federal courts for years thereafter.[61] Travel and business negotiations taxed Littlejohn's personal resources and highlighted the value of his social ones. His network provided a much larger pool of social and economic resources than he commanded personally. His "temporal business" required regular visits to Frankfort. He had no love for the commercial town, finding it "a place like all the Metropolises[,] where Religion is more in name than power," but he was comfortably received there. Just as he stayed with the Hunters and Respesses, when in Frankfort he found an open door at "Brother and Sister Trigg's where I am always at home." "This home is a real home for the feeble Pilgrims," he remarked. "Let God's blessing be on it forever." Having such a resting place allowed Littlejohn to combine his work as minister and land agent, a model he described in his journal: "After doing what business I could, Preeching occasionally at Frankfort and other places in my rout[e]." But this was no humble accommodation, for William Trigg was among the largest slaveholders residing in Frankfort as of 1810. The preacher's network, however much he protested the moral priorities of the "Metropolises," gave him access to the economic elite of this hub of commercial and civic life. Susannah and William Trigg were valuable associates, and they were not his only contacts around the capital.[62] He occasionally visited his "old friend & Brother Col. George Thompson." Thompson was the sort of dignified figure whose acquaintance held earthly value. He had been a Virginia militia officer during the Revolution. In Kentucky, he was a member of a prominent family associated with Methodism in Harrodsburg and Mercer County. The relationship dated to 1776 and 1777 when Thompson hosted Littlejohn several times as an itinerant preacher in Fluvanna County, Virginia. In later years, the family remained a resource for Littlejohn, as when Thompson gave the preacher "a Letter of Introduction to his only Son, the then speaker of the [Kentucky] House of representatives," which read, "I introduce to you your Mother's preecher." Thompson was also likely one of Littlejohn's clients in his land agency business.[63] As the letter of introduction states and as historians have established, preachers typically ministered to families by way of wives and mothers, but the husbands and fathers represented to the community the social and economic value of families. In his relationship with the Thompsons, Littlejohn leveraged both facets of the patriarchal household and capitalized on the gendered nature of evangelical social relations.

Littlejohn's relationships cannot be reduced to any one description. They were based on business, politeness, and religion, and no one of these trumped the others. He maintained friendships despite differences in religious principles. Captain Hunter was not a member of the MEC and had in fact split from the body during the O'Kelly schism over episcopal authority in the 1790s. While Littlejohn lamented the falling away from Methodism of Colonel Thompson and Captain Hunter, whom he alleged had been seduced, respectively, by wealth and by the Campbellites, he maintained their friendship.[64] Other ties bound them together, such as the fact that Littlejohn's granddaughter was growing up in Hunter's home.

These relationships were especially important to Littlejohn as he aged. At times during the 1820s, he suffered sickness and debility. When his physical state worsened after his seventieth birthday, he considered that his "span of life might [be] coming to a close." This thought "excited serious reflection on the past, present & future." But the delays of illness were temporary, and he traveled through his seventies thanks to the care of his friends. For example, he once arrived at the Triggs' home several days after tumbling down a flight of stairs. Brother Trigg "applied without my knowledge to Doctor Majors of Frankfort who sent me some Medicine with a request that if I got worse he would visit me as a friend." Littlejohn remarked, "This was very kind in a stranger." Yet stranger was not the best term for the relationship. Dr. Majors was what we might call an indirect tie, a person known to Littlejohn through an intermediary. Majors's medical knowledge was one of the resources within the preacher's social network. Littlejohn apparently paid no fee and implied the care was offered freely. It would be easy to interpret the favor as charity to a poor, old preacher. However, the evidence supports that conclusion no more than an alternative: that Littlejohn repaid the social debt by spreading news of the benevolence of Brother Trigg and Dr. Majors. The former conclusion suggests dependency; the latter, interdependence. At another time, Littlejohn was recovering from an illness that made him too weak to leave home. After his pain subsided and with the only remaining symptom being a weak voice that "could not be heard the length of a large room," he traveled to a camp meeting. There, sickness returned, and he collapsed. Other attendees, including doctors, rushed to his aid. Under the care of a Methodist sister, he recuperated after several days.[65] In a period lacking institutional healthcare, Littlejohn's community of friends provided vital help as he struggled with debility while pursuing his obligations away from home.

Illustrating how Littlejohn gained from his social ties is easier than measuring those gains. The scattered data he recorded in his journal and almanacs do not allow a close accounting of his success as a land agent. But by 1830, Littlejohn's economic situation appears to have improved, which accompanied other important changes. He had moved his family to Logan County, and he had buried his wife. He had lost children as well. As Littlejohn aged, his household followed the broader trend in western Kentucky, shifting from free labor to that of enslaved people.[66] Littlejohn did not explain this last change in his journal, even though in previous years' entries he had expressed pity at their worldly status.[67] Perhaps an explanation of his household's turn to slavery seemed unnecessary. As a financial strategy, purchasing slaves was in line with his society's increasing reliance on slavery for labor, as an investment, and as collateral. Middling whites found property in slaves to be an accessible, liquid, and flexible instrument compared with real estate. However, this shift puts Littlejohn's social exchanges into their broader context, showing the intersection of (and likely conversion of) social and economic capital. His investment in slavery reveals the limits of social exchange as a liberal, market-oriented activity but also its practical economic power in the lives of people like Littlejohn. Social exchange was a practice for the preacher, not a moral commitment. He relied on social exchange not because it allowed him to operate according to voluntary principles like reciprocity but because it was a valuable product of good standing in the MEC, one of the young nation's largest systems of voluntary association and network opportunities. Methodism's social capital connected Littlejohn to the southern elite, the landowning and slaveholding families who controlled economic capital in the region. What he gained from voluntary exchanges, he perhaps invested during his twilight years in the involuntary form of capital that dominated his society.[68] What is clear is that travel, vocational status, and social exchanges provided access to traditional resources of land and labor to form Littlejohn's personal economy in Kentucky.

In 1830, on a final trip east to Virginia and Maryland, Littlejohn began to arrange his affairs. He had outlived much of his family. His journal entries increasingly turned to the relationship among his body, his spirit, and God. He meditated on disability, which he understood would slow and eventually end his travels. Returning to Baltimore, he visited friends and settled family affairs. He rejoined the Baltimore Annual Conference in a superannuated status so that he could die a member of his old preaching fraternity. This was a symbolic gesture toward his lifelong connection to the Methodist itinerancy.[69] However, the access to resources that Littlejohn gained from his association with the itinerancy was very real. Littlejohn had traveled in an official capacity for two years before retiring to local life, but during the decades that followed he was frequently on the move. Wherever he traveled, he preached, visited friends, and managed a portfolio of work that brought money into his household, extended his contacts, and allowed him to establish his family in the western lands of Kentucky. His piety and usefulness worked to his advantage in all of these pursuits. In death, which came in the spring of 1836, he was remembered for those qualities.[70] Doubtless his network of hosts and clients valued his reputation, availability, and knowledge, each tied to his experience as a traveler and religious leader. Where religion, occupation, and status met, Littlejohn found opportunity. His accumulation of resources was not aggressive, but it was sustained over eight decades and countless miles. Littlejohn's was a story of personal progress, and his use of social exchange took advantage of existing social structures rather than combatting them. His middling success depended on respecting and promoting consensus and stability within the church and in his personal relationships. Whether or not southern evangelicals traveled the arc from "dissent to cultural dominance," it was the mundane social practices like those of Littlejohn's travels that established evangelicals' place in southern society.[71] Littlejohn's life represents a stratum of the southern and western social order that was shifting after the Revolution, and his connections provide a view of how some individuals harnessed mobility to achieve stability in the churning middle of that order.

Stability eluded many, however. The enslaved woman who greeted Littlejohn in Louisville and those he purchased buttressed his stability while living under the paternalist presumption of being unfit for independent stability. The Native Americans who had used and claimed the lands that Littlejohn traveled and transacted were largely expelled from the land and expunged from settler memory. Many white women, despite sponsoring preachers like Littlejohn, found their stability within the MEC tenuous.

5

THE SETTLING AND UNSETTLING OF ANN HULME PRICE

Women and the Limits of Methodist Sacred Capital

Ann Hulme Price lived a comfortable, settled life in 1820s Cincinnati. Moving to that burgeoning city on the Ohio River marked the beginning of happy stability for Price; her husband, John; and their children. Beforehand her family had been in "an unsettled situation" in the nearby town of Lebanon, she wrote. To feel unsettled was to feel alienated from the ideal of settler society. Settlers were deemed respectable migrants because their mobility was temporary and contributed to a stable European American community.[1] To feel unsettled was to feel as people not deemed respectable: homeless (even placeless), contingent, overly dependent, out of control. The norms of settler society tried to relegate those feelings to the lower class, the enslaved, Natives, rogues. Little wonder then that on settling in Cincinnati Price exulted, "I feel my self more at home than I have ever done since I left New Jersey," her native state.[2] For several years she had regularly and faithfully counted her blessings and praised God for them. But in the summer of 1832, on the brink of the city's cholera epidemic, she lost her husband. She called him "my earthly support protection guide comforter and truly loving Husband."[3] They had lived in love and mutual support. This was not the only loss in Ann's life, but the loss of her partner was profound and unsettled her domestic life.

Ann Price wrote to New Jersey friends and family throughout the years. Her correspondence answers questions about the limits of Methodist sacred capital. The previous chapters have shown how social connections within the MEC aided Anglo-American settlers of the trans-Appalachian

West. But those social connections had limits. Considering those limits shows the boundaries of social capital in Methodism, and Ann Price's story is particularly illuminating in that regard.

Women guided the early Methodist movement. From the 1760s through the first half of the nineteenth century, women led Methodist band meetings and class meetings. They gave room and board to traveling preachers in their homes, providing the domestic work that sustained the traveling ministry. They introduced preachers to new people, extending the itinerancy. In addition to economic and social resources, women provided moral inspiration. They ministered to male and female Methodists, praying publicly, testifying to their own spiritual experiences, and exhorting fellow Christians to turn from sinfulness and continually pursue holiness. The MEC consistently opposed female preaching, meaning women could speak publicly but were not allowed to teach from biblical texts. That was the preserve of men (though a small number of women in Methodist denominations are known to have preached). More commonly, preachers' wives traveled with their husbands, supporting and complementing them as ministers of the Gospel. Normally, the wives of preachers anchored the household while their husbands traveled. All those "mothers in Israel"—ministering women—imbued early American Methodism with much of its countercultural power. With time women's public participation waned as patriarchal society embraced the ideology of domesticity. Amid this elaboration of domesticity, notable women, in the tradition of mothers in Israel, continued to press the gendered boundaries of mainstream Christianity in the early republic by performing public roles in the MEC. Nevertheless, those women remained exceptional.[4] Most women's religious work developed the itinerancy and, in turn, settlement.

In her early years, Price performed a similar role as a preacher's wife, but with time she transitioned from a mother in Israel to a mother in Cincinnati. Methodist sources herald mothers in Israel but say little of the everyday mothers consumed at once by their spirituality and earthly chores. White Methodist women might be expected to have fared much better than groups kept on the margins of the institution. Historians well know that African Americans and Native Americans did not receive the full benefits of the predominantly white MEC. Neither did white women. In a church constituted mostly by women, men filled the local and itinerant offices. This was key, for women's access to Methodist social capital was often indirect, occurring through male relatives. The result for Ann Price, like many Methodist women, was that her connection to Methodism was deeply felt, indeed foundational to her identity, and yet was vulnerable. Her life as captured in her letters allows an intimate history of that paradox.

Evangelical religion was not a path out of domesticity. Understanding this is important for understanding the boundaries of the Second Great Awakening. Some women used evangelical churches for social bonds and political action. Especially in the towns of the Northeast, some middling women founded their identities on their domestic virtue but also forged relationships with other pious women, stretching their social lives beyond husbands, children, and extended family. They participated in the public sphere through associations for reform and charity.[5] Most women did not fit that model, however, nor did Ann Price. Her story describes the history of evangelical women in important ways. Occupied by the physical and emotional labor of domestic life—what historians have recently called "embodied motherhood"—she was relatively bound to her home.[6] Her confinement resulted not from Methodism's domestication in the 1820s and 1830s as it shifted its basic disciplinary practices from class meetings to homes.[7] Rather, it resulted from the draw of settlement and the accompanying demands of marriage and motherhood. Even though she lived in an urban area where opportunities for association were bountiful, Price did not invest substantially in associational activity with other evangelical women. She had neither the time nor energy. In that regard, she was like the many white evangelical mothers who were more numerous than the associating women of the Northeast but who have received less attention. Price's experience, even though she lived in Cincinnati, better represents western and rural evangelical women and mothers, for whom the Second Great Awakening and capitalism did not provide great physical or social mobility.[8]

Settling: A Pilgrim Finds Repose

Born in 1784, Ann Hulme was one of two children of a religious family of Burlington, New Jersey.[9] A devout upbringing laid the foundation for a life of devotion. From her father she descended from members of the Philadelphia Yearly Meeting of the Society of Friends. Her mother was Episcopalian. There within the small Hulme family on the banks of the Delaware River about twenty miles upstream of Philadelphia was a meeting of two sides of the English Reformation, the radical piety of Quakerism converging with the postrevolutionary remnant of the Church of England. Ann's brother, John, hewed to the Quaker sentiments of their father, but not Ann.[10] Years later, Ann credited her "dear mother" for teaching her and John the importance of "laying up treasure in heaven" and training their own children to do the same.[11] It is difficult to say why any individual chose one religious group over another from the vibrant spiritualities of postrevolutionary America, but Ann's choice of Methodism makes sense in two ways. First, Methodism was a synthesis of the radical piety of the Protestant Reformation and the episcopal Protestantism of the Church of England in which it originated as a religious society. Second, she met a Methodist preacher, whom she married.[12]

Ann Hulme likely met John Price in 1813, when he was assigned to the Burlington Circuit of the Philadelphia Annual Conference. John had been a traveling preacher since 1810 and by the time he worked in Burlington had been fully admitted to the itinerancy, ordained, and named to the office of deacon. That role required election by his annual conference and conferred the authority to baptize and officiate marriages. The following year he progressed to the position of elder. At thirty-two years of age, Ann married John in September 1816, the year he had sole charge of the newly formed St. John's Church in Philadelphia. She accompanied her husband to his 1817 appointment to the Dauphin Circuit surrounding Harrisburg, Pennsylvania, about 125 miles west of Burlington.[13] There she lodged with the McAllisters, parents of another Methodist itinerant, and occasionally traveled along the circuit with John. Daily details of her life are scant, but she was likely an emotional and intellectual support for her husband in his ministry. She had been baptized fifteen years earlier.¹⁴ Her formative years in a pious home imparted to her a deep faith that she drew on throughout her life to urge her loved ones toward holiness, the work of motivation and accountability being essential Methodist practice. The one letter from this time does not nominate her contributions to the itinerancy but it is suggestive. From her long experience with evangelical piety, she understood the requirements of clerical success and confirmed them in her husband. "Mr. Price," she wrote, "is very much respected, which affords me great satisfaction. He is indeed worthy of it." Methodist itinerants craved that kind of emotional support amid their sometimes solitary travel, and so it must be accounted in Ann's connection to the church's mission. Much as an official Methodist preacher would, she identified as a "pilgrim and sojourner" and "desire[d] to be useful to our fellow creatures." She spoke admiringly of her husband's performance in his work but rarely explicated the tie to her own. The omission perhaps marked humility and admiration, but it was also a product of the patriarchal domesticity that concealed women's work value in the early nineteenth century.¹⁵ She contributed to Methodist society in ways similar to her contributions to the McAllister home, where she encouraged Mrs. McAllister's quest "for that change of heart which she is deeply convinced as necessary to prepare her for death," and where she consoled family members after an elderly relative was found dead and fallen into a fireplace.¹⁶

Ann remained attached to the itinerancy for at least three more years as her husband filled assignments. His appointments were to the circuits of Bristol and Freehold in the Schuylkill and Jersey Districts of the Philadelphia Annual Conference. Without evidence to the contrary, we can assume that Ann accompanied him and continued contributing to the work of Methodism in those areas. By May 1822, John had stepped down from the Methodist itinerancy.¹⁷ Within about a year and a half, he and Ann were living near Lebanon, Ohio, a town approximately thirty miles northeast of Cincinnati along the Little Miami River, which flows into the Ohio River just east of that city.¹⁸ For preachers and their partners, marriage commonly brought transition from full-time itinerancy to the settler mode of domestic life. Lebanon was a country town in the prosperous hinterland that had emerged from the troubled Symmes Purchase to turn Cincinnati into the "Queen City of the West." As settlement went,

Ann and John Price would have found much to their liking in this part of a state called "the garden of the world."[19] However, Ann wrote, "many circumstances conceived to effect" their move downstream to Cincinnati in the spring of 1824, and the reasons read nearly like timeless considerations of middling people searching for stability: "The loss of society, distance from [Methodist] meeting and the want of suitable schools for the children were our principal inducements to leave." Precipitating the decision was the death of the family horse, who perished after delivering them home from a quarterly meeting. "His equal we never expected to find," she wrote.[20] Instead, Ann and John decided to move to Cincinnati where they would not need a horse.

For Ann, this transition marked the end of the mobility that had occasioned to separate her from John. This kind of transition was what Francis Asbury had discouraged. He wanted a mobile corps of single, male preachers who would follow migrants and avoid the local entanglements of settled life. He might as well have tried to stop the process of settlement itself. Ann, John, and many others connected to the itinerancy did not think primarily in Asbury's terms. Rather, they desired to locate themselves amid the streams of commerce fanning out over North America with the expansion of the Market Revolution. Ann and John's choice of Cincinnati matched that of many Methodists. Cincinnati was becoming famous as "Porkopolis" in this era, but it was also a burgeoning hub of Methodism, hosting in time the MEC's western publishing house and a growing population of church members. Ann's story during this settling phase aligns with a main trend of the Methodist Age.

In Cincinnati Ann found the settled feeling she desired. Circuit life had been unsettled; Lebanon had not seemed like the final destination, but in less than a month of living in Cincinnati, Ann felt "my self more at home than I have ever done since I left New Jersey."[21] In an era of US history made possible by forced migrations, she found worldly repose. Owing to old Christian narratives, Ann identified spiritually as a pilgrim, but she also conceived of herself obliquely in terms of Christian settlement. In fact, she combined her dual desires to sojourn in spiritual terms and to settle in worldly terms. In her correspondence, the pilgrimage narrative allowed Ann, like other Methodists, to think of herself as a spiritual traveler passing through a world that she was called both to improve and transcend. That construction fit nicely within the Anglo-American discourse of colonization and settlement, which, in steps, claimed the earth and condemned it. Methodists reinforced this view of the world through frequent recitation and sharing of hymns.

In a letter to her cousin Martha Neale, Ann addressed the combination of problems confronting Methodist settlers: the dislocations of migration and settlement distant from family, the impermanence of life sharpened by those dislocations, and the pursuit of the transcendence of the world, which would reunite Christians in everlasting life. Moving to "this western country" limited their correspondence. Ann continued to press her friend toward salvation, toward transcendence of this "vale of tears," despite the belief that "I do not calculate to ever see you again."[22] She thus quoted a stanza from *The Pilgrimage of the Saints; or, Earth and Heaven*, by the prolific English hymnist Isaac Watts:

> Where on a Green and flowery mount
>   Our weary Souls shall sit
> And with transporting joys recount
>   The Labours of our feet
> Eternal Glories to the King
>   Who brought us safely through
> Our Souls shall never cease to sing
>   And endless praises renew.

Methodists interpreted the world through the text of hymns. The point of hymns was spiritual but the metaphors used were natural. In this case, Ann quoted a hymn that connects earth and heaven. The stanza describes weary pilgrims. The close reader can imagine the soreness of feet, the fatigue of body and soul, and the joyous rest on a verdant hill felt by the traveler upon safe passage. Ann's focus was on the pilgrim's rest, but the stanzas that she did not quote help us understand the relationship of spiritual pilgrimage and temporal settlement in her mind. She could hardly quote this pastoral stanza of deliverance without knowing that most of the hymn denigrates the earth. "Lord! what a wretched land is this," it begins. The earth is "horrid" and full of "terrors." Its features are "pricking thorns," "mortal poisons," "savage beasts of prey," all shrouded in "long nights and darkness."²³ The unregenerate would succumb to such snares, but Ann and Martha would transcend the forlorn world and reach "our Fathers House above."²⁴ That was the prize for the daily pursuit of holiness for Methodists, and that transcendence of the world is why they wrote and spoke and sang so much of holiness.

Ann Price's pursuit of holiness and transcendence of the world was premised on a practical awareness of the imminence of death. In that way, she was no different from other Christians connected to England's Puritan tradition, which reminded adherents that due to original sin, death was stalking them. Unsurprisingly, then, death was a recurrent, foundational theme in Price's writing. Two deaths threatened all humans. She called them "Death temporal and Death eternal." All Methodists would experience death temporal, but a good Methodist would escape death eternal by pursuing holiness rather than the "evil course" of the world's dissipations.²⁵ In both forms death created urgency, and Price urged her loved ones to prepare themselves. She implored her niece to "not forget that she is to die and that the time is all uncertain." "What is our life," she asked, "but as a vapour that appeareth but for a little time and vanisheth away!"²⁶ Her loved ones should pursue heartfelt religion, which would make them "useful and happy in life and qualify them for Heaven when this life shall end." She was "still striving to do the will of God and to be prepared to die." "The longer I live," she wrote, "the more important it appears to me to be ready to die—for my childrens sake I would wish if it is the will of God to live a few years longer but not for any worldly good wich we may possibly enjoy."²⁷ These words show Price's sincere attention to transcending the world, compelled by the realities of temporal and eternal death. This was the pilgrim's progress through life and over death.

However, even as she denigrated the world and hoped to transcend it, she could not avoid measuring her life in worldly terms. This was the settler's progress, a thread in her correspondence as important as her thoughts on pilgrimage. After several years of mobility, Price evaluated her settlement in Cincinnati in terms of family and friendships and the economic productivity of her family and of the city generally.

Pilgrim and Settler: Home and Improvement in the Queen City of the West

Price generally favored life in Cincinnati in the 1820s. Her pilgrimage values and her settler values were entangled in subtle ways. As a pilgrim, she criticized the worldliness she perceived, much as John Littlejohn had done of the Kentucky towns he visited to conduct business. "The Ladies," she wrote, "are as fine as Butterflies or tulips," sporting fashionable hats, "Gipsy Leghorns loaded with ribbons and Artificials." (Leghorns had been a sure sign that on the "farmer's frontier," the age of "capital and enterprise" had come to the West.)[28] The ladies "appear as if they did not know they have a Soul that must live for ever and ever when their poor Bodies are mouldering in the grave and food for worms."[29] Criticizing the short-sighted worldliness of others allowed Methodists to ventilate the tension they felt from living simultaneously as pilgrims and settlers. But making claims about the prioritization of worldly and spiritual matters was itself a way of committing one's energies to the world.

Often Price praised Cincinnati and invited eastern family to settle there. The case she made was economic. Like those trying to lure Edward Dromgoole to Ohio, she compared Cincinnati favorably to the rest of the United States, but she did so with an urban spin. "Any family with even a little money may live better and cheaper in this town than in any other in the united States," she wrote in May 1824.[30] Eight months later, she felt largely the same even as financial pressures had arrived for her family. The town was "the cheapest place to live in and live well too." Price's boosterism focused on the city's market, which, she related, "is said to be equal to any in the United States." It was full of "very cheap fine fat fowls" and sundry other goods. She listed their prices as evidence of the accessible abundance in which she lived.[31]

Price and her husband had arrived in Cincinnati during the canal era. By the 1830s, canal construction amplified the city's connection to its agricultural hinterland even beyond its beneficial riverine situation. It brought economic growth and social change, including class turmoil.[32] But Price saw improvement, "the cultivation of personal faculties and the development of national resources," as defined by its leading historian—a main theme of the nineteenth-century settler discourse.[33] "Cincinnati is improving very fast," she wrote her family.³⁴ The Prices had purchased a lot near the future canal path, and the area bustled with construction.³⁵ "Houses are building this summer in every direction," she wrote three years into the canal era. She described a new aesthetic. Where she once viewed the countryside, she now viewed houses. If she risked losing sight of the "beautiful high green Hills," she now took in "the Beautiful Bridges under which the Boats pass." Price was aware that not all progress was improvement. The Miami Canal boosted the region's economy, "but it has not made it any pleasanter living here[.] By some it is thought it will make it unhealthy[.] That we are yet to [prove]."³⁶ That last sentence proved ominous regarding her family's health, but for the time being Price attended to settling her family in the growing city. If Cincinnati were no longer "the cheapest place to live in" after three years of canal-powered growth, her family was among those riding the waters toward prosperity. One result of the canal was increased property values, which rose generally as much as 25 percent in under five years.³⁷ Price confirmed that "property greatly raised in consequence of" local business activity. Four years after moving to Cincinnati, the Prices purchased the lot next to theirs. The first lot had cost $100, the second, $300.75.³⁸ Ann compared the prices as evidence of real-estate appreciation, suggesting that the lots were of similar character, but the family was able to afford the rising costs.

Salvation and holiness promised Methodist pilgrims final deliverance from the world, but in a booming western city, a house was a helpful comfort to a settler. In a tradition stretching to seventeenth-century Puritan poet Anne Bradstreet, Ann Price thought deeply of her house. She chronicled construction plans and imbued those plans with aspirations of worldly pleasantness and stability. She wrote in 1828, "I endeavour to be thankful every day for what we have of this world['s] goods and if I shall live to see our House completely finished I hope I shall be humble and with gratitude enjoy it but if I should not I hope to rest with God above this world of toil affliction and Sorrow."³⁹ Her words show that she viewed her house as the meeting point of "this world" and the world above. It was at once a stopping point on a spiritual pilgrimage and the seat of Price family settlement. Judging by her surviving letters, Price's house ranked in value only below faith and family. As she thought of laying up treasure in heaven, her house contained the worldly goods her family accumulated. Because of construction delays, her thoughts on her house can be read as an index of her family's settlement in Cincinnati from 1824 through 1829.[40]

Price was not simply thankful for her house; it was she who propelled its construction. A carpenter boarding with the Prices in a rented home had offered to build them a house in exchange for future boarding. "This offer," Price wrote, "I urged Mr Price to accept."[41] John Price followed his wife's wish and purchased a lot for the house. When the carpenter, scorned in love, decamped to Natchez, Mississippi, the Prices had to hire a replacement to make the house habitable. That brought indebtedness and extended the construction timeline. The Prices lived in the incomplete house for several years. The debt provided enough pressure that Ann occasionally measured the stability of homeownership against it.

Her house was a place to pursue the ideology of improvement personally as the city around her bustled with improvement collectively. She strived to make it comfortable and pleasant, the standard units of her assessment. Early in her residence, she led an epistolary tour for her brother in New Jersey, using words to walk him through the house, downstairs and upstairs, measuring rooms, noting materials that "comfortably lined" the walls, pointing out windows. The unfinished house nicely contained their furnishings. There were well-lighted rooms and a porch for taking air, gathering rainwater, and relieving the kitchen of heat. She boasted, "I think my [Brother] could not [have planned] an House for comfort and convenience better than we have and I know you are good at planning."[42] About half a year later, she related to her niece that construction was set to resume and would make the house "of course more comfortable."[43] More than two years after moving into the house, it remained unfinished, but she still found that they "have a pleasant situation and live very comfortably."[44] In fact, Price's tone changed little over time, even as the four-year mark passed and she wrote thankfully, "Our partly finished house hath hitherto been the seat of peace and plenty!"[45]

Completion was not needed for the house to be a studio for improvement. Piece by piece the Prices added to the house. A new kitchen and new oven, for instance, supplied an opportunity to measure her improvement. She suggested as much to her niece, recalling, "I was saying yesterday when I set in my bread and pie I wisht your dear Mother could see me thus employed[.] I think she would smile to see how I have improved in housekeeping."⁴⁶ Modern readers might pass over "improved" as a common secular word. To Price, it meant more. From the Elizabethan era, improvement was a providential theme of colonization, justifying possession of lands from those whom settler colonists had displaced. The word grounded the discourse of settlement, having layers of meaning that were agricultural, moral, religious, collective, and individual. Through the language of improvement settlers told themselves they were fulfilling biblical dictates of productivity and stewardship. By Price's time, the term's deep cultural meaning had entered the field of partisan politics by way of John Quincy Adams, evangelicals, and future Whigs. Day to day, hardly could Price have participated more fundamentally in the acts of settlement than through domestic improvement, by building her house and baking her "bread and pie" there.⁴⁷

"Forty Big Apples": Domestic Labor and the Marketplace

Early in 1829, Ann Price wrote, "So bountifully hath a gracious providence dealt with me that I have lacked no good thing whatever[.] All I have to do is to take care of what is brought to the house and for endeavouring to do this I have the approbation of the best of husbands and the satisfaction of my own mind."⁴⁸ She described the separate spheres—home and market—of nineteenth-century culture. This was one of several times when Price differentiated her husband's business from her work. Hers inside the house she envisioned, instigated, and improved. It was godly, providential, and satisfying to her. In fact, the material foundation of John's business was the house and lot Ann had led her husband to acquire. Cincinnati's moniker Porkopolis pointed to its signature trade, and Ann wrote, "Our first lot was about entirely covered with Buildings absolutely necessary for carrying on the *Pork Business* as it is calld in this town." Pork came to town from hinterland farms, and John Price had put away the itinerant's saddle and picked up a cleaver. The yard surrounding the house was given over to "cutting up Hogs into Ham shoulders, Pork Lard, and Sausage Meat."⁴⁹ But as historian Jeanne Boydston described, there was "a widespread dissociation of wives and wives' work from the symbols of economic value" in the early republic, and one can see this in Ann's thinking.⁵⁰ As Boydston further explained, women's and men's work remained connected, but the connection was not acknowledged at the societal level. Ann, however, felt valued and shared the feeling for John. "I am not good for much," she self-deprecated, "tho Mr Price says he would not sell me for forty big Apples."[51] She rarely—perhaps never—spoke of her domestic labor as having economic value, that is, as being part of the Price family business, but it was.[52] Women's historians have described how domestic labor intersected with husbands' marketable productivity, and this was the case for the Price family. John hinted that much by accounting that he would not sell her "for forty big Apples." If not meaning it literally, here still was a man who sold food at market stating the value of his wife in terms of trade—a commodification she appreciated. If he did not mean to tie his wife to the market, he did so nonetheless.

Even in a family of mutual respect, domesticity as a social fact was powerful. Rather than relative work value, probably the main point about domesticity for Ann's life was mobility. John went out and Ann stayed in. John built reputation and Ann valued it. She focused on her housework, and that limited her connections.

John Price built his reputation quickly and converted social capital to financial capital with relative ease. At the beginning of 1825, Ann noted that all that hindered speedy completion of their house was that John lacked funds to grow his business, "the advantage wich many men have."[53] But not six months later, she related, "he has many friends in this place who have already lent him several hundred (and without interest)." As Ann boasted more than once, this was due in part to the fact that "his Bacon Pork Lard and Sausage meat bring the first price."[54] It was also a function of social capital. His lenders were friends. Ann worried that John would labor himself to death, and his friends likely admired that work ethic. His Methodism helped too. He remained a local preacher, and that was a model of respectability. Whether his loans came through a Methodist network Ann did not say, but John had little trouble raising capital for his meat business.

Both as a vendor of pork and as a Methodist local preacher, John moved within Cincinnati and traveled into the surrounding countryside, delivering sermons and buying stock to purvey in the city. Ann did not begrudge him his mobility, but it was a different course than her own.

It is hard to know all the work Ann did because she did not always describe it nor denominate it as work. Her work was similar to other middle-class mothers of her time: hard, constant, and exhausting. (Nonetheless, she continued to express satisfaction with it.) Like most middle-class mothers of her time, her work kept her close to home and precluded the public activities of civil society such as moral reform activism.[55]

From the home, Ann supported the pork business by investing substantial emotional labor into supporting John. Her letters are replete with praise. She crowned him the "best of husbands" and credited his work: "he labours very hard" and "toils with pleasure to make us comfortable." Moreover, she praised him with the language of the market, reciting weights to the pound and prices and margins to the cent. "How kind," she remarked, "was Providence to me to thus provide for me and bless me with a Companion in every respect so suitable." But she was well aware of the cost of his work: "He suffers much with pain in his legs." She understood that "he has been well repaid for his hard toiling[,] loss of sleep &cc," yet that understanding did not diminish the stress she felt for her companion.[56] She engaged closely intellectually and emotionally with market relations and their impact on her husband, but she engaged them from a distance.

Within the house was a range of daily tasks that consumed her attention. There was always sewing to be done. She loved to sew, remarking that one daughter "is like poor me she wants to do nothing else but sew," but it was labor still. Not only did Ann sew as part of her housework; she occasionally taught sewing for money. She was also teaching her daughters to sew. Not uncommon for middling housewives, she occasionally (and reluctantly) hired help with her sewing, but this was no sign of luxury or leisure.[57] Ann's housework was a daily cycle. These and other domestic tasks took their toll on her health—to such an extent that periodically, if reliable help could be found, she had to hire out all of her washing in order to complete the remainder of the work.[58] The cycle was incessant and tied her to her home. In this she differed little from other nonelite white mothers.

Motherhood and Immobility in "This Vale of Tears"

In large part, Ann Price's housework exhausted her because every task was performed amid the constant work of rearing her young children. She put her children to housework as she could, but they did not always reach the heights of efficiency. She had to teach them to be workers on top of teaching them how to be people. She was laden with the demands of childcare. Her youngest daughter clung to her: "the Girls can not keep Ann from me," she wrote. "She has awakend from her morning Nap and wants my paper pen and Ink[.] She walks around my lap on wich I am writing."[59] The cumulating demands of childcare, especially when nursing young or sick children, and housework left her at times "very weak and poorly" and "unable to go down stairs [and she] could some days just get across the room."[60] Ann's work was located throughout the house and, in the form of childcare, moved through the house with her, demanding her mind and her body. She was likely not the only mother of her day to recite the book of Lamentations: "O the Goodness of God to me ... mercy endureth forever and his compassion fails not[;] therefore am I not consumed."[61]

Ann also cared for her children spiritually. This was no light task. Devout Methodists believed in the long road of holiness—the necessity of sustained devotional effort and vigilance against backsliding into sin and damnation. As she reminded her brother, "We have a great [charge] devolving upon us[.] our Childrens Bodies and Souls too are consigned to our care over them[.] we are appointed to watch continually[.] O let us be careful to instruct them aright in the important principles of Religion and morality[.] let us try to do our duty by them as our Dear Honored Mother did by us that we may have no cause to reflect on ourselves if after all they will take the downward road."[62] Arminian theology kept front and center the prospect of eternal damnation. This religion was no opiate for earnest mothers.

Amid all of her physical and spiritual labor, however, Price did find in Methodism refuge and strength if not escape. As her niece prepared to marry, Price explained the role, which promised "duties" and "crosses" to bear. "You will feel," she counseled, "if rightly exercised[,] your daily need of divine grace." Quoting a psalm, she confided that she "still hide[s] beneath the shadow of his wings until all these calamities are over." Marriage and motherhood were joyful courses, but the work and fatigue attendant were among the "calamities" of a fallen world, "this vale of tears."[63] She did not only look to God's wings but valued church society. "When the Sabbath comes," she told another correspondent, again thinking of a psalm and Isaac Watts's take on it, "I am glad to hasten with my little Family to the house of the Lord. . . . I still love his Earthly Courts[,] the places of his Sanctuary more than any place." She could not always mobilize her young and sometimes sick children to go out to places "Where God resorts," however.[64] In those instances, she remained home, and John, still serving as a local preacher, went out to fill pulpits.[65] Even as women were the majority of evangelical churchgoers, the demands of motherhood still hindered them from going to meetings.

Between family and friends, near and far, Ann led a meaningful social life, but it was not a mobile one. She rarely wrote of calling on neighbors or stepping out to shop or attend meetings. She went to religious services on the Sabbath when able. She had little time for reform societies, auxiliary groups, or the like. It is true that her surviving papers are letters to eastern kith and kin, but we need not assume that the correspondence shows only a sliver of her world. Ann's letters were registers of recent life. They suggest that her social network comprised, for the most part, the members of her household and her distant correspondents.

Marriage and motherhood supplied most of her society. She adored her husband and children and enjoyed their presence. The children were in constant proximity and enriched her life, peopling the stories that fill her letters. Her husband was devoted, but as we have seen, his preaching and marketing took him from the home. From her home, Ann tended to the relations she had left behind. In this she was like many women who had migrated away from loved ones.[66] Regularly she reflected to relatives, "I do not expect to see you in this life." The belief that life was merely a pilgrimage provided comfort from permanent worldly separation so long as loved ones pressed after "the pearl of great price namely heartfelt Religion wich alone can bear you above the trials of this life and prepare you for Heaven." If they did not, she could not "bear the thought of not meeting you with Joy in that world of Spirits to wich we are all hastening."[67]

Price was thankful for letter-writing, a mode of converse available to the middling and elite.[68] Literacy, combined with the social or economic resources necessary for postage, allowed "interchanging thoughts and expressing the feeling of my heart."[69] Her letters reveal two levels of family life. She wrote to express love, relate local goings-on, and inquire about family and friends. But her letters also show that she led her children in an imaginative enactment of kinship. She wrote to her niece, "We talk every day more or less about you or some one of the relatives connexions or friends with whom the days of my youth were spent."[70] "You would laugh to hear them talk about coming to see you."[71] Price and her daughters planned trips they knew might never happen. They rehearsed introductions and conversations with kin they knew they might never meet. Even the youngest "has all your names as correct as if she saw you all but Yesterday."[72] Letter-writing allowed an exchange of feeling and news for which she was thankful and which was especially invigorating to the powerful imaginations of her children.

Locally, Price had "connexions" as well, but she wrote less about them. One of the tragedies of her life showed a community gathering around her. In early 1827, she suffered the demise of her newborn son. She fought bodily weakness, painful gathering of the breasts (likely lactation mastitis), and the torment of watching a weak baby alternate between "spasms," "strong convulsions," and "screaming intermissions" between them. Before three months, on a Sabbath day, she prayed for God to "take the dear little suffering babe to rest." The child died in its father's lap as he recited a Wesleyan hymn:

> Happy babe thy days are ended,
>   All thy painful days below
> Go by angel guards attended
>   To the Arms of Jesus Go!

The lyrics were the death knell tolling to those gathered, for "the room was crowded with neighbors and solemnity filled the place."[73] Ann's postpartum travails brought her neighbors to comfort her and pay respects. That fact shows that Ann was not wholly homebound, but it is telling that the moment she was most surrounded by local friends occurred at a rare time of crisis and within her home.

Ann was not without visitors. Beyond the occasional woman kept to help with sewing, washing, or childcare, there were relatives. John's sister stayed for a stretch, and Ann's nephew George lodged with them after traveling from the East heading for New Orleans. Houseguests brought Ann joy. Even George—a moody, drunken, lying cuss who complained of his father's (and benefactor's) overbearing ways and carped at his hosts—was a welcome presence.[74] And because Ann tried to occupy George by taking him visiting, it is clear that she could leave the house to socialize.

But these were exceptions, limited by the confinement of domesticity, and that is why her correspondence meant so much. Her brother wrote infrequently, though she asked more of him.[75] Her faithful correspondent, and main connection to her native world, was her niece Sarah.[76] However, the claims of domesticity, through Sarah's becoming a wife, threatened that exchange. "Mr Price tells me," she lamented, "I must not expect Sarah to write so frequent as she used to now she is Married... but I hope she will not forget or neglect to write for her Letters have been for these last three years (more especially) a source of pleasure and satisfaction I cannot express." A comparison of community produced Ann's concern: "Tho I have many kind friends and agreeable acquaintances in this place yet none of them feel so united to my affection as the friends and acquaintance of my youthful days."[77] If Ann's words were sincere—and there is little reason to doubt them—she had not reproduced the fullness of society she had come from. The problem was on her mind in 1828, the year following her son's death. Perhaps the loss caused reflection. She turned to poetry to illustrate her feelings, quoting an unsurprising poet, the popular and evangelical William Cowper. The particular poem, however, is revealing. Of all Cowper's verse and hymns, Ann thought of his speculation on the experience of Alexander Selkirk, the seventeenth-century castaway and inspiration for Robinson Crusoe. Resonating for her was the most famous story of isolation in the Anglo-American world, particularly the stanza imagining "native home":

> How fleet is the glance of mind
> > Compared to the spread of its flight
> The tempest itself lags behind
> > And the swift winged arrows of light
> When I think of [our] Native home,
> > In a moment I seem to be there.

Ann interjected before the stanza's final line: "I will not add 'but alas recollection at hand soon hurries me back to dispair,' No blessed be God I am not in dispair[.] I am happy!" In fact, she continued, "I feel this night a degree of Peace I would not barter for the Gold of Indies." The tension in her commentary was the result of settlement. She felt at once isolation and peace. She was thankful for her domestic context, but it left her "generally fatigued enough to retire to bed as soon as the business of my family will admit."[78] The business of her family did not admit much time for society beyond the home.

Ann's faith in pilgrimage sustained her because it promised a resolution to this tension. She could feel both isolation and peace because she had "a good hope that through Grace I shall gain the port of endless rest myself and that I shall meet many now dear to my heart by the ties of Nature Grace & friendship on that peaceful Shore."[79] Moreover, she was in fact mostly settling successfully by 1828. She had ceased the mobility of an itinerant's wife, built most of a home and found satisfying work within it, and begun to rear a generally healthy family. Her pilgrimage narrative actually sustained her faith in settlement. The earth was a vale of tears and affliction, as she often wrote. Life in the world, she knew, was meant to be a struggle with death. (To a Christian, of course, this life was death, and death was the beginning of true life.) Comparatively, successful settlement was comfortable, but its stakes were not high.

"Little Congenial Society": The Unsettling of Ann Price

In 1827 and 1828, then, the strains of motherhood mounted for Ann Price. The work and the trials paced neck and neck. Much as Janet Moore Lindman has shown of Quaker women, the bodily and emotional stresses of motherhood increased Ann's piety but also decreased her access to her network and specifically her church.[80] Not only had Price borne and lost a newborn amid postpartum discomfort, but in the surrounding months two of her three daughters had sickened near to death. "I endeavour to hold her very loose," she wrote of the youngest, "ready to relinquish her at my heavenly Father's call for I know not the day nor the hour." At the same time, her own feebleness had her weighing whether "it would be a far greater trial for me to die and leave them my children than for them to die first." Although a contemplation of this kind was nearly ordinary for early American mothers, that did not render it less grave in the asking. On the physical plane, if Price's daughters were on top of her when they were well, they were when sick nearly immovable from her lap. It is no wonder she reported that "a little exertion makes me tremble and pant for breath."[81] Being a migrant and settler compounded the difficulty. Whereas some women were surrounded by a network of mothers, sisters, cousins, servants, or slaves to help with childbirth and young children, this was not the case for Price.

Given Methodism's emphasis on social religion and the opportunities for bonds within the "connexion," one might expect Price to have found sisters and mothers in Christ to help her. They are not prominent in her letters. Domestic life and church politics contributed to the absence. In the late 1820s, calls for episcopal reform came to a head and led to schism in the MEC, creating the Methodist Protestant Church (MPC). The reformers demanded lay representation in MEC governance. MEC defenders labeled them radical, expelled some, and caused others to withdraw. It was what Price called "a wonderful day of divisions and Cesessions," and she and her husband took up the "Spirit of Reform."[82]

The issue most evincing Ann's engagement with public affairs was the one that detached her from the nation's largest voluntary association. "I never loved Episcopacy," she declared, "tho [in] every other respect I was a Methodist." She valued Methodism's rejection of predestination and closed communion.[83] She disapproved of the "High handed measure taken by the preacher in charge in this station who expelld from the Society 4 Local preachers and 10 private members for no other cause but reading and approving" the reform periodical *Mutual Rights of the Ministers and Members of the Methodist Episcopal Church*. After she and John joined more than "two hundred and fifty of the most respectable members" in withdrawing locally from the MEC, Ann reported, "For my own part I can say I never have felt my self more at home since I joined the Methodist than I do at this time." John was a leader among the "Seceders," as she called their contingent, having renounced his MEC office and membership as of August 30, 1828.[84] Ann was proud of her new connection. She implored one correspondent, "Try to inform your self upon the subject[.] Your intelligent mind could soon understand the Subject and your views embrace the side of right and the side on wich your Friends John and Ann Price now stand."[85] She was also proud of John. She paid her husband, the former itinerant and now secession organizer, the highest professional compliment: "I never heard him preach with so much life and power."[86] Nevertheless, the Prices had separated from the larger MEC social network.[87] Combined with that, her domestic burdens limited her activity in the MPC network. Despite her interest in ecclesiastical politics, she confessed at times that she had scant opportunity even to think or correspond about the schism, let alone participate outwardly in the new church.[88]

The turn into the 1830s brought hardship to Ann and her family. By 1836, she found herself with "little congenial society" in Cincinnati.[89] Since 1828 at least, in the midst of the Cincinnati secession and following closely the strains of motherhood Ann related, John had endured weakness, swelling, and pain in his legs.[90] Three years later, the disability flared and ended all talk of an overland trip to visit Ann's New Jersey relatives. To appease the disappointed daughters, the family attended the next camp meeting, but there Ann stumbled, broke her ribs, and found herself confined to bed for two weeks. Methodists thought frequently of mortality. Ann's indisposition reminded her of it. She hoped to live a while longer only because of "how much I desire their improvement, and growth in all that's virtuous and good." For resolve, she again quoted the verse of William Cowper:

> Trials make the promise sweet,
>   Trials give new life to prayer,
> Trials bring me to his feet,
>   Lay me low and keep me there.

Dependency, too, came to her mind: "I feel deeply sensible [how] entirely dependent I am on God for Life and health and all the comforts I enjoy." Poor health highlighted her worldly dependency. Hearing the call of housework, Ann reported, "I can get no help," wishing a friend from youth lived near enough to lend a helping hand.⁹¹ That wish testified both to the confinement of domestic life and the limited assistance of Methodist connections.

Nothing stirs feelings of dependency like dependency unfulfilled. Less than a year after Ann's injury, her husband—"my best earthly friend"— died. John had been taking shifts sitting up with their daughter Rebecca through a severe fever, alternating with Ann and a visiting niece. During the days, the June heat was oppressive. On the final Sunday of the month, John took the pulpit but was forced to step away by a profuse nosebleed. For the better part of two weeks he insisted on attending his business at the market until his bowels confined him to the bed where he died. Although his illness is difficult to diagnose, he left Ann and their children in a city that would be ravaged by cholera in the fall.⁹²

If Ann's connection to Methodist society was already tenuous, John's death all but severed the link. His death also increased her burdens, "the many duties *now* devolving upon me," as she wrote. She related, "I have every [assurance] that he who for so many years was my earthly support protection guide comforter and truly loving Husband, and tender Father to my dear children is now forever blest and happy in the Society of God and holy angels." And she expressed faith that God would support her through what would increasingly feel like a lonely pilgrimage. "I trust," she wrote, "I shall still receive the same divine support and comfort."⁹³

Years earlier, Price had nearly rehearsed for this moment. A friend had lost a husband. To encourage her, Price had turned to the book of Isaiah and the Psalms: "Thy Maker is thine Husband the Lord of Hosts is his name the Earth is his and the fulness thereof, the cattle upon a thousand hills are his the hearts of all men are in his Land." What practical use was God as husband? She continued, "He can and will I believe raise up Friends and provide homes for you as long as you continue in this Vale of tears."⁹⁴ This, she believed, was God's promise to a widow. Now the test would come.

John Price was well prepared for death spiritually. "His life was Christian and his end was *Peace,*" Ann wrote. However, he put off writing a will and died intestate. She proceeded to settle his estate and had help.

"Mr. Price had many friends in the City and they are my friends also," she wrote.[95] She worked with or consulted several men about the legal process, including John Wood, who had been John's "endorser in the bank," a neighbor named Mr. Ayers, and Daniel Horne, perhaps an acquaintance in the pork business.[96] The Prices had taken on more debt that year than previously and had a large inventory. Ann needed to sell their stock to recoup the debt. John would have sold at market, but Ann had to hire a man to sell there while she and a neighbor and pork packer named Thomas Barnes sold from her home.[97] Price was well attuned to the intricacies of the business, and her advisers encouraged her to continue running it, but needing to be home, she was dependent on intermediaries for a market presence. Administration of the estate dragged on through 1836. Meanwhile, she took boarders and began teaching, relying on her oldest daughter for assistance with both. This brought "confinement" and concerns about health.[98] Cincinnati was yet under the "awful visitation" of Cholera in the early 1830s. That combined with grief and financial uncertainty to create anxiety and depression. She confessed to her brother in spring 1834, "O if I could only get to feel cheerful and happy as I once was all would be well as to situation[.] I do feel so when I feel well, but when confined to my bed or to my room and the dark side of every thing constantly before me—then I truly feel alone in the world."[99] Earlier, her brother had suggested she return to her native state. Now Price consulted with a physician and friends, receiving conflicting advice, about traveling alone to New Jersey for recuperation—no minor recourse for a parent so devoted to her family. She requested "a respectable pious Widow," who was likely a Methodist Protestant, to watch her children for three months. By the fall of the year, Price had returned from New Jersey. The absence and the caretaker, she found, had been hard on the children, especially Rebecca, who wore the strain physically. Price determined to move her family to New Jersey for social reasons. She had stayed in Cincinnati in part to uphold her husband's vision for the family in that city, but she had become convinced of "how much my dear children lose for want of suitable Society."[100]

Nearly two years more passed without improvement. The estate was not yet settled, and the unsettling of her life had continued. To return to New Jersey, she needed to sell the property and for the court to arrange her support from the estate, but she struggled with indecision. Her adviser, Daniel Horne, would only council her to a point, and she leaned heavily on advice from her distant brother. Friends told her that her plan of selling the home and moving east could ruin her financially. Her boarders and students were declining in number even as they taxed the family's emotional resources. Rebecca, working constantly and having watched her final friend move west, declared that she must go to New Jersey alone for respite from what Price called "the same dull round of all work and no play." "I really feel my mind deeply opresst," Price wrote. Since building her home and praising its urban environs, she now complained of her surroundings: "Our own Neighbourhood has become quite unpleasant—only 7 feet from our side door is nothing heard all day but noise and scolding & crying of children." The change in tone was in part a reaction to urbanization, but it was also a complaint about the failure of Methodism's "social principle" after the death of her husband. In one of her last recorded comments on the subject, she lamented, "I have little congenial society[.] in fact I have none but in a few families and the few I must visit, they come not to see me more than once a year—and my dear Daughters have not that company proper for them nor can they have in this place."[101]

Methodism was at once present and absent in Ann Price's life. This decades-long Methodist and preacher's widow found her faith strong but her society weak. Through the network coursed the language—pilgrimage, improvement, peace, rest, society—that guided and sustained her but not the full advantages of sacred capital. God was with her, but the church was not. Methodism's potential for building social connections made it a valuable mediating institution for the long process of Anglo-American settlement. Price's experience shows that *potential* is the key word. Methodism spread broadly across the burgeoning Empire of Liberty but not evenly. The gendered irony of early American evangelicalism combined with the settler impulse to influence her life. She joined one of the great social movements of the age only to feel isolated after the death of her husband. She followed the main trends of her church and society, building and improving and generally settling into domestic life. Her unsettling too is a story of common relevance. The demands of motherhood limited her contact with a church that lionized preachers and praised a fraction of women as mothers in Israel.

CONCLUSION

Love Thy Neighbor as Thyself

The date June 11, 1844, was widely recognized as a bad day for the United States of America. On that date, after more than a month of debate, the MEC divided finally over the question of slaveholding in its ranks. The largest religious denomination, and one of the largest American institutions generally, split into northern and southern churches. This was the culmination of a decade of periodic conflict over whether the MEC would countenance slaveholding among its members. Over the years, each side had its champions within the church—abolitionists from the North hectored intransigent representatives of the South while moderates leaning to one side or the other tried to keep the body in union.[1] The question that sheared the cloth in two centered on one man, Bishop James Osgood Andrew. The case was full of the irony and complex irrationality that marked so much of the nation's broader sectional conflict. Andrew had inherited two enslaved people late in life from his spouse. One of the slaves was a child; the other allegedly objected to leaving Andrew.[2] Manumitting them was illegal in Georgia; owning them, as a bishop, was untenable in his church. The simplest solution, to resign, was acceptable to him, as he had already contemplated retirement, but was not an option for his fellow southerners, who would not accept his resignation. That slavery was the cause of the schism seemed obvious; that the schism portended a larger rupture was clear. Editors north and south prophesied darkly, politicians Democratic and Whig rehearsed eulogies. Looking back from 1850, John C. Calhoun expressed the prevailing judgment that the division was significant because it occurred in one of the strongest of national cultural institutions. The schism was an "explosive force," and now the "numerous and strong ties which held it together, are all broken, and its unity gone. They now form separate churches; and, instead of that feeling of attachment and devotion to the interests of the whole church which was formerly felt, they are now arrayed into two hostile bodies." One of the nation's most important "bonds of union" had snapped.[3]

The Social Principle, Sacred Capital, and Settler Colonialism

Why were well-informed Americans like Calhoun convinced that the MEC was critical to the union's health? They perceived that the religious organization was deeply tied to the middling settler communities of the expanded nation. They glimpsed what this book has described. The MEC organized and amplified the social processes of white settlement. Connected by a fluid and disciplined itinerancy, Methodists carried forward the religious discourse that had justified possession and settlement since the Elizabethan era. As settlers, they pursued practices of social exchange, living the Methodist social principle. They formed meetings where they worshipped, held one another accountable, and, straying from the movement's discipline, traded news of worldly things. Methodists, preachers and laity, exchanged numerous letters in which they poured forth their godly love for one another, confessed their struggles and weaknesses, devoted their lives to the pursuit of holiness and their souls to God's mercy—and then traded the latest intelligence on lands, jobs, and spouses. The efficient networks of religion and settlement benefited antislavery Methodists in Ohio as well as proslavery Methodists in Mississippi. Those networks helped young men like Henry Matthews in their quests to establish themselves, as well as older men like John Littlejohn. Presiding elders such as James Finley and William Winans preached the Gospel, tended to the flock and to the shepherds, and gained reputations for their knowledge and usefulness in addition to their holiness. The legion of white women constituting Methodist societies also reaped the rewards of the social principle, even as Methodism's patriarchal values made women's connections to the church tenuous. Contemporaries and historians often judged the MEC remarkable in its time; it is little wonder that close observers held it essential to the nation of settlers that had barreled out of the American Revolution and seized a vast territory.

The Methodist social principle and the sacred capital it produced helped construct that settler nation. During the "Long War for the

CONCLUSION

West," white settlers seized lands as they were vacated by Native Americans in response to violence and political pressure.[4] The practices of taking—military campaigns, settler violence, removal politics, missionary projects—were one aspect of US settler colonialism; the MEC's main impact was in the arena of social reproduction. The day-to-day networking practices along preaching circuits developed American settler society in the trans-Appalachian West in ways that violence and politics did not. The first set of practices was for clearing, the second for building.

Love, Localism, and Sectionalization

From one perspective the MEC seemed a truly national body. It thrived in every state of the union, spreading a popular Protestant culture across the nation. Nevertheless, cultural similarity did not create a strong national society. Beneath the surface were many fissures. Methodist organizing combined print and oral communications with associational life to create "a common world of experience." The MEC and the other major popular churches were "socializing institutions" that created "a more integrated American society as opposed to a confederation of provincial societies." The MEC had a "nationalizing influence." That influence was founded on local social religion. While national organizations created uniformity of experience, local religious societies were the centers of people's interests. A national American community, as far as religion goes, emerged more from "strong local churches that shared common values and norms with their counterparts" than from the "power of a national institution."[5] Few high-level contemporary observers doubted that those bonds were powerful and held together a truly national religious community. That the slavery issue could sever them testified to its sharpness and fearsomeness as a threat to perpetual union. Viewing the MEC's print culture and shared norms, the organization fits well within the framework for nationalism, especially Benedict Anderson's "imagined communities."[6]

Too much can be made of that perspective. The national denominations had deeply local roots. We must remember how much Francis Asbury feared localism. Localism was to Asbury what faction was to James Madison, that is, natural but dangerous. Methodism was beset by local impulses that battled the episcopacy for control of the itinerancy and the basic identity of the church, and, most concerning to Asbury, distracted Methodists from their quests for holiness and mission to save souls.

Methodism's language of love enfolded those local impulses in emotion. Below the national level flowed powerful undercurrents of localism. The national Protestant consensus, despite skepticism and doubt, exercised substantial moral hegemony over American society, but it did not translate effectively into national bonding.[7] Despite observers' claims in the 1840s and 1850s, national denominations failed to subordinate local connections. Methodist organizing did as much, if not more, to strengthen local connections than national ones. Within an expanding nation, Methodism's language of Christian love created intense local bonds that overrode the national likenesses reflected in common Protestant experiences. Nationally, common experience might have worked for reviling Catholics, skeptics, libertines, and Native Americans, and for confirming ideologies of family and refinement, but it did not hegemonize personal social networks.

The social principle gradually localized and sectionalized. Although the history of emotions often deals with print culture, for Methodists and other evangelicals daily, in-person expressions of emotions were powerful bonding agents. The MEC was a national voluntary association, and it comprised important networks at the scales of region and nation, but the most intense bonds were formed through local, personal interactions. Indeed, displays of emotions helped draw the attention of contemporaries to Methodism. Detractors called those displays enthusiasm, which was typically associated with public revivalism in camp meetings or in barely veiled private meetings such as classes and love feasts. Enthusiastic emotion, however, was but one form in a spectrum of intense feelings and expressions. The most important emotions were experienced locally by way of spoken testimonies, prayers, and songs performed among spiritual family members—and, if we take their language seriously, through the routine and loving encouragements for brothers' and sisters' spiritual pilgrimages to holiness that framed nearly all Methodist correspondence. When Methodists came into conflict over matters of principle, feelings of betrayal ran high, as seen in the language of longtime Ohio itinerant Adjet McGuire before joining the MPC, who wrote, "I find that there is

CONCLUSION

no peace to be enjoyed in the MEC, By any one, who dare to have an opinion of their own, unless they will suffer themselves to be gaged [gagged] and treated with contempt, by Old & young men in Power."[8] Another area of intensity was conflict between local influence and episcopal control, which occurred frequently in the day-to-day functions of the MEC. Those conflicts inspired numerous disciplinary proceedings. An example is the case of former itinerant John W. Langdon, who was charged, tried, and expelled for violating the Methodist discipline by organizing the purchase of a Presbyterian meetinghouse for the use of the Methodists in defiance of the stationed preacher of Cincinnati. Langdon's feelings of betrayal were clear as he wrote to the quarterly conference: "How often in those days of Religious prosperity has Bishops Asbury & Whatcoat Sheltered under my roof and [concerted] ways and means for the furtherance of the Blessed work. And now I am old and grey headed, and still feeling the same love and attachment to the cause of my divine master, as well as to the Doctrines & Discipline of the Methodist Episcopal Church. To be thus treated, is to [me] grievous indeed." The aggrieved Methodist went so far as to compare the violence he experienced at the hands of mobs during the Revolution favorably to the treatment his fellow Methodists dealt him during his trial in Cincinnati.[9] Langdon and McGuire tell only one side of their respective stories, but what is clear is the emotional intensity Methodism contained.

The Methodist language of love had many tones and could lead to embarrassment or shame as concerned individuals watched and reproved one another, but the objective was fellowship of spiritually improved selves. The connections of Methodism were based on interpersonal exchanges and intensified by emotions. Those connections occurred not primarily through the distance-conquering technologies of religious print culture but through the primitive forms of association that Methodists traced to the apostolic age refracted through the Reformation, that is, the band meeting, the class meeting, the love feast, the watch night, and the hand-delivered personal letter. Referring to the context of the class meeting, itinerant John Kobler called those connections Methodism's "bond of union"—a label related but not equivalent to the "bonds of union" that John C. Calhoun mourned in his 1850 address to Congress over slavery and the sectional crisis. But Calhoun's faith in the national strength of the popular denominations was misplaced, for the power of emotion as a bonding agent was intensely personal. Whatever power the common experiences of religion possessed, their greatest effect was local.[10]

The history of Methodist love played out amid geographic mobility that was sectionalizing the MEC decades before the 1844 schism. Those Methodists who took seriously Jesus's command to love thy neighbor as thyself did so in shrinking religious neighborhoods among neighbors sharing local self-interests. If common Methodist culture, transmitted through print, held the promise of linking distant believers through the neighborly love of the New Testament, it had to battle against latent, erosive division. Sectionalization due to distance was a demographic process more basic and grinding than the better known history of periodic denominational schisms in the MEC which included the O'Kelly schism of the 1790s that produced the Republican Methodists; the separations of the African Methodist Episcopal Church and the African Methodist Episcopal Zion Church in 1816 and 1821; the formation of the MPC in 1830; the departure of the New England itinerant Orange Scott with a portion of abolitionist Methodists in 1843; and finally the 1844 rupture. Observing the new nation's territorial size and expansionism, contemporaries and historians alike have linked the questions of distance and disunion. Benjamin Rush said in 1787 that "there is but one path that can lead the united states to destruction, and that is their extent of territory."[11] Writing in 1847, Connecticut minister Horace Bushnell made clear that the margins were still worrisome for the nation when he wrote of the "wild race of nomads roaming over the vast western territories of our land" (and he was referring to white settlers).[12] For Rush and Bushnell, institutions would solve the problems of migration. Rush placed his faith in the postal service and communications, Bushnell in the large denominations, especially the Methodist itinerancy. Many historians who have considered similar questions for the period have found in popular religion the institutional development necessary to integrate a centrifugal society.[13]

But national integration was not the main theme of Methodism's institutional expansion and development though Francis Asbury hoped it was. In 1797, he wrote, "Methodism is Union all over; Union in exchange of preachers; Union and exchange of sentiment; Union and exchange of interests."[14] This was the bishop in a hopeful moment of aspiration, but as the preceding chapters have shown, he had his terms somewhat reversed. Methodism was exchange all over but not always union. In language befitting a Federalist in a ratification convention, Asbury regularly belittled and bemoaned the divisiveness of local interests. There was good reason to fear. The threat he sensed came from the self-interestedness of emerging democracy and capitalism.

Also menacing Methodist union was the expansiveness of a settler-colonial nation. By the end of the first decade of the nineteenth century, organized Methodism had thickened in areas of early settlement. It had extended to the Mississippi River and in some cases crossed it, organizing under one Western Annual Conference that included Methodist societies from the highlands of eastern Tennessee and the hills of southeastern Ohio to the old French settlements of the Louisiana Territory in the Upper and the Lower Mississippi Valley. Asbury's vision "to extend our ministry to the very utmost bounds of the empire" proceeded toward fulfillment, keeping pace with Thomas Jefferson's parallel vision to achieve a vast agricultural republic, an Empire of Liberty. But this unification of Methodists across a thousand miles was administrative and felt mostly by circuit preachers, required to gather each year to report at nonlocal conferences. Even so, they did not always comply, begging off because of distance and circuit obligations.

As the Methodist itinerancy expanded, the scope of ordinary Methodists' actual associations constricted. Although the earliest circuits had carved the West into large arcs along which Methodists gathered for fellowship in their two-day quarterly meetings, the passage of time saw those circuits subdivide like early counties. The old circuits encompassed less territory even as they included more people. The pattern repeated with the formation of new circuits. Quarterly circuit meetings were supposed to host the fullness of Methodist social religion, but they brought together Methodists and other Christians for fellowship from increasingly small areas. Preachers once frequently worked across political and regional boundaries; with time the borders of their home states constrained their travels. Perhaps the most telling example is that after 1820, conference realignments meant that antislavery Methodists north of the Ohio River had few pressing reasons to fellowship with their neighbors in the slave states to their south. In this regard, diversity of experience in terms of how Methodists associated with each other was the cost of organizational efficiency.[15] The religious social network of average western Methodists, then, was becoming more populous but also more local as the circuits in which they resided shrank in area. The logic of circuit growth brought sectionalization. As circuits constricted, the practice of loving thy neighbor as thyself constricted. Methodists still drew on connections afar when motivated to, say, learn of land, retrieve a stolen horse, or find a spouse, but less and less were they regularly linked to people beyond their shrinking spheres.

Above the circuits, the Western Conference itself subdivided. For fifteen years after its organization, circuit preachers presided over a large area of the continent. Young men rose to the itinerancy from villages and towns along the circuits of the Western Conference and took traveling assignments from a roving bishop. This process subordinated local concerns. An itinerant might spend a year in the heart of middle Tennessee, a society growing with an economy based on slavery, and the next year find himself traveling through the communities of southern Ohio, where Methodists had fled slavery's reach. This changed in 1812 when the Western split into the Tennessee and Ohio Conferences. The two new conferences split the state of Kentucky in half. The western annual conferences continued to subdivide. The Missouri Conference formed four years later, followed by the creation of the Mississippi Conference in 1817. In 1820, the Kentucky circuits got their own conference. And so the process of sectionalization played out: Illinois and Holston in 1824, Alabama in 1832, Memphis in 1840. In 1839, itinerant and historian Nathan Bangs commented on the unifying influence of Methodism: "Its extensive spread in this country, the hallowing influence it has exerted on society in uniting in one compact body so many members, through the medium of an itinerant ministry, interchanging from north to south, and from east to west, has contributed not a little to the union and prosperity of the nation."[16] The functions Bangs described—the spreading, uniting, and interchanging—had continued but not across the geography he sketched. Within five years the MEC was in crisis. In 1844, the issue of slavery cleaved the great body of American Methodists, creating the Methodist Episcopal Church and the Methodist Episcopal Church, South. The

CONCLUSION

Methodists were not the only denomination divided: the Baptists and Presbyterians also split along sectional lines, leaving Henry Clay to lament "the greatest source of danger to our country," and John C. Calhoun to remark, "Nothing will be left to hold the States together except force."[17]

These statesmen saw only the end of a longer process. The MEC had been experiencing sectionalization for decades. Slavery was the immediate cause of national rupture, but the demographic forces of migration and settlement had always caused circuits and conferences to subdivide. In the late eighteenth century, localized conferences were the norm because of a lack of organization. And although the MEC reformed their system in 1796, the church grew far too large to keep Methodists united in a handful of conferences, much less the "compact body" of Nathan Bangs's wishful thinking.[18]

The division of the early republic's largest religious denomination was not simply the 1844 General Conference meeting in New York where Bishop Andrew was tried, nor the debates in the church between abolitionists and southern hardliners, but rather a long history of emotional bonding within increasingly regional and local social networks. Within that context the question of slavery turned Methodists against one another, sometimes violently.[19] Methodists had built a great national institution but failed to build national unity. As settlement patterns shrank Methodists' networks, Methodist settlers continued to think of themselves as pilgrims hastening to "that peaceful shore."[20] They exhorted their loved ones to practice holiness and transcend this vale of tears, ardent for reunion amid perpetual peace. Meanwhile, they conducted their daily business, exchanging with those like them, thinking little of those who were not, benefiting from an institution that helped with both.

NOTES

Abbreviations

AHP   Ann Hulme Price Papers, Ohio History Center, Columbus
DD   *Doctrines and Discipline of the Methodist Episcopal Church, in America,* 10th ed. Philadelphia: John Dickens, 1798.
JBF   James Bradley Finley Letters, Archives of Ohio Methodism, Ohio Wesleyan University, Delaware
JLFA Asbury, Francis. *The Journal and Letters of Francis Asbury.* 3 vols. Edited by Elmer T. Clark et al. Nashville, TN: Abingdon Press, 1958.
PP   Littlejohn, John. *Preecher and Patriot: The Journal and Memorandums of the Rev. John Littlejohn, A Pioneer Preacher of American Methodism.* Edited by Richard A. Weiss. Utica, KY: McDowell, 2005.
SHC   Edward Dromgoole Papers, Southern Historical Collection, University of North Carolina–Chapel Hill
WW   William Winans Papers, J. B. Cain Archives of Mississippi Methodism, Millsaps College, Jackson

Introduction

1. Goen, "The 'Methodist Age' in American Church History"; Hudson, "The Methodist Age in America." Additionally, see Ahlstrom, *Religious History of the American People,* 436–39; Hatch, "The Puzzle of American Methodism"; McLoughlin, *Revivals, Awakenings, and Reform,* 131–36; Miller, *Life of the Mind in America,* 51; and Noll, *America's God,* 169, 181.

2. Turner, *Frontier in American History,* 36.

3. William Warren Sweet, introduction, in Sweet, *Religion on the American Frontier,* 3, 50.

4. Tweed, "After the Quotidian Turn."

5. The representative books are Hatch, *Democratization of American Christianity,* and Johnson, *Shopkeeper's Millennium.* The dichotomy of social control and democratization is reflective of the tension between Marxist and Weberian interpretations

of popular religion; see Wigger, *Taking Heaven by Storm*, 190–91. Methodism's functional adaptability is a major theme of Hempton, *Methodism*.

6. The concept of movement has informed much of the recent work on early American Methodism; see, for example, Mathews, "Second Great Awakening as an Organizing Process," 23–43; Hatch, *Democratization of American Christianity*; Richey, *Early American Methodism*; Heyrman, *Southern Cross*; Lyerly, *Methodism and the Southern Mind*; Owen, *Sacred Flame of Love*; Wigger, *Taking Heaven by Storm*; Andrews, *Methodists and Revolutionary America*; Hatch and Wigger, *Methodism and the Shaping of American Culture*; Mulder, *Controversial Spirit*; and Hempton, *Methodism*.

7. The quotation refers to Edward Eggleston, *The Circuit Rider: A Tale of the Heroic Age* (New York: J. B. Ford, 1874). This began in nineteenth-century church histories, and the influence is seen in the later work of Methodist historian of American religion William Warren Sweet; see Sweet, *Religion in the Development of American Culture*.

8. Onuf, *Jefferson's Empire*, 2.

9. Bowes, *Land Too Good for Indians*, 11–12, points to the nuances of settler participation in colonialism. See also Bruyneel, *Settler Memory*, 3.

10. Representative approaches to settler colonialism are Belich, *Replenishing the Earth;* Wolfe, "Settler Colonialism and the Elimination of the Native"; Wolfe, *Settler Colonialism and the Transformation of Anthropology;* Ford, *Settler Sovereignty;* Tomlins, *Freedom Bound;* Veracini, *Settler Colonialism;* and Faragher, "Settler Colonial Studies and the North American Frontier." On religion and settler colonialism, see Saler, *Settlers' Empire*, chap. 5, and Conroy-Krutz, *Christian Imperialism*, esp. chap. 4.

11. Griffin, *American Leviathan*, 11.

12. Wiebe, *Search for Order*, xiii.

13. Ostler and Shoemaker, "Forum: Settler Colonialism in Early American History: Introduction," 362; Veracini, *Settler Colonialism*, 15.

14. Bowes, *Land Too Good for Indians*, 11.

15. The latter is a key theme in Ostler, *Surviving Genocide*. On pietism and politics, see Carwardine, *Evangelicals and Politics in Antebellum America*, 14, 27. One could argue that Methodism fit partially in the category of "good religion," as theorized by scholars of secularization; see Fitzgerald, "Critical Religion and Critical Research on Religion," 306, and Josephson-Storm, "Superstition, Secularism, and Religion Trinary," 3.

16. A large literature addresses the timing and effects of the transition to capitalism; see, for example, Sellers, *Market Revolution;* Lamoreaux, "Rethinking the Transition to Capitalism"; and Larson, *Market Revolution in America*.

17. Isaac, *Transformation of Virginia;* Wood, *Radicalism of the American Revolution;* Hatch, *Democratization of American Christianity*.

18. *JLFA*, 1:ix; Wigger, *American Saint*, 8–9, 215–16.

19. *DD*, 14, 151–53. Although inspired in part by a free-will theology adopted from Calvinism critic Jacobus Arminius, orthodox Methodists understood the flesh cynically. Their greater regard for what theologians often called human ability in the process of salvation rarely tempered their belief in the inheritance of original sin. On the social institutions of the Methodist movement, in addition to works cited above, see Wigger, *Taking Heaven by Storm*, chap. 4; Richey, *Methodist Conference in America*; and Ruth, *Little Heaven Below*.

20. Francis Asbury to William McKendree, August 5, 1813, in *JLFA*, 3:481–82, 476.

21. *JLFA*, 1:440 (April 5, 1783); 681 (June 16, 1791); Zephaniah 1:12–13. All biblical cites are to the King James Version unless otherwise noted.

22. Finley, *Sketches of Western Methodism*, 239–40.

23. Here I build on Mathews, "Second Great Awakening as an Organizing Process," 23.

24. On the relationship of social networks to social capital, see Kadushin, *Understanding Social Networks*, chap. 10. On social capital, see Putnam, Leonardi, and Nanetti, *Making Democracy Work*; Putnam, *Bowling Alone*; Lin, *Social Capital*; and McLean, Schultz, and Steger, *Social Capital*. For a collective assessment of these themes, see the two-part roundtable "Patterns of Social Capital: Stability and Change in Comparative Perspective," *Journal of Interdisciplinary History* 29, nos. 3–4 (1999). Particularly helpful have been Rotberg, "Social Capital and Political Culture," and Greene, "Social and Cultural Capital."

25. *DD*, 118.

26. Itinerancy and communications are major themes of the popular awakenings. See, for example, Mathews, "Second Great Awakening as an Organizing Process"; Stout, "Religion, Communications, and the Ideological Origins of the American Revolution"; Nord, "Evangelical Origins of Mass Media in America"; Hatch, *Democratization of American Christianity*, chap. 5; Lambert, "Great Awakening as Artifact"; and Breen and Hall, "Structuring Provincial Imagination."

27. Wigger, *Taking Heaven by Storm*, 8; Hempton, *Methodism*, 18, 23, 202.

28. Bourdieu, "Forms of Capital."

29. Rockman, *Scraping By*, 75–99; Sachs, *Home Rule*, 41–70.

30. Historians have shown that some Methodists and other evangelicals critiqued patriarchal authority during the revolutionary era; however, like the rest of society, relatively few Methodists repudiated or replaced the patriarchal household. See Johnson and Wilentz, *Kingdom of Matthias*, chap. 1; Lyerly, *Methodism and the Southern Mind*, 7; Heyrman, *Southern Cross*, chap. 3; and Lawrence, *One Family under God*, 8–10.

31. Carwardine, *Evangelicals and Politics in Antebellum America*, xv.

32. Wigger, *Taking Heaven by Storm*, 1. For a sample of the variety of histories that focus on the social value of early American evangelical religion, see Johnson,

Shopkeeper's Millennium; Raboteau, *Slave Religion;* Eslinger, *Citizens of Zion;* Najar, *Evangelizing the South;* Lindman, *Bodies of Belief;* and Dennis, *Seneca Possessed.*

33. Sweet, *Religion in the Development of American Culture;* Boles, *Great Revival;* Eslinger, *Citizens of Zion;* Miller, *Life of the Mind in America,* 72, 95; McLoughlin, *Revivals, Awakenings, and Reform,* chap. 4.

34. John, "Governmental Institutions as Agents of Change"; John, "Why Institutions Matter." Greater attention is devoted to Protestant institutions in the later antebellum period; see Schweiger, *Gospel Working Up.*

35. Ann Braude, "Women's History Is American Religious History," in Tweed, *Retelling U.S. Religious History,* 89–90.

1. The Structures of Western Methodism in the Empire of Liberty

1. *JLFA,* 2:8 (July 25, 1807); Numbers 23:23.

2. Francis Asbury to Thornton Fleming, December 2, 1802, in *JLFA,* 3:251. On Asbury's health and administrative talent, see Wigger, *American Saint,* 5, 8.

3. Francis Asbury to Stith Mead, January 20, 1801, in *JLFA,* 3:196.

4. Francis Asbury to Daniel Hitt, January 26, 1805, in *JLFA,* 3:306.

5. Francis Asbury to Zachariah Myles, August 16, 1804, in *JLFA,* 3:298.

6. Francis Asbury to Jacob Gruber, January 29, 1813, in *JLFA,* 3:469.

7. On Methodism and symbiosis, see Hempton, *Methodism,* chap. 1.

8. The literature on Indigenous expulsion and resistance is vibrant and growing. Important recent works include Edmunds, *Enduring Nations;* Jortner, *Gods of Prophetstown;* Bowes, *Land Too Good for Indians;* Snyder, *Great Crossings;* Sleeper-Smith, *Indigenous Prosperity and American Conquest;* Ostler, *Surviving Genocide;* Witgen, "Nation of Settlers"; Saunt, *Unworthy Republic;* and Witgen, *Seeing Red.*

9. Turner, *Frontier in American History,* 12.

10. Furstenberg, "Significance of the Trans-Appalachian Frontier," 647–50. For a critical examination of the Empire of Liberty in the Ohio Valley, see Hinderaker, *Elusive Empires,* chaps. 5–6. On warfare and violence as the context for Indian removals, see Bowes, *Land Too Good for Indians,* chap. 1.

11. Smith, "Congregation, State, and Denomination."

12. Carté, *Religion and the American Revolution,* 31–36. My thinking on magisterial and radical traditions is indebted to Brooke, *Refiner's Fire.*

13. Mathews, "Second Great Awakening as an Organizing Process," 23–43; Hatch, "The Puzzle of American Methodism"; Eslinger, *Citizens of Zion;* Wills, *Democratic Religion;* Najar, *Evangelizing the South.*

14. Heitzenrater, *Wesley and the People Called Methodists,* chaps. 1–2; Andrews, *Methodists and Revolutionary America,* 5, 15–26; Sirota, *Christian Monitors,* 24–32; Hammond, *John Wesley in America,* chap. 3; Engel, *Religion and Profit,* 13–22; Watson, *Pursuing Social Holiness,* 17–38; Ward, *Protestant Evangelical Awakening,* 121–26; Ward, "Legacy of John Wesley," 347; Kisker, *Foundation for Revival,* 162–64;

Mack, *Heart Religion in the British Enlightenment*, chap. 1; Marsden, *Jonathan Edwards*, 173; Knott, *Sensibility and the American Revolution*.

15. Carté, *Religion and the American Revolution*, 219, 223, 226, 289, 307–13, 315, 377.

16. On the composite character of Methodism, see Andrews, *Methodists and Revolutionary America*, 17. On the combined influence of European pietism and English reactions to Restoration-era social immorality as predecessors of the Methodist organizing impulse, see Heitzenrater, *Wesley and the People Called Methodists*, 19–25. On the familial forms of Methodist networks in a transatlantic study, see Lawrence, *One Family under God*, 1–2, 7–8, 79–82.

17. Michael Woolcock, "Civil Society and Social Capital," in *The Oxford Handbook of Civil Society*, ed. Michael Edwards (New York: Oxford University Press, 2011), 197–98.

18. Kadushin, *Understanding Social Networks*, 162.

19. John, *Spreading the News*.

20. Noll, *Civil War as a Theological Crisis*, 12.

21. Francis Asbury to Thomas Coke, May 7, 1806, in *JLFA*, 3:343.

22. Bushnell, *Barbarism the First Danger*, 31.

23. In contrast, Heyrman, *Southern Cross*, 226–30, argues that Methodism suffered serious setbacks during the Revolution.

24. Belich, *Replenishing the Earth*, 4.

25. Increasing population within Britain beginning in the middle of the sixteenth century led to Anglo outmigration. Belich, *Replenishing the Earth*, 126–27. Belich notes that "this vast Anglo exodus" was similar in size to global migrations of continental Europeans, Russians, Indians, and Chinese during the long nineteenth century. According to Belich, however, the "Anglo diaspora" was unique because it "began earlier, was more permanent, and its migrants went to reproductions of their own society, not someone else's." On the variety of economic "pushes" behind British emigration, see James Horn, "British Diaspora," in Marshall, *Oxford History of the British Empire*, 28–52, and on the prevalence of skilled workers, see pages 36–37.

26. Alison Games, "Migration," in Armitage and Braddick, *British Atlantic World*, 31; Bailyn, *Voyagers to the West*, 3. Several scholars have quantified immigration to British North America. Bailyn judged that between the beginning of British settlement and 1760, some 700,000 individuals of various origins had come to the thirteen original colonies and Nova Scotia; see Bailyn, *Voyagers to the West*, 25. Benjamin, *The Atlantic World*, 259 (table 5.3), provides a broader view, estimating that between 1500 and 1700, 390,000 individuals from what became the British Isles migrated to the Americas. Historian James Horn estimates that between the years 1700 and 1760, 173,200 immigrants to the thirteen colonies (excluding Nova Scotia) were of British extraction. Over the next fifteen years, immigrants of all stripes arrived in British North America at a rate of 15,000 per year, totaling over 220,000. Horn's estimate suggests that over 43,000 British immigrants came to the colonies from

1760 to 1775; see Horn, "British Diaspora," 32 (table 2.2). Migration continued to impact the character of North America during and after the American Revolution. In the final quarter of the eighteenth century, more than a quarter million Europeans departed for Britain's remaining North American possessions and for the newly independent United States; see Games, "Migration," 48. In 1780, there were 2 million British American settlers in the Caribbean, Nova Scotia, Newfoundland, and the rebel colonies; see Belich, *Replenishing the Earth*, 36.

27. Anglo-American migration to the West by 1815 was no longer simply a function of British emigration. After 1815, the Atlantic states were, in James Belich's terms, both a "settler" society and a "settling" society, still receiving migrants as well as sending them forth. Belich, *Replenishing the Earth*, 57.

28. A synthesis of this contested history is Griffin, *American Leviathan*, chaps. 1–3.

29. Bailyn, *Voyagers to the West*, 3, 7.

30. Rohrbough, *Trans-Appalachian Frontier*, 3, 19, 23–25; Roth, *Democratic Dilemma*, 15–17; Hofstra, *Planting of New Virginia*, 1–5; Eslinger, *Citizens of Zion*, chap. 1.

31. Rohrbough, *Trans-Appalachian Frontier*, 30; Greene and Harrington, *American Population*, 192.

32. Horn, "British Diaspora," 50. James Belich argues that the year 1780 roughly marked the beginning of an "Anglo divergence" in global demographic history. See Belich, *Replenishing the Earth*, 40, 49.

33. Belich, *Replenishing the Earth*, 79, 82–83; Rohrbough, *Trans-Appalachian Frontier*, 113.

34. Rohrbough, *Trans-Appalachian Frontier*, 224.

35. Belich, *Replenishing the Earth*, 91.

36. Rohrbough, *Trans-Appalachian Frontier*, 13.

37. It is important to place this spectacular growth of the late eighteenth and early nineteenth centuries in appropriate context. The burgeoning West was not unique to early America. As James Belich notes, while the Anglo-American West boomed under Anglo migration, so too did Australia and other provinces and colonies of Britain. Much of that growth, especially in Australasia, occurred in the second half of the nineteenth century. The American West itself continued to grow after the end of the Civil War. Another 6.5 million men and women moved west from the eastern states between 1870 and 1920. Over the long term, roughly 1815 to 1930, an estimated 12 million native-born Americans moved west. This era saw the rise of the great cities of the American West: Cincinnati, St. Louis, Chicago, and their hinterlands. The main trend through the first third of the twentieth century was dizzying growth. But those who lived through the early phases of growth were dizzied no less because their descendants lived amid even more explosive years. Belich, *Replenishing the Earth*, 65–66, 84, 94.

38. Belich, *Replenishing the Earth*, 91.

39. Methodist men could be found in various political parties and performing various styles of masculinity, but in contrast to the rugged frontier masculinity portrayed in Methodist print culture, many Methodist men fit the profile of "restrained manhood" described in Greenberg, *Manifest Manhood*, 11–12.

40. Wigger, *American Saint*, 8; Sweet, introduction, 5–6.

41. Hempton, *Methodism*, 92–93; Andrews, *Methodists and Revolutionary America*, 7, 49–55, 60–61 (quotation); Wigger, *American Saint*, 90, 111–22; Heyrman, *Southern Cross*, 226–30; Mathews, *Religion in the Old South*, 46–47; Mulder, *Controversial Spirit*, 90, 101–2, 150; Lyerly, *Methodism and the Southern Mind*, 10, 12, 18–26; Butler, *Awash in a Sea of Faith*, 195, 207; McDonnell, *Politics of War*, 30; Carté, *Religion and the American Revolution*, 31–36.

42. Hempton, *Methodism*, chap. 1.

43. Francis Asbury to Zachariah Myles, August 16, 1804, in *JLFA*, 3:298.

44. Francis Asbury to Thornton Fleming, November 7, 1806, in *JLFA*, 3:357.

45. For context, see Onuf, *Jefferson's Empire*.

46. Gaustad and Barlow, *New Historical Atlas of Religion in America*, 358, figure C.2.

47. Sweet, introduction, 51.

48. The relationship of Methodism to democratization is briskly argued in Hatch, *Democratization of American Christianity*. A succeeding generation of historians of Methodism heeded Hatch's call to study Methodism but have not been wholly bound to his democratization thesis; see Wigger, *Taking Heaven by Storm*; Wigger, *American Saint*; Andrews, *Methodists and Revolutionary America*; and Lyerly, *Methodism and the Southern Mind*.

49. Elliott, *Empires of the Atlantic World*, 184; Armitage, *Ideological Origins of the British Empire*, chap. 3; Douglas Bradburn, "Eschatological Origins of the English Empire," in Bradburn and Coombs, *Early Modern Virginia*, 15–56; Stanwood, *Empire Reformed*; Steve Pincus, *1688: The First Modern Revolution* (New Haven, CT: Yale University Press, 2009); Nicholas Canny, *Making Ireland British, 1580–1650* (New York: Oxford University Press, 2001).

50. Williams, *Religion and Violence*, 2–10; Horn, *Adapting to a New World*, 127–28.

51. Ezra Booth to the Editors of the *Methodist Magazine*, 1819, JBF. The final sentence of the Booth quotation recalls Isaiah 35:1: "The wilderness and the solitary place shall be glad for them; and the desert shall rejoice, and blossom as the rose." Because writers such as Richard Hakluyt the younger and Samuel Purchas struggled to fix English imperial claims, settlement would increasingly find justification in the "agriculturalist" arguments, which relied less on theological concepts such as grace as the justification for taking possession of land and more on criticism of Indians' alleged wastefulness and on praise of settlers' improvement, elaborated most clearly by John Locke; see Armitage, *Ideological Origins of the British Empire*, 90–91, 97–98.

52. An excellent modern biography of Peter Cartwright is Bray, *Peter Cartwright*.

53. On the development of a racial discourse of settler expansion out of mid-eighteenth-century warfare, see Silver, *Our Savage Neighbors*.

54. On language and western expansion, with a focus on erasure of Indigenous history, see Buss, *Winning the West with Words*.

55. Cartwright, *Autobiography*, 17–19.

56. Cartwright, *Autobiography*, 22.

57. Cartwright, *Autobiography*, 22–23.

58. Seed, *Ceremonies of Possession*, chap. 1.

59. Cartwright, *Autobiography*, 26–27.

60. Francis Asbury to [Thomas Sargent], December 28, 1805, in *JLFA*, 3:332.

61. For a summary of the geopolitics, see Furstenberg, "Significance of the Trans-Appalachian Frontier," 647–77.

62. Gibson and Jung, *Historical Census Statistics*, 50, 68, 75.

63. To compile these membership numbers, I compared the total society membership of the Western Conference in 1810 with the size of circuits existing in 1800 that in later years were categorized under the Western Conference. See *Minutes of the Annual Conferences*, 1:92, 183.

64. Sweet, *Rise of Methodism in the West*, 5.

65. *Minutes of the Annual Conferences*, 1:18, 23, 26, 28–64.

66. Finley, *Sketches of Western Methodism*, 17–18. "Waste, howling wilderness" is a direct reference to Deuteronomy 32:10.

67. Turner, *Frontier in American History*.

68. On the link between religion and state formation, see Saler, *Settlers' Empire*, esp. chap. 5.

69. Aron, *How the West Was Lost*, 20–21.

70. Tanner, *Atlas of Great Lakes Indian History*, 79–87.

71. For Native American "subsistence crises," see Aron, *How the West Was Lost*, 50. Nancy O'Malley, "Frontier Defenses and Pioneer Strategies in the Historic Settlement Era," in Friend, *Buzzel about Kentuck*, 63–65, explains the role of raids in frontier security, noting that most conducted by Native Americans in the 1770s were small and could be withstood by settlers inside a fortification, though crops and livestock remained vulnerable; settlers risked death as they ventured outside of settlements and as they conducted their own raids against Indians.

72. Prucha, *Sword of the Republic*, 26–40; Calloway, *Victory with No Name*; Rohrbough, *Trans-Appalachian Frontier*, 19 (first quotation); Tiro, "New Narratives," 550 (second quotation).

73. M'Ferrin, *History of Methodism in Tennessee*, 189.

74. Francis Asbury to Jacob Gruber, September 3, 1812, in *JLFA*, 3:463.

75. Francis Asbury to [William McKendree], September 15, 1809, in *JLFA*, 3:415.

76. *Minutes of the Annual Conferences*, 1:3. On statistics in the early republic, see Patricia Cline Cohen, "Statistics and the State: Changing Social Thought and the

Emergence of a Quantitative Mentality in America, 1790 to 1820," *William and Mary Quarterly*, 3rd series, 38, no. 1 (January 1981): 35–55, and Cohen, *A Calculating People*.

77. Lee, *Short History of the Methodists*, 78–79, 118, 134, 140–41, 159, 193–95; *Journals of the General Conference*, 11–12 (quotations).

78. Circuits in the western reaches of the seaboard states, such as Redstone, often remained in the eastern conferences. In 1797, two districts constituted the Methodist organization on the Upper South's frontier. Together the districts contained ten circuits and eighteen traveling preachers. Kentucky had the most circuits and the greatest membership west of the mountains, followed by Tennessee and, distantly, Ohio. Sweet, *Rise of Methodism in the West*, 11–22; *Minutes of the Annual Conferences*; Barclay, *Early American Methodism*, 140–44.

79. Boles, *Great Revival*, 46–47.

80. Conkin, *Cane Ridge*; Westerkamp, *Triumph of the Laity*; Schmidt, *Holy Fairs*; Johnson, *Frontier Camp Meeting*. The importance of interdenominational cooperation in the early stages of southern revivalism is an important theme in Boles, *Great Revival*, 25–35, 55, which argues that outpourings of religious activity occurred because of an evangelical theology common to Baptists, Methodists, and Presbyterians, which posited belief in an omnipotent God who would deliver his people from religious decline.

81. *Minutes of the Annual Conferences*, 1:93; 3:63.

82. Finke and Stark, *Churching of America*, 71.

83. The civilization theme is prominent in the works of influential Methodist historian William Warren Sweet.

84. *DD*, 147.

85. Barclay, *Early American Methodism*, 264–65.

86. Howe, *What Hath God Wrought*, chap. 6.

87. *Minutes of the Annual Conferences*, 1:74, 209, 451; Barclay, *Early American Methodism*, 226. For perspective on travel time, the Albany District of New York was two hundred miles shorter and required of the presiding elder from eight to nine consecutive weeks of travel to round; see Barclay, *Early American Methodism*, 123.

88. Tigert, *Constitutional History*, 264–65; Bucke et al., *History of American Methodism*, 439, 465–66; M'Caine, *Letters*, 163; *DD*, 46–47, 49.

89. *JLFA*, 1:620 (January 12, 1790).

90. Francis Asbury to James Quinn, September 24, 1812, in *JLFA*, 3:466.

91. Francis Asbury to Jacob Gruber, September 1, 1811, in *JLFA*, 3:453.

92. Francis Asbury to Jacob Gruber, August 30, 1810, in *JLFA*, 3:438.

93. *DD*, 50–52.

94. Francis Asbury to Thomas Coke, May 12, 1811, in *JLFA*, 3:449.

95. Francis Asbury to George Roberts, February 11, 1797, in *JLFA*, 3:160.

96. Francis Asbury to Joseph Benson, January 15, 1816, in *JLFA*, 3:544.

97. Francis Asbury to Stith Mead, January 20, 1801, in *JLFA*, 3:196; for other instances of this language, see 3:466, 469.

98. Francis Asbury to Thomas L. Douglass, February 24, 1811, in *JLFA*, 3:446–48.

99. On the postal system in early America, see John, *Spreading the News*.

100. M'Ferrin, *History of Methodism in Tennessee*, 66.

101. Barclay, *Early American Methodism*, 101.

102. Redford, *History of Methodism in Kentucky*, 1:62.

103. Finley, *Autobiography*, 268.

104. Barclay, *Early American Methodism*, 123, 226.

105. *DD*, 58, 73.

106. For the differences between Methodist societies, typically comprising around thirty church members, and classes and bands, smaller groups organized within a society according to gender and race and having approximately fifteen and five members, respectively, see Bucke et al., *History of American Methodism*, 115–16.

107. *DD*, 82.

108. *DD*, 71. In the Methodist lexicon, "believer" indicated a mature Christian, at least in relative terms, for devout Methodists considered one's entire course of life to be a transit toward the perfection of God that required constant attention and effort. A believer had experienced God's grace, though their spiritual growth was not complete, rather than merely having been awakened to their own depravity. On Methodist terms, see Ruth, *Little Heaven Below*, 35–38. On the "social religion" of Methodists in the Ohio Valley, see Schneider, *Way of the Cross Leads Home*.

109. *DD*, 151–52. See also *DD*, 78.

110. *DD*, 133, 134–35.

111. Richey, *Early American Methodism*, 21–32; Ruth, *Little Heaven Below*, 22.

112. Schmidt, *Holy Fairs*, chap. 1.

113. The best use of quarterly meeting records is found in Dunn, *Civil War in Southern Appalachian Methodism*.

114. On fraternity in Methodism, see Richey, *Early American Methodism*, 1–20, and Andrews, *Methodists and Revolutionary America*, 56.

2. Pilgrims and Settlers

1. Cartwright, *Autobiography*, 522–23.
2. Stevens, *Dr. Cartwright Portrayed*, 15–17.
3. Cartwright, *Autobiography*, 524–25.
4. Stevens, *Dr. Cartwright Portrayed*, 10.
5. McCabe, *Great Fortunes*, 5.
6. Peter Cartwright, *The Backwoods Preacher: An Autobiography of Peter Cartwright, for More Than Fifty Years a Preacher in the Backwoods and Western Wilds of America*, ed. W. P. Strickland (London: Alexander Heylin, 1858); Peter Cartwright, *Autobiography of Peter Cartwright, the Backwoods Preacher: The Birth, Fortunes, and*

General Experiences of the Oldest American Methodist Travelling Preacher, ed. W. P. Strickland (London: Arthur, Hall, Virtue, 1862), iv (quotations).

7. On the language of colonization and its endurance, see Merrell, "Second Thoughts." See also "Hunters of Kentucky; or, Half Horse and Half Alligator" (Boston: William Rutler, n.d.), American Song Sheets, Rare Books and Special Collections, Library of Congress, Washington, DC.

8. "Settlerism" is borrowed from Belich, *Replenishing the Earth*, 153.

9. Bourdieu, "Forms of Capital," 243–48.

10. Casper, *Constructing American Lives*, 1–10.

11. The classic work on the myth of Jackson is Ward, *Andrew Jackson*.

12. On satirical portrayals of Methodism, see Lyles, *Methodism Mocked*.

13. *Proceedings of the Board of Managers of the Western Methodist Historical Society in the Mississippi Valley; Containing an Account of the Origin of the Society, Its Organization, Constitution, Address, Circular, &c.* (Cincinnati: Methodist Book Room, 1839), 7–10.

14. "Address of the Ohio Annual Conference, to the Members & Friends of the M. E. Church in the West," [1835], box 1, folder 1, Methodist Episcopal Church, Ohio Records, Ohio Historical Society.

15. Putney, *Muscular Christianity*; Byrne, *No Foot of Land*.

16. Reverend John F. Wright, "Public Thoroughfares—Pioneers of Methodism," *Northwestern Christian Advocate*, March 7, 1866, in "Early Methodist Newsclippings," 25–27, Archives of Ohio United Methodism, Ohio Wesleyan University.

17. Wright, "Public Thoroughfares—Pioneers of Methodism," 25–27.

18. "Letter from the Venerable Rev. Henry Smith," in "Early Methodist Newsclippings," 65–67.

19. Ahlstrom, *Religious History of the American People*, 443. This approach is most evident in Sweet's later writing; see Sweet, *Religion in the Development of American Culture*. On Sweet's influence on the study of religion in America, see Ash, "American Religion and the Academy," and Billington and Ridge, *Westward Expansion*, 1–7. Ray Allen Billington and Martin Ridge note that Turner's formulation was not as rigid as many of his "disciples" or critics have indicated. Billington and Ridge provide their own schema that collapses each of Turner's "types" into "users" (traders, herders, and miners) and "subduers" (farmers and other "settlers").

20. Schneider, "Ritual of Happy Dying."

21. Hatch, *Democratization of American Christianity*, 87. On the itinerants' "distinctive social age," defined as departing from the normal schedule of attaining manhood by not being the head of a household, see Andrews, *Methodists and Revolutionary America*, 208–9. A study that interprets Methodism through the lens of age is Ellis, "The Confused, the Curious, and the Reborn."

22. Details for the early history of the Western Annual Conference are found in Sweet, *Rise of Methodism in the West*.

23. Some birthplaces are approximate: circuit rider Lewis Garrett, for example, is included here in the Virginia count based on his enumeration in the 1850 US Census, but William B. Sprague, *Annals of the American Methodist Pulpit* (New York: Robert Carter, 1861), 7:429n, included that he "was born in Pennsylvania, April 24, 1772. Shortly after his birth, his father removed to Virginia." Such a discrepancy in the census may indicate Garrett's cultural identification with a Virginia homeland or the census enumerator's presumption, but because Garrett spent most of his first years in Virginia, the variation does not disrupt the contours of migration.

24. The data in this and the preceding paragraph are compiled from a variety of sources, including *Minutes of the Annual Conferences*, vols. 1 and 2; Sweet, *Rise of Methodism in the West*; Sweet, *Circuit-Rider Days*; and a number of genealogical sources accessed via Ancestry.com.

25. See Ward, "Legacy of John Wesley," 347; Hatch, *Democratization of American Christianity*, 87–88.

26. Bangs, *History of the Methodist Episcopal Church*, 2:421–54.

27. Hatch, *Democratization of American Christianity*, 86–87.

28. Sprague, *Annals of the American Pulpit*, 7:324–27; Harmon, *Encyclopedia of World Methodism*, 1:281; "Tennessee State Marriages, 1780–2002," Tennessee Historical Society, Tennessee State Library and Archives; "Index to the Compiled Military Service Records for the Volunteer Soldiers Who Served during the War of 1812," microfilm roll M602, box 18, National Archives and Records Administration, Washington, DC.

29. Sprague, *Annals of the American Pulpit*, 7:326.

30. This data was compiled from *Minutes of the Annual Conferences*, vols. 1 and 2; Sweet, *Rise of Methodism in the West*; Sweet, *Circuit-Rider Days*; and a number of genealogical sources accessed via Ancestry.com.

31. For critical analysis of "religion" and "secularism" in American history, see Fitzgerald, "Critical Religion and Critical Research on Religion"; Jordan, "Secularism and Empire," 117; and Josephson-Storm, "Superstition, Secularism, and Religion Trinary."

32. Hatch, *Democratization of American Christianity*, 88.

33. *JLFA*, 1:567, 602, 628; 2:33, 65, 102, 104, 196, 237, 638; 3:386. Regular deficiencies in salaries for the Western Annual Conference are given in Sweet, *Rise of Methodism in the West*.

34. *JLFA*, 2:102.

35. Sprague, *Annals of the American Pulpit*, 7:257, 272, 429n; US Census, 1840, Davidson County, TN, roll 520, 336; US Census, 1850, Madison County, MS, roll M432_376, 173B.

36. US Census, 1840, Blount County, TN, roll 517, 78; US Census, 1850, Monroe County, TN, M432_891, 98A; "Sketch of the Life of Rev. Samuel Douthit," in Samuel Evans Massengill, *The Massengills, Massengales and Variants, 1472–1931* (Bristol,

TN: King Printing, 1931), 254; R. N. Price, *Holston Methodism: From Its Origin to the Present Time*, 4 vols. (Nashville, TN: Methodist Episcopal Church, South, 1906), 2:35–37.

37. Yates Snowden, ed., *History of South Carolina*, 5 vols. (Chicago: Lewis, 1920), 3:163.

38. Sweet, *Circuit-Rider Days*, 53–54; Finley, *Sketches of Western Methodism*, 92; Matthew Simpson, ed., *Cyclopedia of Methodism*, 4th ed. (Philadelphia: Louis H. Everts, 1881), 146.

39. Lewis Garrett owned four slaves in 1840 (US Census, 1840, Davidson County, TN, roll 520, 336); Ezekiel Burdine, five in 1820 and three in 1840 (US Census, 1820, Lebanon, Russell County, VA, roll M33_141, 133; US Census, 1840, Russell County, VA, roll 577, 23); Samuel Douthit, six in 1830 and 1840 (US Census, 1830, Western Division, Blount, TN, roll 178, 276; US Census, 1840, Blount County, TN, roll 517, 78); James Douthit, one in 1820 and eight in 1840 (US Census, 1820, Pendleton, SC, roll M33_120, 181; US Census, 1840, Anderson County, SC, roll 507, 147); John Page, seven in 1820 and fourteen by 1840 (US Census, 1820, Smith County, TN, roll M33_125, 40; US Census, 1840, Smith County, TN, roll 534, 254); Thomas Wilkerson, fifteen slaves in 1850 (US Census, 1850, Washington County, VA, roll M432_980, 148B).

40. Lyerly, *Methodism and the Southern Mind*, 5.

41. Miller, *Life of the Mind in America*, 7; Hurt, *Ohio Frontier*, 286–87 ("ignorant"). Noteworthy contrasts to the accounts cited above are Johnson, *Frontier Camp Meeting*, chap. 8, and Boles, *Great Revival*, 70. More recently, Farrelly, "'God Is the Author of Both,'" agrees that Methodists were not anti-intellectual but examines the years after 1830.

42. Benjamin Lakin Notebooks, box 4, folders 2 and 4, series 3: Methodists, Church History Documents Collection, Special Collections Research Center, Regenstein Library, University of Chicago; A. G. Thompson to Daniel Hitt, n.d.; Thompson to Hitt, May 25, 1790; Seely Bunn to Hitt, October 21, December 7, 1792; May 22, September 14, 1793; August 26, 1794; Thomas Scott to Hitt, April 17, 1795, Daniel Hitt Letters, Archives of Ohio United Methodism, Ohio Wesleyan University.

43. *JLFA*, 3:164.

44. Farish, *Circuit Rider Dismounts*.

45. Henry Smith to Samuel Williams Esq., October 2, 1840, *Western Christian Advocate*, in "Early Methodist Newsclippings," 64–65.

46. Wigger, *American Saint*, 5. The hardship of life in the traveling connection was significant enough to become firmly a part of the Methodist frontier mythology. As historian Nathan O. Hatch has noted, Methodist ministerial commitment often came at a high price to the physical body; see Hatch, *Democratization of American Christianity*, 81–93, which provides a brief survey emphasizing the strains of circuit travel.

47. "Critical Notices," *Methodist Quarterly Review* 30 (April 1848): 324.

48. "Our Heroic Inheritance," *Methodist Review* 21, no. 5 (1905): 787.

49. Cartwright, *Autobiography*, 5, 61, 231, 332.

50. [John Cennick], ["The Pilgrims' Song"], in *A Collection of Hymns for the Use of the Methodist Episcopal Church* (New York: B. Waugh and T. Mason, 1836), 328–29.

51. Historians have convincingly shown that American Methodism, especially at the end of the eighteenth century, appealed to middling white men and women and African Americans, but the nature of this appeal was complicated. For the southeastern context, in which Methodism offered means for resisting gentry values and paralleled republican critiques of wealth, see Lyerly, *Methodism and the Southern Mind*, chap. 4, esp. 80–86. For analysis of class dynamics in the Mid-Atlantic cities of New York, Philadelphia, and Baltimore, see Andrews, *Methodists and Revolutionary America*, chap. 6, which finds that Methodists came from diverse social backgrounds and that Methodist societies were often "plebian institutions" but relied on wealthy members for support, which created tension between itinerant ministers and influential local members. Migrants from throughout the eastern seaboard filled the early West, which brought a complex mixture of regional and social affiliations to the western itinerancy and the societies to which it ministered. For issues of support in the Methodist itinerancy, see Hatch, *Democratization of American Christianity*, 86–88.

52. Itinerancy was not the only such travel occupation; sail allowed some non-elite people travel experiences that combined danger and expansiveness; see Rouleau, "Maritime Destiny as Manifest Destiny," and Will B. Mackintosh, *Selling the Sights: The Invention of the Tourist in American Culture* (New York: New York University Press, 2019).

53. Learner Blackman, Journal Manuscript, 1800–1804, typescript, 2–3, Learner Blackman Papers, United Methodist Archives Center, Drew University (hereafter Blackman Journal).

54. Blackman Journal, 3–4.

55. Blackman Journal, 4–5, 15.

56. If evangelicalism promoted exceptional attention to one's self, perhaps in the case of young men like Blackman it was in part a product of their unique access, based on taking a career in an organization, to broadening experiences, in addition to a process of turning inward for theological reasons, as some have argued; see Boles, *Great Revival*.

57. "The Journal of Benjamin Lakin, 1794–1820," in Sweet, *Religion on the American Frontier*, 207, 212 (hereafter "Journal of Lakin"). Where possible, for reasons of accessibility, I cite Sweet's volume. The majority of Lakin's manuscript material is in the Church History Documents Collection.

58. See, for example, Parrish, *American Curiosity*, chap. 2.

59. King, *Transformations in American Medicine*, 39.

60. Parrish, *American Curiosity*, 80. On nineteenth-century settlers' understanding of the environment, see Valencius, *Health of the Country*.

61. "Journal of Lakin," 233–34.

62. For a discussion of colonists' perceptions of the link between their environment and health, see Trudy Eden, "Food, Assimilation, and the Malleability of the Human Body in Early Virginia," in Lindman and Tarter, *Centre of Wonders*, 29–42.

63. "Journal of Lakin," 234–35.

64. Harold Vanderpool, "The Wesleyan-Methodist Tradition," in Numbers and Amundsen, *Caring and Curing*, 327.

65. "Journal of Lakin," 236–37.

66. "Letter from the Venerable Rev. Henry Smith" in "Early Methodist Newsclippings," 65–67.

67. Blackman Journal, 6–8.

68. Blackman Journal, 9.

69. For a short overview of early Methodist expansion to the southwestern territories, see Posey, "Advance of Methodism into the Lower Southwest."

70. Blackman Journal, 10–11.

71. Blackman Journal, 14.

72. DuVal, *Independence Lost*, chap. 1.

73. Blackman Journal, 14–16.

74. Deloria, *Playing Indian*, 1–9.

75. "Journal of Lakin," 240–41.

76. "Journal of Lakin," 241, 242.

77. "Journal of Lakin," 245.

78. A useful contrast is found in Nenzi, *Excursions in Identity*, 27–33. Important studies of travel include Lefebvre, *Production of Space*; MacCannell, *Tourist*; Leed, *Mind of the Traveler*; Turner and Turner, *Image and Pilgrimage*; and Lane, *Landscapes of the Sacred*. For an introduction to early trans-Appalachian migration, see Eslinger, *Running Mad for Kentucky*, 1–66. For a recent historiographical treatment of travel, see Kilbride, "Travel Writing as Evidence."

79. For an overview of the settlement of the Ohio Valley with an eye toward Methodism, see Sweet, *Circuit-Rider Days*, chap. 1.

80. Nenzi, *Excursions in Identity*, 2. Scholars distinguish among types of travel. For example, recreational travel offers enjoyment and fulfillment and is largely dependent on legal freedom and economic resources. Recreational travelers take little or no direction from authority figures and above all are not coerced. Occupational travel, in contrast, has the purpose of maintaining one's livelihood. Combining elements of both, circuit travel was primarily vocational. It was based on a perceived calling from God, directed at a spiritual goal, and thus bounded by moral obligations.

81. Henry Smith to Samuel Williams Esq., October 2, 1840, *Western Christian Advocate*, in "Early Methodist Newsclippings," 64–65.

82. Samuel Hitt to Daniel Hitt, May 16, 1790, Daniel Hitt Letters.

83. Commonly, the annual conference received a request for an itinerant from a new community and dispatched a circuit rider.

84. Henry Smith to Samuel Williams Esq., October 2, 1840, *Western Christian Advocate,* in "Early Methodist Newsclippings," 64–65.

85. Henry Smith to Samuel Williams Esq., October 2, 1840, *Western Christian Advocate,* in "Early Methodist Newsclippings," 64–65.

86. A similar anecdote is discussed in John Wigger, "Ohio Gospel: Methodist in Early Ohio," in Cayton and Hobbs, *Center of a Great Empire,* 62.

87. Henry Smith to Samuel Williams Esq., October 2, 1840, *Western Christian Advocate,* in "Early Methodist Newsclippings," 64–65.

88. Henry Smith to Samuel Williams Esq., October 2, 1840, *Western Christian Advocate,* in "Early Methodist Newsclippings," 64–65.

3. The Social Principle, Settlement Networks, and Sacred Capital in the Trans-Appalachian West

1. *JLFA,* 2:408 (September 24, 1803); Joseph Addison, *Cato: A Tragedy and Selected Essays,* ed. Christine Dunn Henderson and Mark E. Yellin (Indianapolis, IN: Liberty Fund, 2004), 88. On erasure, see Buss, *Winning the West with Words,* and on representation within settler discourse, see Watts, *In This Remote Country.*

2. *JLFA,* 2:614.

3. The classic article and a foundation for my analytical framework is Mathews, "Second Great Awakening as an Organizing Process."

4. Several American historians have found value applying the insights of scholars of the Enlightenment. For two works that suggest the complex ways that cultures of information exchange shaped both the end products of correspondence—that is, the knowledge produced—and the participants themselves, see Perl-Rosenthal, "Private Letters and Public Diplomacy," and Konstantin Dierks, "Letter Writing, Masculinity, and American Men of Science, 1750–1800," *Pennsylvania History* 65 (1998): 167–98. Important works in the Enlightenment literature are Cook, *Matters of Exchange;* Shapin, *Social History of Truth;* Goodman, *Republic of Letters;* and Goldgar, *Impolite Learning.*

5. Calhoun, *Works,* 557. The work on early American civil society has grown quickly. Representative works include Kelley, *Learning to Stand and Speak;* Koschnik, *"Let a Common Interest Bind Us Together";* Neem, *Creating a Nation of Joiners;* Najar, *Evangelizing the South;* Brooke, *Columbia Rising;* and Roney, *Governed by a Spirit of Opposition.*

6. The seminal work on formal and informal politics in American history is Baker, "Domestication of Politics."

7. Dierks, *In My Power.*

8. John P. Finley to James Bradley Finley, December 15, 1811, JBF.

9. A helpful discussion of the importance of Methodist piety and intimate language to early Ohio political culture is Andrew R. L. Cayton, "'Language Gives Way to Feelings,'" in Brown and Cayton, *Pursuit of Public Power*, 31–48.

10. For scholars' admonition that historians should not assume that communications history is a recent phenomenon associated with industrial technologies and "modern" administration, see Darnton, *Poetry and the Police*, 1–2, and Dierks, *In My Power*. For studies of epistolary networks that emphasize urban settings, see Waterman, *Republic of Intellect*, and Kaplan, *Men of Letters in the Early Republic*. My own work demonstrates that such forms of communication were not uniquely associated with urban contexts. Rather, they were important in frontier and rural settings.

11. See Donald G. Mathews, "Evangelical America—The Methodist Ideology," in Richey, Rowe, and Schmidt, *Perspectives on American Methodism*, 17–30; Hatch, *Democratization*; Nathan O. Hatch, "The Democratization of Christianity and the Character of American Politics," in Noll and Harlow, *Religion and American Politics*, 93–119; and Wigger, *Taking Heaven by Storm*.

12. Befitting an influential leader, Asbury had many detractors and admirers. His recent and best biographer correctly judges him as a firm but good-hearted executive. See Wigger, *American Saint*.

13. Ostler, *Surviving Genocide*, 6–8; Saunt, *Unworthy Republic*, xii–xiv.

14. For the Federalist extension of military power and national authority to Ohio, see Cayton, *Frontier Republic*, 34–39; Rohrbough, *Trans-Appalachian Frontier*, 91; and Aron, *How the West Was Lost*, 50.

15. On migration to Ohio, see Etcheson, *Emerging Midwest*, 3–4, esp. table 2.

16. For a recent discussion of these migrants that places them in a broader history of Protestant migration in early America, see Rohrer, *Wandering Souls*, chap. 5.

17. Harmon, *Encyclopedia of World Methodism*, 2:1800–1801; Sweet, *Circuit-Rider Days*, 109–11.

18. Sweet, *Circuit-Rider Days*, 99–111, 185–95.

19. Sparks, *On Jordan's Stormy Banks*, 10–11.

20. Jones, *Complete History of Methodism*, 33, 40; *Minutes of the Annual Conferences*, 1:93.

21. *Minutes of the Annual Conferences*, 1:344; 2:52–53.

22. Howe, *What Hath God Wrought*, 5–7.

23. On the persistence of unfreedom in the Old Northwest, see Paul Finkelman, "Slavery and the Northwest Ordinance: A Study in Ambiguity," *Journal of the Early Republic* 6, no. 4 (Winter 1986): 343–70; Finkelman, "Almost a Free State: The Indiana Constitution of 1816 and the Problem of Slavery," *Indiana Magazine of History* 111, no. 1 (March 2015): 72; Matthew Salafia, *Slavery's Borderland: Freedom and Bondage along the Ohio River* (Philadelphia: University of Pennsylvania Press, 2017); Tiya Miles, *The Dawn of Detroit: A Chronicle of Slavery and Freedom in the City of the Straits* (New York: New Press, 2017); and M. Scott Heerman, *The Alchemy of Slavery:*

Human Bondage and Emancipation in the Illinois Country, 1730–1865 (Philadelphia: University of Pennsylvania Press, 2018).

24. On Methodism's beginnings in Virginia relevant to this history, see Sweet, *Virginia Methodism,* 46, 48–51, 59–60, 66–68.

25. The two Virginia circuits were Norfolk and Brunswick, with northern Virginia Methodists more closely connected to the Frederick circuit of Maryland. In May 1774, Norfolk (73) and Brunswick (218) had 291 members. In May 1777, the circuits of southern Virginia and the North Carolina Circuit, which Sweet (*Virginia Methodism,* 70n) described as a product of this revival, had the following numbers of members in societies: Hanover (262), Amelia (620), Brunswick (1,360), Sussex (727), Pittsylvania (150), and North Carolina (930), for a total of 4,049. The actual increase was 1,291%. Numbers taken from *Minutes of the Annual Conferences,* 1:6, 8.

26. Putnam, *Bowling Alone,* 22–24.

27. For details on Edward Dromgoole Sr. and slavery, see William B. Bynum, "The Rev. Edward Dromgoole, Sr., Emancipator and Enslaver," presentation, Old Brunswick Circuit Foundation, November 13, 2021, https://doc.vaumc.org/Historical Society/EdwardDromgooleSr._EmancipatorandEnslaver.pdf.

28. McLean, *Sketch of Rev. Philip Gatch,* 96–97.

29. The same year that Gatch's group arrived, the annual conference on request supplied the society with its first itinerant, and the Miami circuit held steady at ninety-nine reported members (ninety-eight white and one Black) for the next three years, until doubling in 1802. *Minutes of the Annual Conferences,* 1:109.

30. Austin M. Patterson, ed., *Greene County, 1803–1908* (Xenia, OH: Aldine, 1908).

31. The Miami circuit held 757 members, making it the fourth largest circuit in the Western Conference, narrowly losing third place to Lexington because of its greater Black membership. Mad River circuit, on which the Bonners and Pelhams resided, held 333. All but six members across both circuits were white. The entire Ohio District, covering southern Ohio and a portion of southwestern Indiana, contained 2,902 members. *Minutes of the Annual Conferences,* 1:147.

32. Philip Gatch to Edward Dromgoole, February 11, 1802, Dromgoole Papers, in Sweet, *Religion on the American Frontier,* 152. Unless noted otherwise, references are for Edward Dromgoole Sr.

33. Philip Gatch to Edward Dromgoole, June 1, 1805, Dromgoole Papers, in Sweet, *Religion on the American Frontier,* 155–57.

34. John Sale to Edward Dromgoole, February 20, 1807, Dromgoole Papers, in Sweet, *Religion on the American Frontier,* 160.

35. Edward Dromgoole Jr. to Rebecca and Edward Dromgoole, June 24, 1807, Dromgoole Papers, in Sweet, *Religion on the American Frontier,* 168–70.

36. Frederick Bonner to Edward Dromgoole, July 19, 1807, Dromgoole Papers, in Sweet, *Religion on the American Frontier,* 170.

37. Peter Pelham to Edward Dromgoole, June 20, 1807, Dromgoole Papers, in Sweet, *Religion on the American Frontier*, 163–68.

38. Unknown to Edward Dromgoole, July 27, 1807, SHC.

39. Beyond the first four pages, the remainder of the letter is missing. As the letter fades out, the writer was beginning the familiar discussion of slavery as a motive to move. Unknown to Edward Dromgoole, July 27, 1807, SHC.

40. Samuel Pelham to Edward Dromgoole Jr., August 24, 1807, SHC. Pelham provided other debt collection instructions in a later letter; see Pelham to Dromgoole, October [21], 1807, SHC.

41. Peter Pelham to Edward Dromgoole, November 19, 1807, Dromgoole Papers, in Sweet, *Religion on the American Frontier*, 177–78.

42. Peter Pelham to Edward Dromgoole, March 8, 1808, Dromgoole Papers, SHC.

43. James Keys to Edward Dromgoole, September 7, 1807; August 20, 1808; January 3, 1809, SHC.

44. Peter Pelham to Edward Dromgoole, April 16, 1810, Dromgoole Papers, in Sweet, *Religion on the American Frontier*, 187–88. Pelham also began corresponding with Edward Jr., in the attempt to persuade him to return to Ohio and bring the Dromgooles, namely his daughter, away from slavery.

45. Lyerly, *Methodism and the Southern Mind*, 82.

46. Barclay, *Early American Methodism*, 151.

47. Jones, *Complete History of Methodism*, 27–28.

48. Drake, "Tobias Gibson," 239.

49. Sparks, *On Jordan's Stormy Banks*, 10–11.

50. Rowland, *Mississippi*, 967, 421.

51. 1805, 1808 Jefferson County, 1810 Warren and Claiborne Counties, 1816 Claiborne County, series 486: Censuses, 1801–1816, Mississippi Territory, Governor, Mississippi Department of Archives and History.

52. Libby, *Slavery and Frontier Mississippi*, 17–22, 29–40; Usner, *Indians, Settlers, and Slaves*; Haynes, *Natchez District*, 91, 92, 133, 134; Haynes, *Mississippi Territory*, 133; Rothman, *Slave Country*, 10, 38–39, 184–85, 217–18; Lowery, "Great Migration to the Mississippi Territory"; Johnson, *Soul by Soul*.

53. Sparks, *On Jordan's Stormy Banks*, 11–12.

54. Gaustad and Barlow, *New Historical Atlas of Religion in America*, 358, figure C.2.

55. Jones, *Complete History of Methodism*, 29, 36–37, 53ff.

56. Jones, *Complete History of Methodism*, 41–42.

57. Jones, *Complete History of Methodism*, 43–44, 51–52.

58. Jones, *Complete History of Methodism*, 32.

59. Jones, *Complete History of Methodism*, 41.

60. Claiborne, *Mississippi*, 107.

61. Jones, *Complete History of Methodism*, 54–55.

62. McBride and McLaurin, *Randall Lee Gibson*, 10.

63. Jordan, *White over Black*, 171–74; Jordan, "American Chiaroscuro"; Berlin, *Many Thousands Gone*, 91, 406–7n38.

64. McBride and McLaurin, *Randall Lee Gibson*, 5–6, 263–64n7; Sharfstein, *Invisible Line*, 188–89.

65. McBride and McLaurin, *Randall Lee Gibson*, 10.

66. Jones, *Complete History of Methodism*, 28.

67. Jones, *Complete History of Methodism*, 41.

68. John Seaton to William Winans, January 24, 1820, WW.

69. John Seaton to William Winans, December 26, 1823, WW.

70. John Seaton to William Winans, April 28, 1821, WW.

71. John Seaton to William Winans, January 24, 1820, WW.

72. John Seaton to William Winans, April 25, 1820, WW.

73. On circuit rider education, see Boase, "Education of a Circuit Rider."

74. John Seaton to William Winans, April 25, 1820, WW.

75. John Seaton to William Winans, April 10, 1821, WW.

76. John Seaton to William Winans, April 10, 1821, WW.

77. John Seaton to William Winans, January 24, 1820, WW.

78. John Seaton to William Winans, February 9, 1823, WW.

79. John Seaton to William Winans, March 25, 1823, WW.

80. Holder, *William Winans*, 44–46.

81. John Seaton to William Winans, March 6, 1820, WW.

82. John Seaton to William Winans, September 26, 1820, WW.

83. John Seaton to William Winans, August 23, September 26, 1820, WW.

84. J. P. Drake to Benjamin Drake, October 10, 1825, Benjamin Drake Papers, Mississippi Department of Archives and History, in Kenneth Stamp, ed., *Records of Antebellum Southern Plantations from the Revolution through the Civil War* (microfilm), series N, roll 7, 00723–26.

85. John Seaton to William Winans, March 15, 1822, WW.

86. See Lyles, *Methodism Mocked*.

87. Holder, *William Winans*, 14.

88. John Seaton to William Winans, April 27, 1822, WW.

89. John Seaton to William Winans, April 27, 1822, WW.

90. John Seaton to William Winans, April 27, 1822, WW.

91. John Seaton to William Winans, April 27, 1822, WW.

92. *Minutes of the Annual Conferences*, 1:428.

93. US Census, 1830, Madison, Mississippi, reel M19, 91, s.v. "John Seaton."

94. On John Irwin's reputation as a Methodist, see Jones, *Complete History of Methodism*, 280–81.

95. John P. Finley to James B. Finley, July 4, 1811, JBF.

96. William P. Finley to James B. Finley, January 9, 1810, JBF.

97. *Minutes of the Annual Conferences,* 2:82.

98. Gray, *Yankee West.*

99. James W. Finley to James B. Finley, January 31, 1830, JBF.

100. The use of the Methodist tactic of deploying a son of thunder is suggested by William P. Finley to James B. Finley, March 1, 1811, JBF, describing local conditions: "Our prospect of religion is but very indifferent yet I look for better times in the warm season[.] our preachers are very negligent[.] we have had but one circuit sermon[.] the reason we are neglected I know not but my prayer is Lord send us a son of thunder who [values] neither heat nor cold men nor devils but being filled with the power of God so that he may cry aloud and spare not."

101. On the exclusive fraternal character of the Methodist itinerancy, see Andrews, *Methodists and Revolutionary America,* 93, 209, 297n116.

102. The following description draws on Samuel Baker to James B. Finley, February 2, 1823; Alfred Brunson to Finley, February 20, 1823; Baker to Finley, March 19, 1823; Brunson to Finley, April 27, May 28, June 11, 1823, JBF.

103. Alfred Brunson to James B. Finley, May 28, 1823, JBF.

104. *JLFA,* 2:614 (September 10, 1809).

105. George W. Maley to James B. Finley, March 6, 1830, JBF.

106. George W. Maley to James B. Finley, March 13, 1830, JBF.

107. For an example from the history of the Wyandot Mission at Upper Sandusky, see Charles Elliott to James B. Finley, May 28, 1823, JBF.

108. For an example, see "Communication from Wesley Smith," *Pittsburgh Christian Advocate,* November 18, 1856. Thanks to the inimitable research of Matthew Foulds for this reference.

109. Henry Matthews to Nathaniel Little, May 8, 1818, Henry Matthews Diaries, vol. 2, Special Collections, A. Frank Smith, Jr. Library, Southwestern University.

110. Henry Matthews to Nathaniel Little, May 8, 1818, Henry Matthews Diaries, vol. 2.

111. Reciprocity in epistolary networks is an important theme in Dierks, "Letter Writing, Masculinity, and American Men of Science."

112. Sweet, *Circuit-Rider Days,* 164, 171, 173, 183, 187, 218.

113. Henry Matthews to Hiram Matthews, April 23, 1818, Henry Matthews Diaries, vol. 2.

114. Henry Matthews to Nathaniel Little, May 8, 1818, Henry Matthews Diaries, vol. 2.

115. Henry Matthews to Russell Bigelow Sr., April 24, 1818, Henry Matthews Diaries, vol. 2.

116. *DD,* 151–53.

117. John C. Brooke to James B. Finley, May 12, 1823, JBF.

118. William Blair to James B. Finley, May 13, 1823; May 21, 1823, JBF.

119. William Blair to James B. Finley, June 19, 1823, JBF.

120. The phrase is from William W. Sweet, "The Churches as Moral Courts of the Frontier," *Church History* 2 (1933): 3–21. Recent works examining churches' extra-judicial practices are Najar, *Evangelizing the South,* and Jeffrey Thomas Perry, *Law in American Meetinghouses: Church Discipline and Civil Authority in Kentucky, 1780–1845* (Baltimore, MD: Johns Hopkins University Press, 2022). On sexual violence and law in early America, see Sharon Block, "How Should We Look at Rape in Early America?" *History Compass* 4, no. 3 (2006): 603–14, and Mary R. Block, "Rape Law in 19th-Century America: Some Thoughts and Reflections on the State of the Field," *History Compass* 7, no. 5 (2009): 1391–99.

121. Trial Proceedings, Charles Waddell, 1826–1835, 1, box 1, folder 23, MSS 231, Methodist Episcopal Church, Ohio Records.

122. Trial Proceedings, Charles Waddell, 13, 9, MSS 231, Methodist Episcopal Church, Ohio Records.

123. Trial Proceedings, Charles Waddell, 15, MSS 231, Methodist Episcopal Church, Ohio Records.

124. *DD,* 32, 59, 91.

125. John W. Blassingame, *The Slave Community: Plantation Life in the Antebellum South,* rev. ed. (1972; New York: Oxford University Press, 1979), chap. 3; Eugene D. Genovese, *Roll, Jordan, Roll: The World the Slaves Made* (New York: Vintage, 1976); Lawrence W. Levine, *Black Culture and Black Consciousness: Afro-American Folk Thought from Slavery to Freedom,* rev. ed. (1977; New York: Oxford University Press, 2007); Raboteau, *Slave Religion;* Mechal Sobel, *Trabelin' On: The Slave Journey to an Afro-Baptist Faith* (Westport, CT: Greenwood Press, 1979); Richard S. Newman, *Freedom's Prophet: Bishop Richard Allen, the AME Church, and the Black Founding Fathers* (New York: New York University Press, 2008); Alexis Wells-Oghoghomeh, *The Souls of Womenfolk: The Religious Cultures of Enslaved Women in the Lower South* (Chapel Hill: University of North Carolina Press, 2021).

126. Interview with Siney Bonner, in *Born in Slavery: Slave Narratives from the Federal Writers' Project, 1936–1938,* vol. 1, Alabama Narratives, 39–40, Digital Collection, Library of Congress, Manuscript Division, http://memory.loc.gov/ammem/snhtml/snhome.html.

127. Orsamus L. Nash to Benjamin Drake, July 31, 1832, Benjamin Drake Papers, in Stamp, *Records of Ante-bellum Southern Plantations,* series N, roll 7, 00832–35. On the history of sexuality and race in New Orleans, see Jennifer M. Spear, *Race, Sex, and Social Order in Early New Orleans* (Baltimore, MD: Johns Hopkins University Press, 2009). On disproportionate discipline of Black and enslaved marriage and sexuality in Baptist congregations, see Najar, *Evangelizing the South,* 71–72, 86.

128. "Woodrow" to Benjamin Drake, March 27, 1828, Benjamin Drake Papers, in Stamp, *Records of Ante-bellum Southern Plantations,* series N, roll 7, 00748–51.

129. Settler conscience is a theme in Bruyneel, *Settler Memory,* and Saunt, *Unworthy Republic.*

130. Michael Leonard Cox, "The Ohio Wyandots: Religion and Society on the Sandusky River, 1795–1843" (Ph.D. diss., University of California, Riverside, 2016), 91–92; Nathan Emory to James B. Finley, April 16, 1823, JBF.

131. Seeley, *Race, Removal, and the Right to Remain,* 281. On Wyandot religion, see Bontrager, "'From a Nation of Drunkards,'" 632 (quotation), and Cox, "Ohio Wyandots," esp. chaps. 2 and 3.

4. The Traveling Life of John Littlejohn

1. *PP,* 130–31. To define social exchanges, I borrow a simple formulation from sociology: "interactions between two or more individuals where valued goods are exchanged." See Katie E. Corcoran, "Divine Exchanges: Applying Social Exchange Theory to Religious Behavior," *Rationality and Society* 25 (August 2013): 335–69, 335 (quotations). A number of fine works have discussed kinship (blood, legal, and fictive) in the Old South; this article emphasizes that exchanges constituted relationships, especially with regard to fictive kinship. On kinship, see especially Billingsley, *Communities of Kinship,* and Glover, *All Our Relations.* Essays on religious exchange that differ in focus from my own are Catherine L. Albanese, "Exchanging Selves, Exchanging Souls: Contact, Combination, and American Religious History," in Tweed, *Retelling U.S. Religious History,* 200–226, and Leigh Eric Schmidt, "Practices of Exchange: From Market Culture to Gift Economy in the Interpretation of American Religion," in Hall, *Lived Religion in America,* 69–91. On evangelical Christianity in frontier Kentucky, see Boles, *Great Revival,* and Eslinger, *Citizens of Zion.*

2. Recent studies of connection through social and trade networks in the West are Winship, "Land of Connected Men," 88; Gitlin, *Bourgeois Frontier;* and Hyde, *Empires, Nations, and Families.*

3. Tanner, *Atlas of Great Lakes Indian History,* 79–87.

4. Demographic and commercial expansion refashioned American social conditions from the mid-eighteenth to the mid-nineteenth century. According to Gordon S. Wood's influential interpretation, these social forces surged during the revolutionary period, tumbling patriarchal hierarchy and leaving a more democratic social structure. Evangelical religion participated in that process through opposing elite authority, as described by Rhys Isaac about revolutionary Virginia. I take issue with two particulars of these descriptions of religion and the American Revolution. First, according to Wood and others who focus on political language, this democratization was due to Protestantism's emphasis on the individual conscience, in direct communication with God, as the proper seat of moral reasoning. However, the individualism that historians have found in Protestant theology and evangelical rhetoric, while not irrelevant to revolutionary events, does not reflect how Protestants maintained social ties within, between, and even outside their churches. Second, Wood argues that the revivalism of the Second Great Awakening, itself buffeted by the destabilizing social forces of revolution, bred sectarian competition and "actually did

not bring people together as much as it helped to legitimate their separation and make morally possible their new participation in an impersonal marketplace." Yet a finer-grained view than that taken by Wood reveals that in daily social and business interactions, religious affiliations remained flexible and useful means for building social networks. These facts of social life brought people together as much as separated them. Evangelicalism helped topple some hierarchies just as it promoted the creation of new ones. Revolutionary religion was leveling, but it only appeared radical from certain vantage points in the social structure. See Wood, *Radicalism of the American Revolution*, 144–45, 308–11, 331–33, 331n (quotation). Akin to Wood's perspective are Hatch, *Democratization of American Christianity*, and Isaac, *Transformation of Virginia*.

Littlejohn felt the full force of revolutionary politics because of his religious affiliation. During the war, Methodists suffered accusations of Toryism and bouts of harassment due to John Wesley's notorious opposition to the American cause and the belief of Patriot leaders and parts of the populace that Wesley's preachers were bent on undermining it. In fact, Methodists were split on the question of independence (with those recruited to the sect while in Britain tending toward Loyalist views) and on the morality of Christians participating in combat. Littlejohn endured indictments, arrests, and popular resentment from both Patriots and Loyalists because of his reticence to pledge allegiance officially to either side (though in his journal he claimed to be against Toryism), and he witnessed similar trials among his associates. Time and geography, however, mended the reputation of Methodists. The persecution faced by Littlejohn and his colleagues burned hottest between 1775 and 1778. Yet, as Dee Andrews has observed, by the time the war entered its southern campaign in 1778, most Loyalist itinerants had emigrated or sought British protection, and the theater of war shifted to locales where the remaining Methodist preachers had won many hearts and minds through revival preaching. Revolutionary politics troubled but did not thwart American Methodism. *PP,* 12–13, 23, 62–63, 66, 70, 101–2, 104–7. On Methodism and wartime revolutionary society, see Andrews, *Methodists and Revolutionary America*, 47–62, and McDonnell, *Politics of War,* 30; and on Littlejohn particularly, see Wigger, *American Saint*, 93–94, 97, 101–2. On mobs, oaths, and religious tests, see Wood, *Radicalism of the American Revolution*, 214–15, and Edwin S. Gaustad, "Religious Tests, Constitutions, and 'Christian Nation,'" in Hoffman and Albert, *Religion in a Revolutionary Age*, 218–35.

5. Helpful introductions to trans-Appalachian travel to Kentucky are Eslinger, *Running Mad for Kentucky*, 1–66, and Friend, *Along the Maysville Road*, 43–58. On Virginians' migrating to Kentucky, see Fischer and Kelly, *Bound Away*, 152–58, 216. Summaries of scholarship on nineteenth-century mobility are found in Stephan Thernstrom and Peter R. Knights, "Men in Motion: Some Data and Speculations about Urban Population Mobility in Nineteenth-Century America," in Hareven, *Anonymous Americans*, 17–47, esp. 18–19, and Henkin, *Postal Age*, 27–30.

6. Sociologists, in contrast, place "particular emphasis on the resources that come with religious affiliation and membership"; see Nancy Foner and Richard Alba, "Immigrant Religion in the U.S. and Western Europe: Bridge or Barrier to Inclusion?" *International Migration Review* 42 (Summer 2008): 360–92, 362 (quotation). See also Stark and Bainbridge, *Future of Religion*, 178–83, 323–24.

7. On the personal costs of itinerancy, see Hatch, *Democratization of American Christianity*, 82–85; Heyrman, *Southern Cross*, 87–88; Wigger, *Taking Heaven by Storm*, 57–62; Andrews, *Methodists and Revolutionary America*, 214–15; Wigger, *American Saint*, 84, 101–2; and Carney, *Ministers and Masters*, chap. 3. Hatch, Heyrman, and Carney mischaracterize as essentially negative the practice of itinerants' "locating" from the traveling ministry. Nineteenth-century Methodists too emphasized the worldly costs of itinerancy; see, for example, Redford, *History of Methodism in Kentucky*, 1:213, 275–76.

8. Beth Barton Schweiger, in *Gospel Working Up*, offers an important contrast to historians who focus on sacrifice and suffering, arguing that Baptist and Methodist institutions of the early nineteenth century were important environments of social mobility. Schweiger examines formal denominational structures rather than personal ties and begins her story in the 1830s.

9. Insurgent or heretical organization through social and communication networks is found across time and space, though Christianity is the framework for this study. For a network-based explanation of the spread of early Christianity, see Stark, *Rise of Christianity*. For the late medieval period, the Waldensians and Lollards are instructive examples; see the brief description in Euan Cameron, "Dissent and Heresy," in *A Companion to the Reformation World*, ed. R. Po-chia Hsia (Malden, MA: Blackwell, 2004), 3–21, esp. 5–7. On radical network formation in the Protestant Reformation, see Dailey, "Itinerant Preacher and the Social Network," 37–48, esp. 37–38. Such religious networks achieved greater evangelical reach after the emergence of print in Europe in the fifteenth century, which added value to preceding elements of orality, interpersonal relationships, and travel. For a recent study of the methods of spreading Reformation doctrine, see Pettegree, *Reformation and the Culture of Persuasion*. Communication networks have received attention in several studies of early American religion that focus on the role of media—preaching, hymnody, and print—in the spread of revivalism; see Hatch, *Democratization of American Christianity*, and Sweet, *Communication and Change*. For select works on regional and transatlantic networks in the eighteenth century, see O'Brien, "Transatlantic Community of Saints"; Susan O'Brien, "Eighteenth-Century Publishing Networks in the First Years of Transatlantic Evangelicalism," in Noll, Bebbington, and Rawlyk, *Evangelicalism*, 38–57; Lambert, *"Pedlar in Divinity"*; Lambert, *Inventing the "Great Awakening"*; Fea, "Wheelock's World"; Brown, *Knowledge Is Power*, chap. 3; and Lawrence, *One Family under God*.

10. Littlejohn's manuscript journal is in the John Littlejohn Papers, United Methodist Heritage Center, Kentucky Wesleyan College. Scholars often cite the "Journal

of John Littlejohn" transcribed by Annie L. Winstead, located in the archives. For accessibility, I cite the more recent edition compiled by Kentucky Wesleyan College archivist Richard A. Weiss, *Preecher and Patriot*. When I have found that text ambiguous, I have consulted the manuscript version, cited herein as "Littlejohn Journal."

11. Andrews, *Methodists and Revolutionary America;* Lyerly, *Methodism and the Southern Mind;* Wigger, *Taking Heaven by Storm;* Wigger, *American Saint*.

12. *JLFA*, 2:551. This accounting was a reduction from his August 16, 1804, estimate of more than two thousand local preachers. Francis Asbury to Zachariah Myles, August 16, 1804, in *JLFA*, 3:298–99.

13. *PP*, 2. Littlejohn was identified as a tax collector in Edward D. Ingraham, *A Sketch of the Events Which Preceded the Capture of Washington, by the British, on the Twenty-Fourth of August, 1814* (Philadelphia: Carey and Hart, 1849), 48. Studies that emphasize the factor of youth in evangelicalism are Hatch, *Democratization of American Christianity*, 87; Heyrman, *Southern Cross*, esp. chap. 2; and Ellis, "The Confused, the Curious, and the Reborn."

14. Several fine studies of the Baptists confirm the importance of social networks for southern evangelicals. On religious conversions as a product of networks, see Jewel L. Spangler, "Becoming Baptists: Conversion in Colonial and Early National Virginia," *Journal of Southern History* 67 (May 2001): 243–86, esp. 268–77, and Spangler, *Virginians Reborn*, 224–27. On the use of networks (local, regional, and transatlantic) by white, male Baptists to develop the denomination and its leaders, see Lindman, *Bodies of Belief*, 164–78. For the Baptists' use of church-to-church communication networks "to supervise people during migrations and to provide a framework for the construction of orderly new communities," see Najar, *Evangelizing the South*, 89–114, 99 (quotation). Lindman and Najar in particular discuss socioeconomic aspects of Baptist networks, specifically education, upward mobility, poor relief, and oversight of market transactions.

15. Counted among the evidence of sincere pursuit of salvation and holiness was "doing good, especially to them that are of the household of faith, or groaning so to be; employing them preferably to others, buying one of another, helping each other in business: and so much the more, because the world will love its own and them *only*." *DD*, 134. Two Baptist preachers who migrated from Virginia to Kentucky confirm the relevance of Littlejohn's experiences for understanding middling evangelicals. John Taylor traveled and preached while gaining wealth through land acquisitions in Kentucky and Indiana. Henry Toler found in Baptist associational life the means for social mobility, though he prospered less in Kentucky than did Taylor and Littlejohn. On Taylor's land speculations, see Taylor, *Baptists on the American Frontier*, 25–29, 34–38, 42–43, 83. On Toler, see Lindman, *Bodies of Belief*, 163, 168–69, and Taylor, *Baptists on the American Frontier*, 212n145.

16. Charles Hirschman, "The Role of Religion in the Origins and Adaptation of Immigrant Groups in the United States," *International Migration Review* 38 (Fall

2004): 1206–33, 1210 (first quotation), 1208 (second quotation). Where religious affiliation benefits migrants, it does so by providing "refuge from the trauma of loss and separation," "respectability, and resources." Hirschman, "Role of Religion," 1228. Many factors determine how religion influences migration experiences, but social scientists point especially to the nature of the societies into which migrants integrate. In his youth, John Littlejohn migrated to colonial America, where religion was being reorganized into voluntary associations and was relatively pluralistic. That environment resembled what sociologists Phillip Connor and Matthias Koenig have termed a "Tocquevillian religious field" in which they find religion to be especially beneficial to migrants as a bridge to integration. It should be noted that in other contexts, namely present-day Western Europe, religion can serve as a barrier to integration. On context in receiving societies, see Connor and Koenig, "Bridges and Barriers: Religion and Immigrant Occupational Attainment across Integration Contexts," *International Migration Review* 47 (Spring 2013): 3–38, 5 (quotation), and Foner and Alba, "Immigrant Religion in the U.S. and Western Europe." These studies support the view of Stephan Thernstrom and Peter R. Knights that a relationship existed between mobility and nineteenth-century Americans' having been "frantic joiners of voluntary associations." Thernstrom and Knights, "Men in Motion," 41. On pluralism in the revolutionary era and early republic expressed as a religious marketplace, see Hatch, *Democratization of American Christianity*, and Finke and Stark, *Churching of America*.

17. Corcoran, "Divine Exchanges," 335, 338–39. It is important to note that social and economic exchange can be decoupled theoretically, but in practice they remain entangled, as Littlejohn's life shows. On social exchange, see also Coleman, *Foundations of Social Theory*, 37–43, and Lin, *Social Capital*, 143–64. Exchange theorists accept several premises that shed light on Littlejohn's interactions. One assumption is that individuals occupy specific (but not static) positions in a social network that influence their access to resources. While exchange theory is common in the social sciences, American historians have employed it sporadically. An important exception is the work of historians of Native Americans and Native American–European interactions, who examine intercultural exchanges in trade and diplomacy. Representative histories on the South are Alan Gallay, *The Indian Slave Trade: The Rise of the English Empire in the American South, 1670–1717* (New Haven, CT: Yale University Press, 2003), and Hall, *Zamumo's Gifts*.

18. Scholars argue that the rise of commercialism in the eighteenth century changed the meaning of *friendship* from the instrumental relationships of alliances and patronage to ones based on affection between equals. Fittingly for an era of transition, Littlejohn's relations bore signs of both the old definition and the new. Further, relations inside the itinerant hierarchy resembled the common patronage model; that framework retains little value once one begins to consider the many local preachers and lay organizers (men and women) who surrounded the itinerancy.

Friendship and *kinship* are also problematic. Like his evangelical contemporaries, Littlejohn used *friend* for some associates and the *brother* and *sister* of fictive kinship for others. At times he used those terms interchangeably. To adopt friendship, kinship, or patronage over social exchange as an analytical framework is to flatten the textures of Littlejohn's social network. On definitions of friendship, see Allan Silver, "Friendship in Commercial Society: Eighteenth-Century Social Theory and Modern Sociology," *American Journal of Sociology* 95 (May 1990): 1474–504; Godbeer, *Overflowing of Friendship*, 156–57; Loiselle, *Brotherly Love*, 1–7; and importantly Tadmor, *Family and Friends*, 167–72, which demonstrates the great flexibility and, I argue, imprecision of the terms *friend* and *friendship*.

19. On Methodist dependency, see, for example, Carney, *Ministers and Masters*, 65–90, esp. 70, 79, 81–82. Skeptical of the independence of individuals generally is Barry Wellman and S. D. Berkowitz, eds., *Social Structures: A Network Approach* (New York: Cambridge University Press, 1988), 1–7.

20. *PP*, 1–2; John Littlejohn, obituary, in *Minutes of the Annual Conferences*, 2:486–87, hereafter cited as Littlejohn obituary.

21. Rohrbough, *Trans-Appalachian Frontier*, 224. On transatlantic migration, see Games, *Migration and the Origins of the English Atlantic World*, 1–12, and Bailyn, *Voyagers to the West*, esp. chap. 1. The seminal work on push and pull factors in migration is Everett S. Lee, "A Theory of Migration," *Demography* 3, no. 1 (1966): 47–57.

22. *PP*, 1–3; Littlejohn obituary, 486. On the Methodist appeal to artisans, see Wigger, *Taking Heaven by Storm*, 48–49. On the relationship of Methodist growth to social and economic change, see Hempton, *Methodism*, 22–23. The classic account of instability in migration is Handlin, *The Uprooted*. For vivid description of the transient, the downwardly mobile, and the unfree in the early national Chesapeake, see Rockman, *Scraping By*.

23. *PP*, 3–9, 9 (quotation); Lednum, *History of the Rise of Methodism*, 198–99. On youth vacillating between frivolity and devotion in Puritan and Quaker writings, see Shea, *Spiritual Autobiography*, 48. On dreams in early American religion, see Hall, *Worlds of Wonder*, 87–91, 106–9; Butler, *Awash in a Sea of Faith*, 222–23, 238–39; and Heyrman, *Southern Cross*, 61–62. Dreams and visions are explored in Atlantic contexts in Gerona, *Night Journeys*, and Plane and Tuttle, *Dreams, Dreamers, and Visions*. On dreams as tools of self-fashioning, see Sobel, *Teach Me Dreams*, esp. 29–32, regarding Methodism. On dream reporting, see Plane, *Dreams and the Invisible World*, 2–12. Lyerly interprets Littlejohn's dreams not only as examples of mysticism that separated evangelicals from the broader culture but also as forms of "interpretive and moral autonomy" from family members, religious associates, and secular authorities. Lyerly, *Methodism and the Southern Mind*, 36–37. Doubt too is common in contemporary spiritual autobiographies. Placing religious doubt in a broader political context is Porterfield, *Conceived in Doubt*.

24. Sociologists of religion find that individuals are drawn to religious groups because of social ties more so than religious ideology or individuals' feelings of deprivation; see Stark and Bainbridge, *Future of Religion*, 307–24. Heyrman, *Southern Cross*, 81, notes that relationships may have drawn youths into evangelical churches in the Second Great Awakening. For similar forces at work on eighteenth-century Virginia Baptists, see Spangler, "Becoming Baptists," 268–77.

25. *PP*, 9–11. On recruitment, see Heyrman, *Southern Cross*, 83; Schweiger, *Gospel Working Up*, 21–22; and Wigger, *Taking Heaven by Storm*, 48–49, 52, 74. On exhorting, see Ruth, *Little Heaven Below*, 57–67. For examples of the suicidal thoughts of other early American evangelicals, see Heyrman, *Southern Cross*, 30–31, 33, 36, 282n54 (for the controversial use of claims about suicide by competing religious groups), and Brekus, *Sarah Osborn's World*, 65–71, 109–10.

26. On strained family relationships, see Heyrman, *Southern Cross*, 140–41, and Lyerly, *Methodism and the Southern Mind*, 111.

27. He gained probationary admission to the annual conference in May 1777. *Minutes of the Annual Conferences*, 1:8.

28. Wigger, *Taking Heaven by Storm*, 35; Bucke et al., *History of American Methodism*, 117–18, 156.

29. On the Methodist itinerancy as a form of apprenticeship, see Wigger, *Taking Heaven by Storm*, 71.

30. Lednum, *History of the Rise of Methodism*, 151.

31. *PP*, 13–15.

32. Heyrman, *Southern Cross*, 186–87; Elder, "Twice Sacred Circle," esp. 612–13; Friedman, *Enclosed Garden*; Lyerly, *Methodism and the Southern Mind*, 94–118, 157–60; Andrews, *Methodists and Revolutionary America*, 99–122, esp. 112; Wigger, *Taking Heaven by Storm*, 151–72. The preponderance of women was common in evangelical groups; see Noll, *America's God*, 501n48.

33. *PP*, 11–12. Methodist preachers often assessed their performances in terms of whether they received "Liberty & Power" from God, and they connected that success to their sensitivity to the spirit of God before and during their delivery of sermons and exhortations. As Randolph Ferguson Scully writes, *liberty* took on multiple meanings amid the discourses of revolution, servitude, and spirituality that intermingled in eighteenth- and nineteenth-century Virginia. Littlejohn's coupling of "Liberty & Power" confirms Scully's interpretation that when applied to preaching, the term signified "ability"—one's gaining temporary freedom from the restrictions of the sinful flesh along with the power to transmit God's inspiration to an audience. Scully, "'Somewhat Liberated,'" esp. 330, 344–50.

34. *PP*, 14–15.

35. *PP*, 14–15. Littlejohn recorded his preaching text as Luke 4:18–19.

36. *PP*, 15–16; "Littlejohn Journal," September 25, 1776.

37. Littlejohn thought of locating in the terms of temptation by the domestic comforts of settled life but not necessarily of sin, as has been suggested regarding other Methodist itinerants. See *PP,* 20, and, in contrast, Carney, *Ministers and Masters,* 75.

38. *PP,* 14, 105, 109, 123.

39. *PP,* 123–24.

40. *PP,* 123–25. On Thomas and Bryan Fairfax, see Brown, *Virginia Baron,* and Polzin, "Reverend Bryan Fairfax."

41. *PP,* 124.

42. On Devereux Jarratt's cooperation and conflicts with non-Anglican evangelicals, see Sweet, *Virginia Methodism,* 59–70; Andrews, *Methodists and Revolutionary America,* 203–4; Irons, *Origins of Proslavery Christianity,* 42, 67–68; Lindman, *Bodies of Belief,* 50; Lyerly, *Methodism and the Southern Mind,* 147–48; and Wigger, *Taking Heaven by Storm,* 10–11.

43. Bucke et al., *History of American Methodism,* 232.

44. Robert Ayres, Journal, October 28, 1788, Papers of Robert Ayres, Detre Library and Archives, Heinz History Center. Ayres's journal confirms Bryan Fairfax's cooperation with Methodists. When Ayres left the Methodist itinerancy in 1789 for ordination in the Protestant Episcopal Church, one Methodist preacher in the area publicly accused him of "serving the Devil." Ayres, Journal, March 14, 1789.

45. *PP,* 129–31. On Kentucky land distribution, see Rohrbough, *Trans-Appalachian Frontier,* 166, and Friend, *Kentucke's Frontiers,* 65–66, 114–16, 215–16, 223.

46. *PP,* 135–36; Jeremiah 9:4; Hirschman, "Role of Religion," 1207. On Methodist encouragement of economic reciprocity and on disciplinary practices, see Lyerly, *Methodism and the Southern Mind,* 92.

47. *PP,* 135, 161. The federal census provides a view of the labor in Littlejohn's household. In 1820, six people—three male and three female, all white and free—lived under Littlejohn's roof. Half were over twenty-five years of age. Of the youth, two were young men between sixteen and twenty-five, and the youngest member of the household was a girl between ten and fifteen years old. Manuscript Census Returns, Fourth Census of the United States, 1820, Warren County, KY, National Archives microfilm series (NAMS), M-33, reel 28, 52. When the enumerator visited the Littlejohns, the patriarch was about sixty-five years old, and his journal suggests he was energetic. The same cannot be said of his wife, who struggled through that summer "with a Rhumatic affection which has deprived her of the use of her hand." The pain so troubled her that she looked to unorthodox methods for a cure, which more than once sent Littlejohn in pursuit of a "Faith Doctor." Despite the doctors' prayers, the "application [for healing] by the Blood kin" of the sick, and the writing of her name on a slip of paper to be stashed in a healer's pocket, she found no relief. *PP,* 145–47.

48. Of the nine people listed under Littlejohn's name in the 1830 US Census, only two were free whites. The remaining seven were enslaved people. Four were over the age of twenty-four (two men and two women); the others were two male youths

between the ages of ten and twenty-three and a girl under the age of ten. Manuscript Census Returns, Fifth Census of the United States, 1830, Russellville, Logan County, KY, NAMS, M-19, reel 39, 68. To place Littlejohn's slaveholdings in context, the Logan County tax lists of 1825 show that about six in ten households owned no slaves at all and more than half of all slaveholders owned fewer than five. In contrast to the Bluegrass region, the Green River watershed had a more equal distribution of wealth. Fewer families owned slaves, and land was less concentrated in the hands of the gentry. Over time, however, the region's economy became more like that of the Bluegrass. Aron, *How the West Was Lost*, 150–69, 209 (table A.9, for Logan County slave ownership statistics). See also Christopher Waldrep, "Opportunity on the Frontier South of the Green," in Friend, *Buzzel about Kentuck*, 153–74.

49. *PP*, 163–65. Many evangelical Christians of Littlejohn's day were wary of the effects of money on the spirit. Francis Asbury advanced this critique among the Methodist preachers. In April 1783, rather than rejoicing at news that the American Revolution was drawing to a close, he feared the coming peace would promote trade over religion in the hearts of Americans. *JLFA*, 1:440.

50. Historians have disagreed about Methodists' views on economics, finding evidence of both aversion and enthusiasm for the market, because Methodist ideas on economy were not simplistic. See Sellers, *Market Revolution*, esp. chap. 5, and Richard Carwardine's critique, "Charles Sellers's 'Antinomians' and 'Arminians': Methodists and the Market Revolution," in Noll, *God and Mammon*, 75–98. For a balanced summary of the relationship between religion and the economy in early America, see Engel, *Religion and Profit*, 7–10.

51. John Littlejohn, "Improve Your Talents," unpaginated typescript, in "Selected Sermons by Reverend John Littlejohn," transcribed by John P. Glover, John Littlejohn Papers. The concept of improvement had roots in both Enlightenment and Christian thought. As a point of convergence of those traditions, it allows us to place Littlejohn in a broader intellectual context and casts doubt on accounts that find a hard separation between Methodism and the Enlightenment. There was a significant "affinity," as Jeremy Gregory has described it, between the British Enlightenment and Methodism as devised by John Wesley. Moreover, Littlejohn's desire to improve his time on earth placed him in a major cultural trend of the antebellum years. As historian Daniel Walker Howe has explained, Americans up and down the social scale embraced an ethic of improvement aimed at controlling and developing the self. On improvement, see Howe, *Making the American Self*, 107–35; Fea, *Way of Improvement Leads Home*, 5–6; and Sweet, "What Is Improvement?" On the American Enlightenment, see May, *Enlightenment in America*. The classic statement of Methodists as anti-Enlightenment is Thompson, *Making of the English Working Class*, but see also Jeremy Gregory, "The Long Eighteenth Century," in Maddox and Vickers, *Cambridge Companion to John Wesley*, 13–39; Semmel, *Methodist Revolution*, 87–101; and Hempton, *Methodism*, esp. chap. 2. An excellent recent treatment of evangelicalism

and the Enlightenment is found throughout Brekus, *Sarah Osborn's World,* but esp. 7–12.

52. *PP,* 19, 70, 161–62.

53. *PP,* 162–63. For Fleming's service, see *Minutes of the Annual Conferences,* 1:34, 334, 350, 370, 389.

54. *PP,* 133, 137, 139, 140, 144, 164, 170; Bradford, *Kentucky Almanac,* facing 6. All citations are to Littlejohn's personal copy, which he annotated with his schedule, held in the Rare Pamphlet Collection, Filson Historical Society. Citations to these interspersed, unpaginated leaves are noted as "facing" a given page. The comparison of wages is based on Adams, "Some Evidence on English and American Wage Rates," esp. 506, and US Department of Labor, Bureau of Labor Statistics, *History of Wages in the United States,* 127.

55. *PP,* 138–41, 144. Littlejohn referred to Charles Binns Jr., the second clerk of the Loudoun County court, whose father had been Loudoun County's first clerk of court. The junior Charles had been nominated from Loudoun for service as a second lieutenant in the Virginia militia in 1781. Personal library holdings, Wesleyan given names (John, Charles, and Susanna), and Charles Jr.'s burial at the Methodist Old Stone Church in Leesburg suggest the Binns family's Methodist ties. True, "John Binns of Loudoun," esp. 29–30. For Binns's grave at the Old Stone Church Cemetery, see Charles Alexander Binns, *Find a Grave,* https://www.findagrave.com/memorial/22398376/charles-alexander-binns. Littlejohn and his Virginia associates were not unique among Methodists in cooperating to acquire lands and conduct other forms of personal business across the Appalachians. Former itinerant Edward Dromgoole maintained an active correspondence with Methodist friends from Virginia's southern counties after they migrated to southwestern Ohio, a network that helped him purchase and rent out lands there. My analysis of this Virginia-Ohio correspondence network is based on letters in the Edward Dromgoole Papers, Southern Historical Collection, University of North Carolina–Chapel Hill.

56. *PP,* 142–45; Bradford, *Kentucky Almanac,* facing 5. Littlejohn's almanac and the published edition of his journal disagree on the date of his return. Because the almanac lists his travel progress by date, I have followed that source.

57. *PP,* 143, 144, 160; Bradford, *Kentucky Almanac,* facing 7; Littlejohn, "Improve Your Talents." Notices of Littlejohn's representation of Edmund Jennings Lee and Henry Lee are in the Russellville, Kentucky, *Weekly Messenger,* May 20, 27, June 3, July 22, 1820. Binns may have inherited land in Kentucky from his father in 1801; see True, "John Binns of Loudoun," 29. Kentucky land grants for members of the Binns family represented more than eleven thousand acres; see Jillson, *Kentucky Land Grants,* 24, 149.

58. *PP,* 136, 138, 190, 195, 202–4, 207–8, 226. Littlejohn's journal does not provide Respess's full name, but he may have been the Thomas A. Respess who was nominated to the Virginia militia from Loudoun County as a captain in 1777, major in 1781,

and lieutenant colonel in 1782, or that man's son of the same name. The 1810 federal census identifies a Thomas Respess residing in Bourbon County and owning twelve slaves. McAllister, *Virginia Militia,* 212; Crozier, *Virginia County Records,* 9:54–55; Manuscript Census Returns, Third Census of the United States, 1810, Stoner, Bourbon County, KY, NAMS, M-252, reel 5, 209. On James Hunter, see US Census, 1820, Lawrenceburg, Franklin County, KY, NAMS, M-33, reel 22, 118, and US Census, 1830, Southern Division, Franklin County, KY, NAMS, M-19, reel 36, 145.

59. As Littlejohn noted in a March 1777 journal entry, "It was a rule with us to stay with the Families where we preeched at night." *PP,* 29.

60. *PP,* 145 (quotation), 149–58. On conversions of social capital into other forms, see Bourdieu, "Forms of Capital."

61. Bradford, *Kentucky Almanac,* facing 8, 13, 15; *PP,* 172, 182; *Burtis Ringo v. Charles Binns,* 35 US 269 (1836).

62. *PP,* 165, 195, 202, 171–72. William Trigg is listed as owning twenty-nine slaves in Frankfort in 1810, at which point he was the second largest slaveholder in the town and among the top five largest in the county. Quisenberry, "'Heads of Families,'" esp. 85; William E. Robinson, "The Prestons of America," in *Scotch-Irish in America,* 204–20, esp. 218.

63. *PP,* 20, 24–26, 34, 38–41, 45, 48, 52, 79, 165 (quotations), 189–90. Several members of the extended Thompson family held political offices in Kentucky and at the national level, including Littlejohn's main contact, George Claiborne Thompson, and his son of the same name, who was Speaker of the Kentucky House of Representatives. Daviess, *History of Mercer and Boyle Counties,* 159. References to that clan's connection to Methodism are found in Daviess, *History of Mercer and Boyle Counties,* 91, and Johnson, *History of Kentucky and Kentuckians,* 3:1466–67, which includes an apparently autobiographical account by the senior George C. Thompson defending Methodist patriotism during the Revolution and claiming he commanded, as part of his four thousand men, a regiment of five hundred Methodists in Williamsburg, Virginia, in 1777.

64. *PP,* 165, 195, 226. On the O'Kelly schism, see Georgian, "'That Unhappy Division,'" 210–35.

65. *PP,* 191, 194–95, 205–6. On indirect ties, see Lin, *Social Capital,* 44; for the related concept of weak ties, see the seminal article by Mark S. Granovetter, "Strength of Weak Ties." On public recognition and reputation, see Lin, *Social Capital,* 152–53, 157–58, 161.

66. *PP,* 197. Methodists maintained diverse relationships with slavery. Generally opposed to slavery in its earliest days in America, the MEC pursued a course designed not to alienate white Christians. Faced with the choice between, on the one hand, accommodating slavery and being allowed to preach to the enslaved and, on the other hand, opposing slavery and being restricted from preaching to both slaves and proslavery whites, the church decided that pursuing heavenly objectives over

earthly ones was the appropriate path. Further, many Methodists in the southern states owned slaves themselves and were reluctant to manumit them. On the relationship of Methodism and slavery, see Lyerly, *Methodism and the Southern Mind*, 141–44, and Mathews, *Slavery and Methodism*. See also Wolf, *Race and Liberty*, esp. 88–96.

67. For examples of Littlejohn's interactions with "blacks," see *PP*, 31–32, 138.

68. On the uses of slavery beyond labor, see Johnson, *Soul by Soul*, 25–27, 78–116; Rockman, *Scraping By*, 6–7, 57–62, 234–41; Huston, *Calculating the Value of the Union*, chap. 2; and Wright, *Slavery and American Economic Development*, chap. 2.

69. *PP*, 213–25.

70. Littlejohn obituary.

71. The quotation is from the title of the best short treatment of this transition: Boles, "Evangelical Protestantism in the Old South."

5. The Settling and Unsettling of Ann Hulme Price

1. On the language of colonialism, see Merrell, "Some Thoughts," and Merrell "Second Thoughts."

2. Ann Hulme Price to Sarah Hulme, May 2, 1824, AHP.

3. Ann Hulme Price to Sarah Porter, July 29, 1832, AHP.

4. Mathews, *Religion in the Old South*, 47–48, 102; Lyerly, *Methodism and the Southern Mind*, 100–101; Schmidt, *Grace Sufficient*, chap. 2, 23–32, 84–89, 98–116, 132; Wigger, *Taking Heaven by Storm*, 151.

5. Cott, *Bonds of Womanhood*, chaps. 3–4; Ryan, *Cradle of the Middle Class*, chaps. 2–3.

6. Eustace and Little, "'Ineradicably Untidy,'" 403.

7. The shift is the focus of Schneider, *Way of the Cross Leads Home*, 196–208.

8. In her history of northeastern women, Nancy Cott made clear that most mothers did not have time or energy for associational life, but they were not the focus of her study; see Cott, *Bonds of Womanhood*, 57, 136–38.

9. Ann Hulme Price to Sarah Hulme, May 2, 1824, AHP.

10. Hinshaw, *Encyclopedia*, 2:234; Platt, *Life and Letters*, 22–23.

11. Ann Price to John Hulme, October 13, 1817, United Methodist Archives, Lycoming College, quoted in "Rev. Richard McAllister of Fort Hunter," *Chronicle: Journal of the Historical Society of the Central Pennsylvania Conference of the United Methodist Church* 17 (Spring 2006): 80.

12. On relationships of women and ministers, see Mathews, *Religion in the Old South*, 105–6, and Lyerly, *Methodism and the Southern Mind*, 101–2.

13. *Minutes of the Annual Conferences*, 1:176, 204, 232, 237, 285, 300; Ann Price to John Hulme, October 13, 1817, in "Rev. Richard McAllister of Fort Hunter," 82.

14. Ann Hulme Price to Sarah Hulme, May 2, 1824, AHP.

15. Boydston, *Home and Work*, 24.

16. Ann Price to John Hulme, October 13, 1817, in "Rev. Richard McAllister of Fort Hunter," 79–80.

17. *Minutes of the Annual Conferences*, 1:374, 378.

18. Ann Hulme Price to Sarah Hulme, May 2, 1824, AHP.

19. R. Douglas Hurt applies Manasseh Cutler's quotation to Ohio in general; see Hurt, *Ohio Frontier*, 178.

20. Ann Hulme Price to Sarah Hulme, May 2, 1824, AHP.

21. Ann Hulme Price to Sarah Hulme, May 2, 1824, AHP.

22. Ann Hulme Price to Martha Neale, July 22, 1827, AHP.

23. Watts, *Psalms and Hymns*, 275–76.

24. Ann Hulme Price to Martha Neale, July 22, 1827, AHP.

25. Ann Hulme Price to John Hulme, February 1, 1829, AHP.

26. Ann Hulme Price to Sarah Hulme, May 2, 1824, AHP.

27. Ann Hulme Price to Martha Hulme, June 29, 1828, AHP.

28. Turner, *Frontier in American History*, 18; Peck, *New Guide*, 116.

29. Ann Hulme Price to Sarah Hulme, May 2, 1824, AHP.

30. Ann Hulme Price to Sarah Hulme, May 2, 1824, AHP.

31. Ann Hulme Price to John Hulme, January 23, 1825, AHP.

32. Taylor, *Transportation Revolution*, 45–46; Scheiber, *Ohio Canal Era*, 163–64; Ross, *Workers on the Edge*, 10, 28–29.

33. On improvement, see Howe, *What Hath God Wrought*, 244 (quotation); Kerrigan, *Johnny Appleseed*, 140; Fea, *Way of Improvement Leads Home*; and Sweet, "What Is Improvement?" 225–30.

34. Ann Hulme Price to Martha Hulme, June 29, 1828, AHP.

35. Ann Hulme Price to Sarah Hulme, June 4, 1826, AHP.

36. Ann Hulme Price to Martha Hulme, June 29, 1828, AHP.

37. Scheiber, *Ohio Canal Era*, 163.

38. Ann Hulme Price to Sarah Hulme, November 9, 1828, AHP.

39. Ann Hulme Price to Martha Hulme, June 29, 1828, AHP

40. Ann Hulme Price to John Hulme, January 23, 1825, AHP.

41. Ann Hulme Price to John Hulme, January 23, 1825, AHP.

42. Ann Hulme Price to John Hulme, January 23, 1825, AHP.

43. Ann Hulme Price to Sarah Hulme, June 4, 1826, AHP.

44. Ann Hulme Price to Martha Neale, July 22, 1827, AHP.

45. Ann Hulme Price to John Hulme, February 1, 1829, AHP.

46. Ann Hulme Price to Sarah Hulme, November 9, 1828, AHP.

47. "Improvement, n.," OED Online, March 2020, https://doi.org/10.1093/OED/5678745142; Howe, *What Hath God Wrought*, 244; Kerrigan, *Johnny Appleseed*, 140; Fea, *Way of Improvement Leads Home*; Sweet, "What Is Improvement?" 225–30. Ann Price's house-based improvement can be read in a similar line as English acts of

possession; see Seed, *Ceremonies of Possession,* 16–17, and Seed, "Taking Possession and Reading Texts," 191.

48. Ann Hulme Price to John Hulme, February 1, 1829, AHP.

49. Ann Hulme Price to Sarah Hulme, November 9, 1828, AHP.

50. Boydston, *Home and Work,* 24.

51. Ann Hulme Price to Martha Neale, July 22, 1827, AHP.

52. Ann Price exemplified Jeanne Boydston's finding that "the society these women live in—and, in many respects, the women themselves—had come to doubt, even to deny, the economic value of their labors, perceiving . . . that the 'support' of the family came entirely from wages, and especially from the wages of the husband." Boydston, *Home and Work,* xii.

53. Ann Hulme Price to John Hulme, January 23, 1825, AHP.

54. Ann Hulme Price to Sarah Hulme, June 4, 1826, AHP.

55. On the representative experiences of middling women, see Boydston, *Home and Work,* 75–79.

56. Ann Hulme Price to Martha Neale, July 22, 1827; Price to Martha Hulme, June 29, 1828; Price to Sarah Hulme, November 9, 1828; Price to John Hulme, February 1, 1829, AHP.

57. Ann Hulme Price to Sarah Hulme, May 2, 1824; Price to Sarah Hulme, June 4, 1826; Price to Martha Hulme, June 29, 1828, AHP.

58. Ann Hulme Price to Martha Neale, July 22, 1827; Price to Sarah Hulme, April 16, 1827; Price to Martha Hulme, June 29, 1828, AHP.

59. Ann Hulme Price to Sarah Hulme, May 2, 1824, AHP.

60. Ann Hulme Price to Sarah Hulme, June 4, 1826; Price to Sarah Hulme, April 16, 1827, AHP.

61. Ann Hulme Price to Sarah Hulme, April 16, 1827, AHP; Lamentations 3:22.

62. Ann Hulme Price to John Hulme, February 1, 1829, AHP.

63. Ann Hulme Price to Sarah Hulme, February 25, 1828, AHP; Psalm 17:8.

64. Ann Hulme Price to Amy Potts, April 5, 1829, AHP; Psalm 84; Watts, *Psalms of David,* 148–50.

65. Ann Hulme Price to Martha Neale, July 22, 1827, AHP.

66. On women's experiences of migration, see Cashin, *A Family Venture,* and Faragher, *Women and Men.*

67. Ann Hulme Price to Martha Hulme, June 29, 1828, AHP.

68. On correspondence, see Stowe, *Intimacy and Power,* 142–46; Henkin, *Postal Age;* Dierks, *In My Power;* and Schweiger, *Literate South,* 99–103.

69. Ann Hulme Price to John Hulme, February 1, 1829, AHP.

70. Ann Hulme Price to John Hulme, January 23, 1825; Price to Sarah Hulme, November 9, 1828, AHP.

71. Ann Hulme Price to Sarah Hulme, February 25, 1828, AHP.

72. Ann Hulme Price to Martha Hulme, June 29, 1828, AHP.

73. Ann Hulme Price to Sarah Hulme, April 16, 1827, AHP. The hymn, the lyrics of which John Price modified, is "For One Departing," in Wesley and Wesley, *Poetical Works*, 216.

74. Ann Hulme Price to John Hulme, December 24, 1828; February 1, 1829, AHP.

75. Ann Hulme Price to Sarah Hulme, May 2, 1824; Price to John Hulme, January 23, 1825, AHP.

76. Ann Hulme Price to Sarah Hulme, February 25, 1828, AHP.

77. Ann Hulme Price to Martha Hulme, June 29, 1828, AHP.

78. Ann Hulme Price to Sarah Hulme, November 9, 1828, AHP. The poem is "Verses Supposed to Be Written by Alexander Selkirk, during His Solitary Abode in the Island of Juan Fernandez," in Cowper, *Poems*, 339–41.

79. Ann Hulme Price to Sarah Hulme, November 9, 1828, AHP.

80. Lindman, "'To Have a Gradual Weaning.'"

81. Ann Hulme Price to Martha Neale, July 22, 1827. Ann's weakness persisted into the following year; see Price to Sarah Hulme, February 25, 1828, AHP.

82. Ann Hulme Price to Amy Potts, April 5, 1829, AHP.

83. Ann Hulme Price to Sarah Hulme, April 16, 1827, AHP.

84. Quarterly Conference Records for the Cincinnati Circuit, Miami District, Ohio Conference, Methodist Episcopal Church, 1813–1847, September 8, 1828, Archives of Ohio United Methodism.

85. Ann Hulme Price to Amy Potts, April 5, 1829, AHP.

86. Ann Hulme Price to Sarah Hulme, November 9, 1828, AHP.

87. In 1829, Cincinnati reported 392 Methodist Protestant members and 915 white MEC members. The same year, there were just over 1,000 Methodist Protestants in Ohio, while the MEC's Miami District alone had 7,079 white members. John Price was listed as a member and minister at the 1829 annual conference in Ohio of the Methodist Protestants. *Extract from the Journal of the Ohio Annual Conference*, 1, 6; *Minutes of the Annual Conferences*, 2:6.

88. Ann Hulme Price to John Hulme, February 1, 1829, AHP.

89. Ann Hulme Price to John Hulme, July 12, 1836, AHP.

90. Ann Hulme Price to Martha Hulme, June 29, 1828, AHP.

91. Ann Hulme Price to Sarah Porter, October 2, 1831, AHP. The hymn is "Welcome Cross," in Newton and Cowper, *Olney Hymns*, 294.

92. Ann Hulme Price to Sarah Porter, July 29, 1832, AHP. Daniel Drake argued that cholera did not reach Cincinnati until September 30; see "Epidemic Cholera in Cincinnati," *Western Journal of the Medical and Physical Sciences*, October–December 1832, 322.

93. Ann Hulme Price to Sarah Porter, July 29, 1832, AHP.

94. Ann Hulme Price to Amy Potts, April 5, 1829, AHP; Isaiah 54:5, 47:4; Psalms 24:1, 50:10.

95. Ann Hulme Price to John Hulme, August 12, 1832, AHP.

96. Horne was likely the pork merchant listed in the 1836 city directory; see *Cincinnati Directory Advertiser*, 86.

97. The 1836 directory shows Ann Price and Thomas Barnes living on the same block; see *Cincinnati Directory Advertiser*, 16, 138.

98. Ann Hulme Price to Sarah Porter, May 14, 1833, AHP.

99. Ann Hulme Price to John Hulme, April 22, 1834, AHP.

100. Ann Hulme Price to John Hulme, October 6, 1834, AHP.

101. Ann Hulme Price to John Hulme, July 12, 1836, AHP.

Conclusion

1. On the politics of the Protestant schisms over slavery, focused on the border states, see Holm, *Kingdom Divided*.

2. On the conflicting versions of this story and its legacy for race in America, see Mark Auslander, *The Accidental Slaveowner: Revisiting a Myth of Race and Finding an American Family* (Athens: University of Georgia Press, 2011).

3. Calhoun, *Works*, 557–58 (quotations); Norwood, *Schism in the Methodist Episcopal Church*; Mathews, *Slavery and Methodism*, chap. 9; Goen, *Broken Churches, Broken Nation*, 78–90; Snay, *Gospel of Disunion*; Brooke, "Cultures of Nationalism."

4. The term is borrowed from Furstenberg, "Significance of the Trans-Appalachian Frontier," 650.

5. Mathews, "Second Great Awakening as an Organizing Process," 29, 39, 42–43.

6. Anderson, *Imagined Communities*.

7. On skepticism and doubt, see Porterfield, *Conceived in Doubt*, and Grasso, *Skepticism and American Faith*.

8. Adjet McGuire to James B. Finley, January 8, 1829, JBF.

9. John W. Langdon to Quarterly Conference, August 19, 1817, Trial Proceedings, John Langdon, 1817, MSS 231, box 1 folder 19, Methodist Episcopal Church, Ohio Records, Ohio Historical Society.

10. John Kobler, "Annals of Western Methodism: From the Journal of John Kobler," *Western Christian Advocate*, August 1839, 73, quoted in Schneider, *Way of the Cross Leads Home*, 94; Mack, *Heart Religion in the British Enlightenment*; Schneider, *Way of the Cross Leads Home*, chaps. 6–7; Ruth, *Little Heaven Below*, chap. 4. Important treatments of emotion via sensibility in early America are found in Knott, *Sensibility and the American Revolution*, and Kelley, *Learning to Stand and Speak*.

11. Rush, "Address," 8–11.

12. Bushnell, *Barbarism the First Danger*, 6.

13. Classic statements are Berthoff, "American Social Order"; Smith, "Congregation, State, and Denomination"; and Mathews, "Second Great Awakening as an Organizing Process." On the context of home missions, see for example Griffin, "Religious Benevolence as Social Control"; Banner, "Religious Benevolence as Social Control"; Haselby, *Origins of American Religious Nationalism*; Sehat, *Myth of*

American Religious Freedom; and Wyatt-Brown, "Antimission Movement." The concern over social institutions and integration connect to the issue of internal improvement; see Larson, *Internal Improvement.*

14. Francis Asbury to Jesse Lee, September 12, 1797, *JLFA,* in 3:164.

15. Information on the expansion of annual conferences is found in *Minutes of the Annual Conferences,* and Barclay, *Early American Methodism.*

16. Bangs, *History of the Methodist Episcopal Church,* 46.

17. Quoted in Noll, *Civil War as a Theological Crisis,* 26–27.

18. Bangs, *History of the Methodist Episcopal Church,* 46.

19. Methodism became especially violent in border areas where the church was strong, such as western Virginia and the Holston country of eastern Tennessee; see Foulds, "Enemies of the State," and Dunn, *Civil War in Southern Appalachian Methodism.*

20. Ann Hulme Price to Sarah Hulme, November 9, 1828, AHP.

BIBLIOGRAPHY

Unpublished Primary Sources

American Antiquarian Society, Worcester, MA
Archives of Ohio United Methodism, Ohio Wesleyan University, Delaware
    Early Methodist Newsclippings
    James B. Finley Papers
    Daniel Hitt Letters
    Journal and Letters of John Kobler
    Quarterly Conference Records for the Cincinnati Circuit, Miami District, Ohio Conference, Methodist Episcopal Church, 1813–1847
    Samuel Williams Papers
Bridwell Library, Southern Methodist University, Dallas, TX
    Methodism in North America Collection
    William Warren Sweet Papers
J. B. Cain Archives of Mississippi Methodism, Millsaps College, Jackson
    Learner Blackman Papers
    William Winans Papers
Clarke Historical Library, Central Michigan University, Mount Pleasant
    Williams Family Papers
Detre Library and Archives, Heinz History Center, Pittsburgh
    Papers of Robert Ayres
John W. Dickhaut Library, Methodist Theological School in Ohio, Delaware
    Philip Gatch Papers
Filson Historical Society, Louisville, KY
    Corlis-Respess Family Papers
    Rare Pamphlet Collection
Rutherford B. Hayes Presidential Center, Fremont, OH
    Reverend James B. Finley Collection
Lilly Library Manuscript Collections, Indiana University, Bloomington
    Samuel Williams Manuscripts

Manuscript Division, Library of Congress, Washington, DC
   John McLean Papers
Manuscripts, Archives, and Rare Books Library, Emory University, Atlanta, GA
   William M'Kendree Papers
Michigan Conference United Methodist Archives, Adrian College, Adrian
Mississippi Department of Archives and History, Jackson
   Censuses, 1801–16, State Government Records, Series 486
   Benjamin Drake Papers
Ohio Historical Society, Columbus
   Methodist Episcopal Church, Ohio Records
   Ann Hulme Price Papers
   Edward Tiffin Papers
   Samuel Williams Papers
   Thomas Worthington Papers
Princeton Theological Seminary Library, Princeton, NJ
   Benson Collection of Hymnals and Hymnology
Southern Historical Collection, University of North Carolina–Chapel Hill
   Edward Dromgoole Papers
Special Collections, A. Frank Smith Jr. Library, Southwestern University, Georgetown, TX
   Henry Matthews Diaries
Special Collections Research Center, Regenstein Library, University of Chicago
   Church History Documents Collection
   William Warren Sweet Papers
Tennessee Historical Society, Tennessee State Library and Archives, Nashville
   John Lyle Diary
United Methodist Archives, Lycoming College, Williamsport, PA
United Methodist Archives Center, Drew University, Madison, NJ
   Learner Blackman Papers
   James Gilruth Papers
   Thomas C. Nixon Papers
United Methodist Heritage Center, Kentucky Wesleyan College, Owensboro
   John Littlejohn Papers
   Quarterly Conference Minutes, Madison Circuit

Published Primary Sources

Asbury, Francis. *The Journal and Letters of Francis Asbury*. 3 vols. Edited by Elmer T. Clark et al. Nashville, TN: Abingdon Press, 1958.
Bangs, Nathan. *A History of the Methodist Episcopal Church*. 2 vols. New York: T. Mason and G. Lane, 1839.

BIBLIOGRAPHY

Bradford, John. *The Kentucky Almanac for the Year of Our Lord 1820.* Lexington, KY: Thomas Smith, 1819.

Bunyan, John. *The Pilgrim's Progress.* Edited by Cynthia Wall. New York: Norton, 2008.

Bushnell, Horace. *Barbarism the First Danger: A Discourse for Home Missions.* New York: American Home Missionary Society, 1847.

Calhoun, John C. *The Works of John C. Calhoun,* vol. 4, *Speeches of John C. Calhoun, Delivered in the House of Representatives, and in the Senate of the United States.* Edited by Richard K. Crallé. New York: D. Appleton, 1854.

Cartwright, Peter. *Autobiography of Peter Cartwright, the Backwoods Preacher.* Edited by W. P. Strickland. New York: Carlton and Porter, 1856.

Cincinnati Directory Advertiser for the Years 1836–7. Cincinnati: J. H. Woodruff, 1836.

Cowper, William. *The Poems of William Cowper, Esq.* New York: Charles Wells, 1835.

Crozier, William Armstrong, ed. *Virginia County Records.* 11 vols. Hasbrouck Heights, NJ: Genealogical Association, 1905–13.

Doctrines and Discipline of the Methodist Episcopal Church, in America. 10th ed. Philadelphia: John Dickens, 1798.

Extract from the Journal of the Ohio Annual Conference of the Methodist A[ssociated] Churches, Held in Cincinnati, October 15th, 1829. Cincinnati, OH: Whetstone and Buxton, [1829].

Finley, James B. *Autobiography of Rev. James B. Finley; or, Pioneer Life in the West.* Cincinnati, OH: Methodist Book Concern, 1853.

———. *Sketches of Western Methodism: Biographical, Historical, and Miscellaneous. Illustrative of Pioneer Life.* Cincinnati: R. P. Thompson, 1855.

Gibson, Campbell, and Kay Jung. *Historical Census Statistics on Population Totals by Race, 1790 to 1990, and by Hispanic Origin, 1970 to 1990, for the United States, Regions, Divisions, and States.* Washington, DC: US Census Bureau, 2002.

Greene, Evarts B., and Virginia D. Harrington. *American Population before the Federal Census of 1790.* New York: Columbia University Press, 1932.

Jillson, Willard Rouse. *The Kentucky Land Grants: A Systematic Index to All of the Land Grants Recorded in the State Land Office at Frankfort, Kentucky, 1782–1924.* Louisville, KY: Standard Printing, 1925.

Jones, John Griffing. *A Complete History of Methodism as Connected with the Mississippi Conference of the Methodist Episcopal Church, South.* Nashville, TN: Methodist Episcopal Church, South, 1908.

Journals of the General Conference of the Methodist Episcopal Church, vol. 1, *1796–1836.* New York: Carlton and Phillips, 1855.

Lee, Jesse. *A Short History of the Methodists, in the United States of America.* Baltimore, MD: Magill and Clime, 1810.

Littlejohn, John. *Preecher and Patriot: The Journal and Memorandums of the Rev. John Littlejohn, A Pioneer Preacher of American Methodism.* Edited by Richard A. Weiss. Utica, KY: McDowell, 2005.

McCabe, James D., Jr. *Great Fortunes, and How They Were Made; or, The Struggles and Triumphs of Our Self-Made Men.* Philadelphia: George MacLean, 1871.

M'Caine, Alexander. *Letters on the Organization and Early History of the Methodist Episcopal Church.* Boston: Thomas F. Norris, 1850.

M'Ferrin, John B. *History of Methodism in Tennessee,* vol. 1, *From the Year 1783 to the Year 1804.* Nashville, TN: M. E. Church, South, 1888.

McLean, John, ed. *Sketch of Rev. Philip Gatch.* Cincinnati, OH: Swormstedt and Poe, 1854.

Methodist Magazine. New York. 1818–32.

Minutes of the Annual Conferences of the Methodist Episcopal Church. Volumes 1–3. New York: T. Mason and G. Lane, 1840.

[Newton, John, and William Cowper]. *Olney Hymns, in Three Books.* London: T. Wilkins, 1783.

Peck, J. M. *A New Guide for Emigrants to the West, Containing Sketches of Ohio, Indiana, Illinois, Missouri, Michigan, with the Territories of Wisconsin and Arkansas, and the Adjacent Parts.* Boston: Gould, Kendall, and Lincoln, 1836.

Pittsburgh Christian Advocate. Pittsburgh. 1840–1931.

Platt, Jeanette H. *Life and Letters of Jeanette H. Platt.* Compiled by Cyrus Platt. Philadelphia: E. Claxton, 1882.

Redford, A. H. *The History of Methodism in Kentucky.* 3 vols. Nashville, TN: Southern Methodist Publishing, 1868.

Rush, Benjamin. "Address to the People of the United States." *American Museum.* Philadelphia, Mathew Carey. 1787.

Stevens, Abel. *Dr. Cartwright Portrayed, in His Visit to Brooklyn, 1861, Speeches and Anecdotes, and Correspondence with the Devil.* New York: N. Tibbals, 1861.

Sweet, William Warren, ed. *Circuit-Rider Days along the Ohio: Being the Journal of the Ohio Conference from Its Organization in 1812 to 1826.* New York: Methodist Book Concern, 1923.

———, ed. *Religion on the American Frontier, 1783–1840,* vol. 4, *The Methodists.* Chicago: University of Chicago Press, 1946.

———, ed. *The Rise of Methodism in the West: Being the Journal of the Western Conference, 1800–1811.* New York: Methodist Book Concern, 1920.

Taylor, John. *Baptists on the American Frontier: A History of Ten Baptist Churches of Which the Author Has Been Alternately a Member.* Edited by Chester R. Young. Macon, GA: Mercer University Press, 1995.

United States Census. Second Census of the United States, 1800, M32, 52 rolls; Third Census of the United States, 1810, M252, 71 rolls; Fourth Census of the United States, 1820, M33, 142 rolls; Fifth Census of the United States, 1830, M19,

201 rolls; Sixth Census of the United States, 1840, M704, 580 rolls; Seventh Census of the United States, 1850, M432, 1,009 rolls. Records of the Bureau of the Census, Record Group 29, National Archives, Washington, DC.

Watts, Isaac. *The Psalms and Hymns of Dr. Watts, Arranged by Dr. Rippon; with Dr. Rippon's Selection*. Philadelphia: Clark and Lippincott, 1837.

———. *The Psalms of David, Imitated in the Language of the New Testament*. Philadelphia, 1740.

Weekly Messenger. Russellville, KY. 1820.

Wesley, John, and Charles Wesley. *The Poetical Works of John and Charles Wesley*. Vol. 5. Compiled by G. Osborn. London: Wesleyan-Methodist Conference Office, 1869.

Western Christian Advocate. Cincinnati, OH. 1834–1929.

Western Journal of the Medical and Physical Sciences. Cincinnati, OH. 1832.

Secondary Sources

Abelove, Henry. *The Evangelist of Desire: John Wesley and the Methodists*. Stanford, CA: Stanford University Press, 1991.

Adams, Donald R., Jr. "Some Evidence on English and American Wage Rates, 1790–1830." *Journal of Economic History* 30 (September 1970): 499–520.

Ahlstrom, Sydney E. *A Religious History of the American People*, 2nd ed. 1972; New Haven, CT: Yale University Press, 2004.

Anderson, Benedict. *Imagined Communities: Reflections on the Origin and Spread of Nationalism*. New York: Verso, 2006.

Andrews, Dee. *The Methodists and Revolutionary America, 1760–1800: The Shaping of an Evangelical Culture*. Princeton, NJ: Princeton University Press, 2000.

Armitage, David. *The Ideological Origins of the British Empire*. New York: Cambridge University Press, 2000.

Armitage, David, and Michael J. Braddick, eds. *The British Atlantic World, 1500–1800*. New York: Palgrave Macmillan, 2002.

Aron, Stephen. *How the West Was Lost: The Transformation of Kentucky from Daniel Boone to Henry Clay*. Baltimore, MD: Johns Hopkins University Press, 1996.

Ash, James L., Jr. "American Religion and the Academy in the Early Twentieth Century: The Chicago Years of William Warren Sweet." *Church History* 50 (December 1981): 450–64.

Bailyn, Bernard. *Voyagers to the West: A Passage in the Peopling of America on the Eve of the Revolution*. New York: Vintage, 1988.

Baker, Paula. "The Domestication of Politics: Women and American Political Society, 1780–1920." *American Historical Review* 89, no. 3 (June 1984): 620–47.

Banner, Lois W. "Religious Benevolence as Social Control: A Critique of an Interpretation." *Journal of American History* 60, no. 1 (June 1973): 23–41.

Barclay, Wade Crawford. *Early American Methodism, 1769–1844*, vol. 1, *Missionary Motivation and Expansion*. New York: Board of Missions and Church Extension of the Methodist Church, 1949.

Barnhart, John D. *Valley of Democracy: The Frontier versus the Plantation in the Ohio Valley, 1775–1818*. Bloomington: Indiana University Press, 1953.

Beadie, Nancy. *Education and the Creation of Capital in the Early American Republic*. New York: Cambridge University Press, 2010.

Belich, James. *Replenishing the Earth: The Settler Revolution and the Rise of the Anglo-World, 1783–1939*. New York: Oxford University Press, 2009.

Benjamin, Thomas. *The Atlantic World: Europeans, Africans, Indians and Their Shared History, 1400–1900*. New York: Cambridge University Press, 2009.

Berlin, Ira. *Many Thousands Gone: The First Two Centuries of Slavery in North America*. Cambridge, MA: Harvard University Press, 1998.

Berthoff, Rowland. "The American Social Order: A Conservative Hypothesis." *American Historical Review* 65, no. 3 (April 1960): 495–514.

Billingsley, Carolyn Earle. *Communities of Kinship: Antebellum Families and the Settlement of the Cotton Frontier*. Athens: University of Georgia Press, 2004.

Billington, Ray Allen, and Martin Ridge. *Westward Expansion: A History of the American Frontier*. 5th ed. New York: Macmillan, 1982.

Birdsall, Richard D. "The Second Great Awakening and the New England Social Order." *Church History* 39 (1970): 345–64.

Boase, Paul H. "The Education of a Circuit Rider." *Quarterly Journal of Speech* 40, no. 2 (1954): 130–36.

Boles, John B. "Evangelical Protestantism in the Old South: From Religious Dissent to Cultural Dominance." In *Religion in the South*, edited by Charles Reagan Wilson, 13–34. Jackson: University Press of Mississippi, 1985.

———. *The Great Revival, 1787–1805: The Origins of the Southern Evangelical Mind*. Lexington: University Press of Kentucky, 1972.

Bontrager, Shannon. "'From a Nation of Drunkards, We Have Become a Sober People': The Wyandot Experience in the Ohio Valley during the Early Republic." *Journal of the Early Republic* 32 (Winter 2012): 603–32.

Bourdieu, Pierre. "The Forms of Capital." In *Handbook of Theory and Research for the Sociology of Education*, edited by John G. Richardson, 241–58. Westport, CT: Greenwood Press, 1986.

Bowes, John P. *Land Too Good for Indians: Northern Indian Removal*. Norman: University of Oklahoma Press, 2016.

Boydston, Jeanne. *Home and Work: Housework, Wages, and the Ideology of Labor in the Early Republic*. New York: Oxford University Press, 1990.

Bradburn, Douglas, and John C. Coombs, eds. *Early Modern Virginia: Reconsidering the Old Dominion*. Charlottesville: University of Virginia Press, 2011.

Brantley, Richard E. *Locke, Wesley, and the Method of English Romanticism*. Gainesville: University Press of Florida, 1984.
Braun, Willi, and Russell T. McCutcheon, eds. *Guide to the Study of Religion*. New York: Cassell, 2000.
Bray, Robert. *Peter Cartwright, Legendary Frontier Preacher*. Urbana: University of Illinois Press, 2005.
Brekus, Catherine A. *Sarah Osborn's World: The Rise of Evangelical Christianity in Early America*. New Haven, CT: Yale University Press, 2013.
———. *Strangers and Pilgrims: Female Preaching in America, 1740–1845*. Chapel Hill: University of North Carolina Press, 1998.
Breen, Timothy H. "Retrieving Common Sense: Rights, Liberties, and the Religious Public Sphere in Late Eighteenth Century America." In *To Secure the Blessings of Liberty: Rights in American History*, ed. Josephine F. Pacheno, 55–65. Fairfax, VA: George Mason University Press, 1993.
Breen, T. H., and Timothy Hall, "Structuring Provincial Imagination: The Rhetoric and Experience of Social Change in Eighteenth-Century New England." *American Historical Review* 103, no. 5 (Dec. 1998): 1411–39.
Brooke, John L. *Columbia Rising: Civil Life on the Upper Hudson from the Revolution to the Age of Jackson*. Chapel Hill: University of North Carolina Press, 2010.
———. "Consent, Civil Society, and the Public Sphere in the Age of Revolution and the Early American Republic." In *Beyond the Founders: New Approaches to the Political History of the Early American Republic*, edited by Jeffrey L. Pasley, Andrew W. Robertson, and David Waldstreicher, 207–51. Chapel Hill: University of North Carolina Press, 2004.
———. "Cultures of Nationalism, Movements of Reform, and the Composite-Federal Polity: From Revolutionary Settlement to Antebellum Crisis." *Journal of the Early Republic* 29 (Spring 2009): 1–33.
———. *The Refiner's Fire: The Making of Mormon Cosmology, 1644–1844*. New York: Cambridge University Press, 1994.
Brown, Candy Gunther. *The Word in the World: Evangelical Writing, Publishing, and Reading in America, 1789–1880*. Chapel Hill: University of North Carolina Press, 2004.
Brown, Jeffrey P., and Andrew R.L. Cayton, eds. *The Pursuit of Public Power: Political Culture in Ohio, 1787–1861*. Kent, OH: Kent State University Press, 1994.
Brown, Richard D. *Knowledge Is Power: The Diffusion of Information in Early America, 1700–1685*. New York: Oxford University Press, 1989.
Brown, Stuart E., Jr. *Virginia Baron: The Story of Thomas 6th Lord Fairfax*. Berryville, VA: Chesapeake, 1965.
Bruyneel, Kevin. *Settler Memory: The Disavowal of Indigeneity and the Politics of Race in the United States*. Chapel Hill: University of North Carolina Press, 2021.

BIBLIOGRAPHY

Bucke, Emory Stevens, et al., eds. *The History of American Methodism*. Vol. 1. New York: Abingdon Press, 1964.

Buley, R. Carlyle. *The Old Northwest: Pioneer Period, 1815–1840*. 2 vols. Indianapolis: Indiana Historical Society, 1950.

Buskens, Vincent. "The Social Structure of Trust." *Social Networks* 20 (July 1998): 265–89.

Buss, James Joseph. *Winning the West with Words: Language and Conquest in the Lower Great Lakes*. Norman: University of Oklahoma Press, 2011.

Butler, Jon. *Awash in a Sea of Faith: Christianizing the American People*. Cambridge, MA: Harvard University Press, 1990.

Byrne, Donald E., Jr. *No Foot of Land: Folklore of American Methodist Itinerants*. Metuchen, NJ: Scarecrow Press, 1975.

Calhoon, Robert M. *Evangelicals and Conservatives in the Early South, 1740–1861*. Columbia: University of South Carolina Press, 1989.

Calhoun, Craig, ed. *Habermas and the Public Sphere*. Cambridge, MA: MIT Press, 1992.

Calloway, Colin G. *The Victory with No Name: The Native American Defeat of the First American Army*. New York: Oxford University Press, 2015.

Carey, Hilary M. *God's Empire: Religion and Colonialism in the British World, c. 1801–1908*. New York: Cambridge University Press, 2011.

Carney, Charity R. *Ministers and Masters: Methodism, Manhood, and Honor in the Old South*. Baton Rouge: Louisiana State University Press, 2011.

Carté, Katherine. *Religion and the American Revolution: An Imperial History*. Chapel Hill: University of North Carolina Press, 2021.

Carwardine, Richard J. *Evangelicals and Politics in Antebellum America*. New Haven, CT: Yale University Press, 1993.

Cashin, Joan E. *A Family Venture: Men and Women on the Southern Frontier*. New York: Oxford University Press, 1991.

Casper, Scott E. *Constructing American Lives: Biography and Culture in Nineteenth-Century America*. Chapel Hill: University of North Carolina Press, 1999.

Cayton, Andrew R. L. *Frontier Republic: Ideology and Politics in the Ohio Country, 1780–1825*. Kent, OH: Kent State University Press, 1989.

Cayton, Andrew R. L., and Stuart D. Hobbs, eds. *The Center of a Great Empire: The Ohio Country in the Early American Republic*. Athens: Ohio University Press, 2005.

Cayton, Andrew R. L., and Fredrika J. Teute, eds. *Contact Points: American Frontiers from the Mohawk Valley to the Mississippi, 1750–1830*. Chapel Hill: University of North Carolina Press, 1998.

Claiborne, J. F. H. *Mississippi, as a Province, Territory, and State: With Biographical Notices of Eminent Citizens*. Jackson, MS: Power and Barksdale, 1880.

Cohen, Patricia Cline. *A Calculating People: The Spread of Numeracy in Early America*. Chicago: University of Chicago Press, 1992.

Coleman, James S. *Foundations of Social Theory*. Cambridge, MA: Belknap Press, 1990.

Conkin, Paul K. *Cane Ridge: America's Pentecost*. Madison: University of Wisconsin Press, 1990.

Conroy-Krutz, Emily. *Christian Imperialism: Converting the World in the Early American Republic*. Ithaca, NY: Cornell University Press, 2015.

Cook, Harold J. *Matters of Exchange: Commerce, Medicine, and Science in the Dutch Golden Age*. New Haven, CT: Yale University Press, 2007.

Cott, Nancy. *The Bonds of Womanhood: Women's Sphere in New England, 1780–1835*. New Haven, CT: Yale University Press, 1977.

Crothers, A. Glenn. *Quakers Living in the Lion's Mouth: The Society of Friends in Northern Virginia, 1730–1865*. Gainesville: University Press of Florida, 2012.

Dailey, Barbara Ritter. "The Itinerant Preacher and the Social Network in Seventeenth-Century New England." In *Itinerancy in New England and New York*, edited by Peter Benes, 37–48. Boston: Boston University, 1986.

Darnton, Robert. *Poetry and the Police: Communication Networks in Eighteenth-Century Paris*. Cambridge, MA: Belknap Press, 2010.

Daviess, Maria Thompson. *History of Mercer and Boyle Counties*. Harrodsburg, KY: Harrodsburg Herald, 1924.

Deloria, Philip J. *Playing Indian*. New Haven, CT: Yale University Press, 1998.

Dennis, Matthew. *Seneca Possessed: Indians, Witchcraft, and Power in the Early American Republic*. Philadelphia: University of Pennsylvania Press, 2010.

Dierks, Konstantin. *In My Power: Letter Writing and Communications in Early America*. Philadelphia: University of Pennsylvania Press, 2009.

Dochuk, Darren. *From Bible Belt to Sun Belt: Plain-Folk Religion, Grassroots Politics, and the Rise of Evangelical Conservatism*. New York: Norton, 2011.

Drake, Benjamin M. "Tobias Gibson: The First Methodist Missionary to the 'Natchez Country.'" *Southern Methodist Review* 2, no. 2 (May 1887): 238–47.

Dunn, Durwood. *The Civil War in Southern Appalachian Methodism*. Knoxville: University of Tennessee Press, 2013.

DuVal, Kathleen. *Independence Lost: Lives on the Edge of the American Revolution*. New York: Random House, 2016.

Edmunds, R. David, ed. *Enduring Nations: Native Americans in the Midwest*. Urbana: University of Illinois Press, 2008.

Ehrenberg, John. *Civil Society: The Critical History of an Idea*. New York: New York University, 1999.

Elder, Robert. *The Sacred Mirror: Evangelicalism, Honor, and Identity in the Deep South, 1790–1860*. Chapel Hill: University of North Carolina Press, 2016.

———. "A Twice Sacred Circle: Women, Evangelicalism, and Honor in the Deep South, 1784–1860." *Journal of Southern History* 78, no. 3 (August 2012): 579–614.

Eley, Geoff. "Politics, Culture, and the Public Sphere." *Positions* 10, no. 1. (2002): 219–36.

Elliott, J. H. *Empires of the Atlantic World: Britain and Spain in America, 1492–1830.* New Haven, CT: Yale University Press, 2006.

Ellis, John. "The Confused, the Curious, and the Reborn: Methodism as a Youth Movement in the Upper South and Ohio Valley, 1770–1820." *Ohio Valley History* 10 (Spring 2010): 3–31.

Engel, Katherine Carté. *Religion and Profit: Moravians in Early America.* Philadelphia: University of Pennsylvania Press, 2009.

Eslinger, Ellen. *Citizens of Zion: The Social Origins of Camp Meeting Revivalism.* Knoxville: University of Tennessee Press, 1999.

———, ed. *Running Mad for Kentucky: Frontier Travel Accounts.* Lexington: University Press of Kentucky, 2004.

Etcheson, Nicole. *The Emerging Midwest: Upland Southerners and the Political Culture of the Old Northwest, 1787–1861.* Bloomington: Indiana University Press, 1996.

Etherington, Norman, ed. *Missions and Empire.* Oxford: Oxford University Press, 2005.

Eustace, Nicole, and Ann M. Little. "'Ineradicably Untidy': Women and Religion in the Age of Atlantic Empires." *Early American Studies* 17, no. 4 (Fall 2019): 397–413.

Faragher, John Mack. "Settler Colonial Studies and the North American Frontier." *Settler Colonial Studies* 4, no. 2 (2014): 181–91.

———. *Women and Men on the Overland Trail.* New Haven, CT: Yale University Press, 1979.

Farish, Hunter Dickinson. *The Circuit Rider Dismounts: A Social History of Southern Methodism.* Richmond, VA: Dietz Press, 1938.

Farrelly, Maura Jane. "'God Is the Author of Both': Science, Religion, and the Intellectualization of American Methodism." *Church History* 77 (September 2008): 659–87.

Fea, John. *The Way of Improvement Leads Home: Philip Vickers Fithian and the Rural Enlightenment in Early America.* Philadelphia: University of Pennsylvania Press, 2008.

———. "Wheelock's World: Letters and the Communication of Revival in Great Awakening New England." *Proceedings of the American Antiquarian Society* 109 (April 1999): 99–144.

Finke, Roger, and Rodney Stark. *The Churching of America, 1776–1990: Winners and Losers in Our Religious Economy.* 2nd ed. 1992; New Brunswick, NJ: Rutgers University Press, 2005.

Fischer, David Hackett, and James C. Kelly. *Bound Away: Virginia and the Westward Movement.* Charlottesville: University Press of Virginia, 2000.

Fitzgerald, Timothy. "Critical Religion and Critical Research on Religion: Religion and Politics as Modern Fictions." *Critical Research on Religion* 3, no. 3 (2015): 303–19.

Foley, Michael W., and Bob Edwards. "The Paradox of Civil Society." *Journal of Democracy* 7 (1996): 38–52.

Ford, Bridget. *Bonds of Union: Religion, Race, and Politics in a Civil War Borderland.* Chapel Hill: University of North Carolina Press, 2016.

Ford, Lacy K. *Deliver Us from Evil: The Slavery Question in the Old South.* New York: Oxford University Press, 2009.

———. *Origins of Southern Radicalism: The South Carolina Upcountry, 1800–1860.* New York: Oxford University Press, 1988.

Ford, Lisa. *Settler Sovereignty: Jurisdiction and Indigenous People in America and Australia, 1788–1836.* Cambridge, MA: Harvard University Press, 2010.

Foulds, Matthew Tyler. "Enemies of the State: Methodists, Secession, and the Civil War in Western Virginia, 1845–1872." Ph.D. diss., Ohio State University, 2012.

Friedman, Jean E. *The Enclosed Garden: Women and Community in the Evangelical South, 1830–1900.* Chapel Hill: University of North Carolina Press, 1985.

Friend, Craig Thompson. *Along the Maysville Road: The Early American Republic in the Trans-Appalachian West.* Knoxville: University of Tennessee Press, 2005.

———, ed. *The Buzzel about Kentuck: Settling the Promised Land.* Lexington: University Press of Kentucky, 1999.

———. *Kentucke's Frontiers.* Bloomington: Indiana University Press, 2010.

Furstenberg, François. "The Significance of the Trans-Appalachian Frontier in Atlantic History." *American Historical Review* 113, no. 3 (June 2008): 647–77.

Fyfe, Aileen. *Science and Salvation: Evangelical Popular Science Publishing in Victorian Britain.* Chicago: University of Chicago Press, 2004.

Gallay, Alan. *The Formation of a Plantation Elite: Jonathan Bryan and the Southern Colonial Frontier.* Athens: University of Georgia Press, 1989.

Games, Alison. *Migration and the Origins of the English Atlantic World.* Cambridge, MA: Harvard University Press, 1999.

Gaustad, Edwin Scott, and Philip L. Barlow. *New Historical Atlas of Religion in America.* New York: Oxford University Press, 2001.

Georgian, Elizabeth A. "'That Unhappy Division': Reconsidering the Causes and Significance of the O'Kelly Schism in the Methodist Episcopal Church." *Virginia Magazine of History and Biography* 120, no. 3 (2012): 210–35.

Gerona, Carla. *Night Journeys: The Power of Dreams in Transatlantic Quaker Culture.* Charlottesville: University of Virginia Press, 2004.

Gitlin, Jay. *The Bourgeois Frontier: French Towns, French Traders, and American Expansion.* New Haven, CT: Yale University Press, 2010.

Glover, Lorri. *All Our Relations: Blood Ties and Emotional Bonds among the Early South Carolina Gentry.* Baltimore, MD: Johns Hopkins University Press, 2000.

Godbeer, Richard. *The Overflowing of Friendship: Love between Men and the Creation of the American Republic.* Baltimore, MD: Johns Hopkins University Press, 2009.

Goen, C. C. *Broken Churches, Broken Nation: Denominational Schisms and the Coming of the Civil War.* Macon, GA: Mercer University Press, 1985.

———. "The 'Methodist Age' in American Church History." *Religion in Life* 34 (1965): 562–72.

Goff, Philip, Arthur E. Farnsley II, and Peter J. Thuesen. *The Bible in American Life.* New York: Oxford University Press, 2017.

Goldgar, Anne. *Impolite Learning: Conduct and Community in the Republic of Letters, 1680–1750.* New Haven, CT: Yale University Press, 1995.

Good, Cassandra A. *Founding Friendships: Friendships between Men and Women in the Early American Republic.* New York: Oxford University Press, 2015.

Goodman, Dena. *The Republic of Letters: A Cultural History of the French Enlightenment.* Ithaca, NY: Cornell University Press, 1994.

Gould, Eliga H. *Among the Powers of the Earth: The American Revolution and the Making of a New World Empire.* Cambridge, MA: Harvard University Press, 2012.

Grainger, Brett Malcolm. *Church in the Wild: Evangelicals in Antebellum America.* Cambridge, MA: Harvard University Press, 2019.

Granovetter, Mark S. "The Strength of Weak Ties." *American Journal of Sociology* 78 (May 1973): 1360–80.

Grasso, Christopher. *Skepticism and American Faith: From the Revolution to the Civil War.* New York: Oxford University Press, 2018.

———. *Teacher, Preacher, Soldier, Spy: The Civil Wars of John R. Kelso.* New York: Oxford University Press, 2021.

Gray, Susan E. *The Yankee West: Community Life on the Michigan Frontier.* Chapel Hill: University of North Carolina Press, 1996.

Green, Jennifer. *Military Education and the Emerging Middle Class in the Old South.* New York: Cambridge University Press, 2008.

Greenberg, Amy S. *Manifest Manhood and the Antebellum American Empire.* New York: Cambridge University Press, 2005.

Greene, Jack P. "Social and Cultural Capital in Colonial British America: A Case Study." *Journal of Interdisciplinary History* 29, no. 3 (1999): 491–509.

Greene, John C. *American Science in the Age of Jefferson.* Ames: Iowa State University Press, 1984.

Griffin, Clifford S. "Religious Benevolence as Social Control, 1815–1861." *Mississippi Valley Historical Review* 44 (December 1957): 423–44.

Griffin, Patrick. *American Leviathan: Empire, Nation, and Revolutionary Frontier.* New York: Hill and Wang, 2007.

BIBLIOGRAPHY

Gross, Robert A., and Mary Kelley, eds. *A History of the Book in America*, vol. 2, *An Extensive Republic: Print, Culture, and Society in the New Nation, 1790–1840*. Series edited by David D. Hall. Chapel Hill: University of North Carolina Press, 2010.

Habermas, Jürgen. *The Structural Transformation of the Public Sphere: An Inquiry into a Category of Bourgeois Society*. Translated by Thomas Burger. Cambridge, MA: MIT Press, 1991.

Halévy, Elie. *The Birth of Methodism in England*. Edited and translated by Bernard Semmel. Chicago: University of Chicago Press, 1971.

Hall, David D., ed. *Lived Religion in America: Toward a History of Practice*. Princeton, NJ: Princeton University Press, 1997.

———. *Worlds of Wonder, Days of Judgment: Popular Religious Belief in Early New England*. New York: Knopf, 1989.

Hall, Joseph M., Jr. *Zamumo's Gifts: Indian-European Exchange in the Colonial Southeast*. Philadelphia: University of Pennsylvania Press, 2009.

Hammond, Geordan. *John Wesley in America: Restoring Primitive Christianity*. New York: Oxford University Press, 2014.

Handlin, Oscar. *The Uprooted: The Epic Story of the Great Migrations That Made the American People*. Boston: Little, Brown, 1951.

Hareven, Tamara K., ed. *Anonymous Americans: Explorations in Nineteenth-Century Social History*. Englewood Cliffs, NJ: Prentice-Hall, 1971.

Harmon, Nolan B., ed. *The Encyclopedia of World Methodism*. 2 vols. Nashville, TN: United Methodist Publishing, 1974.

Harper, Rob. *Unsettling the West: Violence and State Building the Ohio Valley*. Philadelphia: University of Pennsylvania Press, 2018.

Haselby, Sam. *The Origins of American Religious Nationalism*. New York: Oxford University Press, 2015.

Hatch, Nathan O. *The Democratization of American Christianity*. New Haven, CT: Yale University Press, 1989.

———. "The Puzzle of American Methodism." *Church History* 63, no. 2 (June 1994): 175–89.

Hatch, Nathan O., and John H. Wigger, eds. *Methodism and the Shaping of American Culture*. Nashville, TN: Abingdon Press, 2001.

Haynes, Robert V. *The Mississippi Territory and the Southwest Frontier, 1795–1817*. Lexington: University Press of Kentucky, 2010.

———. *The Natchez District and the American Revolution*. Jackson: University Press of Mississippi, 2008.

Heitzenrater, Richard P. *Wesley and the People Called Methodists*. Nashville, TN: Abingdon Press, 1995.

Hempton, David. *Methodism: Empire of the Spirit*. New Haven, CT: Yale University Press, 2005.

Henkin, David M. *The Postal Age: The Emergence of Modern Communications in Nineteenth-Century America.* Chicago: University of Chicago Press, 2006.

Heyrman, Christine Leigh. *Southern Cross: The Beginnings of the Bible Belt.* Chapel Hill: University of North Carolina Press, 1998.

Hinderaker, Eric. *Elusive Empires: Constructing Colonialism in the Ohio Valley, 1673–1800.* New York: Cambridge University Press, 1997.

Hindmarsh, D. Bruce. *The Evangelical Conversion Narrative: Spiritual Autobiography in Early Modern England.* New York: Oxford University Press, 2005.

———. *The Spirit of Early Evangelicalism: True Religion in a Modern World.* New York: Oxford University Press, 2018.

Hinshaw, William Wade, ed. *Encyclopedia of American Quaker Genealogy.* 7 vols. Ann Arbor, MI: Edwards Brothers, 1938.

Hoffman, Ronald, and Peter J. Albert, eds. *Religion in a Revolutionary Age.* Charlottesville: University Press of Virginia, 1994.

Hofstra, Warren R. *The Planting of New Virginia: Settlement and Landscape in the Shenandoah Valley.* Baltimore, MD: Johns Hopkins University Press, 2004.

Holder, Ray. *William Winans: Methodist Leader in Antebellum Mississippi.* Jackson: University Press of Mississippi, 1977.

Holm, April E. *A Kingdom Divided: Evangelicals, Loyalty, and Sectionalism in the Civil War Era.* Baton Rouge: Louisiana State University Press, 2017.

Horn, James P. P. *Adapting to a New World: English Society in the Seventeenth-Century Chesapeake.* Chapel Hill: University of North Carolina Press, 1994.

Howe, Daniel Walker. "The Evangelical Movement and Political Culture in the North during the Second Party System." *Journal of American History* 77 (1991): 1216–39.

———. *Making the American Self: Jonathan Edwards to Abraham Lincoln.* Cambridge, MA: Harvard University Press, 1997.

———. *What Hath God Wrought: The Transformation of America, 1815–1848.* New York: Oxford University Press, 2007.

Hudson, Winthrop S. "The Methodist Age in America." *Methodist History* 12, no. 3 (April 1974): 3–15.

Hurt, R. Douglas. *The Ohio Frontier: Crucible of the Old Northwest, 1720–1830.* Bloomington: Indiana University Press, 1998.

Huston, James L. *Calculating the Value of the Union: Slavery, Property Rights, and the Economic Origins of the Civil War.* Chapel Hill: University of North Carolina Press, 2003.

Hyde, Anne F. *Empires, Nations, and Families: A History of the North American West, 1800–1860.* Lincoln: University of Nebraska Press, 2011.

Irons, Charles F. *The Origins of Proslavery Christianity: White and Black Evangelicals in Colonial and Antebellum Virginia.* Chapel Hill: University of North Carolina Press, 2008.

Isaac, Rhys. *The Transformation of Virginia, 1740–1790.* Chapel Hill: University of North Carolina Press, 1982.

John, Richard R. "Governmental Institutions as Agents of Change: Rethinking American Political Development in the Early Republic, 1787–1835." *Studies in American Political Development* 11 (Fall 1997): 347–80.

———. *Spreading the News: The American Postal System from Franklin to Morse.* Cambridge, MA: Harvard University Press, 1995.

———. "Why Institutions Matter." *Common-Place: The Journal of Early American Life* 9 (October 2008), https://commonplace.online/article/why-institutions-matter.

Johnson, Charles A. *The Frontier Camp Meeting: Religion's Harvest Time.* Dallas, TX: Southern Methodist University Press, 1955.

Johnson, Curtis D. *Redeeming America: Evangelicals and the Road to the Civil War.* Chicago: Ivan R. Dee, 1993.

Johnson, E. Polk. *A History of Kentucky and Kentuckians: The Leaders and Representative Men in Commerce, Industry and Modern Activities.* 3 vols. Chicago: Lewis, 1912.

Johnson, Paul E. *A Shopkeeper's Millennium: Society and Revivals in Rochester, New York, 1815–1837.* New York: Hill and Wang, 1978.

Johnson, Paul E., and Sean Wilentz. *The Kingdom of Matthias: A Story of Sex and Salvation in 19th-Century America.* 1994; reprint New York: Oxford University Press, 2012.

Johnson, Walter. *River of Dark Dreams: Slavery and Empire in the Cotton Kingdom.* Cambridge, MA: Belknap Press, 2013.

———. *Soul by Soul: Life Inside the Antebellum Slave Market.* Cambridge, MA: Harvard University Press, 1999.

Jones, Christopher Cannon. "Methodism, Slavery, and Freedom in the Revolutionary Atlantic, 1770–1820." Ph.D. diss., College of William and Mary, 2016.

Jordan, Ryan P. "Secularism and Empire in the United States, 1780–1900." *Religions* 8, no. 7 (July 2017): 117.

Jordan, Winthrop D. "American Chiaroscuro: The Status and Definition of Mulattoes in the British Colonies." *William and Mary Quarterly,* 3rd series, 19, no. 2 (1962): 183–200.

———. *White over Black: American Attitudes toward the Negro, 1550–1812.* Chapel Hill: University of North Carolina Press, 1968.

Jortner, Adam. *The Gods of Prophetstown: The Battle of Tippecanoe and the Holy War for the American Frontier.* New York: Oxford University Press, 2012.

Josephson-Storm, Jason Ānanda. "The Superstition, Secularism, and Religion Trinary; or, Re-Theorizing Secularism." *Method and Theory in the Study of Religion* 30 (2018): 1–20.

Juster, Susan. *Disorderly Women: Sexual Politics and Evangelicalism in Revolutionary New England.* Ithaca, NY: Cornell University Press, 1994.

———. *Doomsayers: Anglo-American Prophecy in the Age of Revolution.* Philadelphia: University of Pennsylvania Press, 2006.

Kadushin, Charles. *Understanding Social Networks: Theories, Concepts, and Findings.* New York: Oxford University Press, 2012.

Kaplan, Benjamin J. "Fictions of Privacy: House Chapels and the Spatial Accommodation of Religious Dissent in Early Modern Europe." *American Historical Review* 107 (2002): 1031–64.

Kaplan, Catherine O'Donnell. *Men of Letters in the Early Republic: Cultivating Forms of Citizenship.* Chapel Hill: University of North Carolina Press, 2008.

Kelley, Mary. *Learning to Stand and Speak: Women, Education, and Public Life in America's Republic.* Chapel Hill: University of North Carolina Press, 2006.

Kennedy, V. Lynn. *Born Southern: Childbirth, Motherhood, and Social Networks in the Old South.* Baltimore, MD: Johns Hopkins University Press, 2012.

Kerrigan, William. *Johnny Appleseed and the American Orchard: A Cultural History.* Baltimore, MD: Johns Hopkins University Press, 2012.

Kidd, Colin. "Civil Theology and Church Establishments in Revolutionary America." *Historical Journal* 42, no. 4 (December 1999): 1007–26.

Kilbride, Daniel. "Travel Writing as Evidence with Special Attention to Nineteenth-Century Anglo-America." *History Compass* 9, no. 4 (2011): 339–50.

King, Lester S. *Transformations in American Medicine: From Benjamin Rush to William Osler.* Baltimore, MD: Johns Hopkins University Press, 1991.

Kisker, Scott Thomas. *Foundation for Revival: Anthony Horneck, the Religious Societies, and the Construction of an Anglican Pietism.* Lanham, MD: Scarecrow Press, 2008.

Klein, Rachel N. *Unification of a Slave State: The Rise of the Planter Class in the South Carolina Backcountry, 1760–1808.* Chapel Hill: University of North Carolina Press, 1990.

Knott, Sarah. *Sensibility and the American Revolution.* Chapel Hill: University of North Carolina Press, 2009.

Koschnik, Albrecht. *"Let a Common Interest Bind Us Together": Associations, Partisanship, and Culture in Philadelphia, 1775–1840.* Charlottesville: University of Virginia Press, 2007.

Lake, Peter, and Steve Pincus. "Rethinking the Public Sphere in Early Modern England." *Journal of British Studies* 45 (April 2006): 270–92.

Lake, Peter, and Michael Questier. "Puritans, Papists, and the 'Public Sphere' in Early Modern England: The Edmund Campion Affair in Context." *Journal of Modern History* 72, no. 3 (2000): 587–627.

Lambert, Frank. "The Great Awakening as Artifact: George Whitefield and the Construction of Intercolonial Revival, 1739–1745." *Church History* 60, no. 2 (June 1991): 223–46.

BIBLIOGRAPHY

———. *Inventing the "Great Awakening."* Princeton, NJ: Princeton University Press, 1999.

———. *"Pedlar in Divinity": George Whitefield and the Transatlantic Revivals.* Princeton, NJ: Princeton University Press, 1994.

Lamoreaux, Naomi R. "Rethinking the Transition to Capitalism in the Early American Northeast." *Journal of American History* 90, no. 2 (September 2003): 437–61.

Lane, Belden C. *Landscapes of the Sacred: Geography and Narrative in American Spirituality.* Enlarged ed. 1988; Baltimore, MD: Johns Hopkins University Press, 2001.

Larson, John Lauritz. *Internal Improvement: National Public Works and the Promise of Popular Government in the Early United States.* Chapel Hill: University of North Carolina Press, 2000.

———. *The Market Revolution in America: Liberty, Ambition, and the Eclipse of the Common Good.* New York: Cambridge University Press, 2009.

Lawrence, Anna M. *One Family under God: Love, Belonging, and Authority in Early Transatlantic Methodism.* Philadelphia: University of Pennsylvania Press, 2011.

Lednum, John. *A History of the Rise of Methodism in America, Containing Sketches of Methodist Itinerant Preachers, from 1736 to 1785.* Philadelphia: John Lednum, 1859.

Leed, Eric J. *The Mind of the Traveler: From Gilgamesh to Global Tourism.* New York: Basic, 1991.

Lefebvre, Henri. *The Production of Space.* Translated by Donald Nicholson-Smith. Malden, MA: Blackwell, 1991.

Lewis, Jan. *The Pursuit of Happiness: Family and Values in Jefferson's Virginia.* New York: Cambridge University Press, 1983.

Libby, David J. *Slavery and Frontier Mississippi, 1720–1835.* Jackson: University Press of Mississippi, 2004.

Lin, Nan. *Social Capital: A Theory of Social Structure and Action.* New York: Cambridge University Press, 2001.

Lindman, Janet Moore. *Bodies of Belief: Baptist Community in Early America.* Philadelphia: University of Pennsylvania Press, 2008.

———. "'To Have a Gradual Weaning and Be Ready and Wiling to Resign All': Maternity, Piety, and Pain among Quaker Women of the Early Mid-Atlantic." *Early American Studies* 17, no. 4 (Fall 2019): 498–518.

Lindman, Janet Moore, and Michele Lise Tarter, eds. *A Centre of Wonders: The Body in Early America.* Ithaca, NY: Cornell University Press, 2001.

Lodge, Martin E. "The Crisis of the Churches in the Middle Colonies, 1720–1750." *Pennsylvania Magazine of History and Biography* 95 (1971): 195–220.

Loiselle, Kenneth. *Brotherly Love: Freemasonry and Male Friendship in Enlightenment France.* Ithaca, NY: Cornell University Press, 2014.

Lowery, Charles D. "The Great Migration to the Mississippi Territory, 1798–1819." *Journal of Mississippi History* 30, no. 3 (1968): 173–92.

Lyerly, Cynthia Lynn. *Methodism and the Southern Mind, 1770–1810.* New York: Oxford University Press, 1998.

Lyles, Albert M. *Methodism Mocked: The Satiric Reaction to Methodism in the Eighteenth Century.* London: Epworth Press, 1960.

MacCannell, Dean. *The Tourist: A New Theory of the Leisure Class.* New York: Schocken, 1976.

Mack, Phyllis. *Heart Religion in the British Enlightenment: Gender and Emotion in Early Methodism.* New York: Cambridge University Press, 2008.

Maddox, Randy L., and Jason E. Vickers, eds. *The Cambridge Companion to John Wesley.* New York: Cambridge University Press, 2010.

Marsden, George. *Jonathan Edwards: A Life.* New Haven, CT: Yale University Press, 2003.

Marshall, P. J., ed. *The Oxford History of the British Empire: The Eighteenth Century.* New York: Oxford University Press, 1998.

Mathews, Donald G. *Religion in the Old South.* Chicago: University of Chicago Press, 1977.

———. "The Second Great Awakening as an Organizing Process, 1780–1830: An Hypothesis." *American Quarterly* 21, no. 1 (Spring 1969): 23–43.

———. *Slavery and Methodism: A Chapter in American Morality, 1780–1845.* Princeton, NJ: Princeton University Press, 1965.

May, Henry F. *The Enlightenment in America.* New York: Oxford University Press, 1976.

McAllister, J. T. *Virginia Militia in the Revolutionary War.* Hot Springs, VA: McAllister, 1913.

McBride, Mary Gorton, and Ann Mathison McLaurin. *Randall Lee Gibson of Louisiana: Confederate General and New South Reformer.* Baton Rouge: Louisiana State University Press, 2007.

McBride, Spencer W. *Pulpit and Nation: Clergymen and the Politics of Revolutionary America.* Charlottesville: University of Virginia Press, 2017.

McCurry, Stephanie. *Masters of Small Worlds: Yeoman Households, Gender Relations, and the Political Culture of the Antebellum South Carolina Low Country.* New York: Oxford University Press, 1995.

McDonnell, Michael A. *The Politics of War: Race, Class, and Conflict in Revolutionary Virginia.* Chapel Hill: University of North Carolina Press, 2007.

McLaren, Scott. *Pulpit, Press, and Politics: Methodists and the Market for Books in Upper Canada.* Toronto: University of Toronto Press, 2019.

McLean, Scott L., David A. Schultz, and Manfred B. Steger, eds. *Social Capital: Critical Perspectives on Community and "Bowling Alone."* New York: New York University Press, 2002.

McLoughlin, William G. *Revivals, Awakenings, and Reform: An Essay on Religion and Social Change in America, 1607–1977.* Chicago: University of Chicago Press, 1978.

Merrell, James H. "Second Thoughts on Colonial Historians and American Indians." *William and Mary Quarterly,* 3rd series, 69, no. 3 (July 2012): 451–512.

———. "Some Thoughts on Colonial Historians and American Indians." *William and Mary Quarterly,* 3rd series, 46, no. 1 (January 1989): 94–119.

Miller, Perry. *The Life of the Mind in America: From the Revolution to the Civil War.* New York: Harcourt, Brace, 1965.

Miller, Randall M., Harry S. Stout, and Charles Reagan Wilson, eds. *Religion and the American Civil War.* New York: Oxford University Press, 1998.

Moreton, Bethany. *To Serve God and Wal-Mart: The Making of Christian Free Enterprise.* Cambridge, MA: Harvard University Press, 2010.

Morgan, Edmund S. *The Puritan Dilemma: The Story of John Winthrop.* Boston: Little, Brown, 1958.

Mulder, Philip N. *A Controversial Spirit: Evangelical Awakenings in the South.* New York: Oxford University Press, 2002.

Mullen, Lincoln A. *The Chance of Salvation: A History of Conversion in America.* Cambridge, MA: Harvard University Press, 2017.

Najar, Monica. *Evangelizing the South: A Social History of Church and State in Early America.* New York: Oxford University Press, 2008.

Neem, Johann N. *Creating a Nation of Joiners: Democracy and Civil Society in Early National Massachusetts.* Cambridge, MA: Harvard University Press, 2008.

———. "The Elusive Common Good: Religion and Civil Society in Massachusetts, 1780–1833." *Journal of the Early Republic* 24 (2004): 381–417.

Nenzi, Laura. *Excursions in Identity: Travel and the Intersection of Place, Gender, and Status in Edo Japan.* Honolulu: University of Hawai'i Press, 2008.

Noll, Mark A. *America's God: From Jonathan Edwards to Abraham Lincoln.* New York: Oxford University Press, 2002.

———. *The Civil War as a Theological Crisis.* Chapel Hill: University of North Carolina Press, 2006.

———, ed. *God and Mammon: Protestants, Money, and the Market, 1790–1860.* New York: Oxford University Press, 2001.

Noll, Mark A., David W. Bebbington, and George A. Rawlyk, eds. *Evangelicalism: Comparative Studies of Popular Protestantism in North America, the British Isles, and Beyond, 1700–1990.* New York: Oxford University Press, 1994.

Noll, Mark A., and Luke E. Harlow, eds. *Religion and American Politics: From the Colonial Period to the Present,* 2nd ed. 1990; New York: Oxford University Press, 2007.

Nord, David P. "The Evangelical Origins of the Mass Media in America, 1815–1835." *Journalism Monographs* 88 (1984): 1–31.

———. *Faith in Reading: Religious Publishing and the Birth of Mass Media in America.* New York: Oxford University Press, 2004.

———. "Free Grace, Free Books, and Free Riders: The Economics of Religious Publishing in Early Nineteenth-Century America." *Proceedings of the American Antiquarian Society* 106 (October 1996): 241–72.

———. "Religious Reading and Readers in Antebellum America." *Journal of the Early Republic* 15 (1995): 241–73.

———. "Teleology and News: The Religious Roots of American Journalism, 1630–1730." *Journal of American History* 77 (1990): 9–38.

Norris, Clive Murray. *The Financing of John Wesley's Methodism, c. 1740–1800.* New York: Oxford University Press, 2017.

Norwood, John Nelson. *The Schism in the Methodist Episcopal Church, 1844: A Study of Slavery and Ecclesiastical Politics.* Alfred, NY: Alfred University Press, 1923.

Numbers, Ronald L., and Darrel W. Amundsen, eds. *Caring and Curing: Health and Medicine in the Western Religious Tradition.* New York: Macmillan, 1986.

O'Brien, Susan. "A Transatlantic Community of Saints: The Great Awakening and the First Evangelical Network, 1735–1755." *American Historical Review* 91 (October 1986): 811–32.

Onuf, Peter S. *Jefferson's Empire: The Language of American Nationhood.* Charlottesville: University Press of Virginia, 2000.

Ostler, Jeffrey. *Surviving Genocide: Native Nations and the United States from the American Revolution to Bleeding Kansas.* New Haven, CT: Yale University Press, 2019.

Ostler, Jeffrey, and Nancy Shoemaker, eds. "Forum: Settler Colonialism in Early American History." *William and Mary Quarterly,* 3rd series, 76, no. 3 (July 2019): 361–68.

Owen, Christopher H. *The Sacred Flame of Love: Methodism and Society in Nineteenth-Century Georgia.* Athens: University of Georgia Press, 1998.

Park, Benjamin E. *American Nationalisms: Imagining Union in the Age of Revolutions, 1783–1833.* New York: Cambridge University Press, 2018.

Parrish, Susan Scott. *American Curiosity: Cultures of Natural History in the Colonial British Atlantic World.* Chapel Hill: University of North Carolina Press, 2006.

Perl-Rosenthal, Nathan. "Private Letters and Public Diplomacy: The Adams Network and the Quasi-War, 1797–1798." *Journal of the Early Republic* 31, no. 2 (Summer 2011): 283–311.

Pestana, Carla Gardina. *Protestant Empire: Religion and the Making of the British Atlantic World.* Philadelphia: University of Pennsylvania Press, 2009.

Pettegree, Andrew. *Reformation and the Culture of Persuasion.* New York: Cambridge University Press, 2005.

Plane, Ann Marie. *Dreams and the Invisible World in Colonial New England: Indians, Colonists, and the Seventeenth Century.* Philadelphia: University of Pennsylvania Press, 2014.

Plane, Ann Marie, and Leslie Tuttle, eds. *Dreams, Dreamers, and Visions: The Early Modern Atlantic World.* Philadelphia: University of Pennsylvania Press, 2013.

Polzin, James Edward. "The Reverend Bryan Fairfax, Eighth Baron of Cameron." M.A. thesis, George Mason University, 1983.

Porterfield, Amanda. *Conceived in Doubt: Religion and Politics in the New American Nation.* Chicago: University of Chicago Press, 2012.

Posey, Warren B. "The Advance of Methodism into the Lower Southwest." *Journal of Southern History* 2 (November 1936): 439–52.

Prucha, Francis Paul. *The Sword of the Republic: The United States Army on the Frontier, 1783–1846.* London: Macmillan, 1969.

Putnam, Robert. *Bowling Alone: The Collapse and Revival of American Community.* New York: Simon and Schuster, 2000.

Putnam, Robert, Roberto Leonardi, and Raffaella Y. Nanetti. *Making Democracy Work: Civic Traditions in Modern Italy.* Princeton, NJ: Princeton University Press, 1993.

Putney, Clifford. *Muscular Christianity: Manhood and Sports in Protestant America, 1880–1920.* Cambridge, MA: Harvard University Press, 2003.

Quisenberry, A. C. "'Heads of Families' in Franklin County: Census of 1810." *Register of the Kentucky State Historical Society* 13 (September 1915): 79–95.

Rable, George C. *God's Almost Chosen Peoples: A Religious History of the American Civil War.* Chapel Hill: University of North Carolina Press, 2010.

Raboteau, Albert J. *Slave Religion: The "Invisible Institution" in the Antebellum South.* New York: Oxford University Press, 1978.

"Rev. Richard McAllister of Fort Hunter." *Chronicle: Journal of the Historical Society of the Central Pennsylvania Conference of the United Methodist Church* 17 (Spring 2006): 78–84.

Richey, Russell E. *Early American Methodism.* Bloomington: Indiana University Press, 1991.

———. *Methodism in the American Forest.* New York: Oxford University Press, 2015.

———. *The Methodist Conference in America: A History.* Nashville, TN: Kingswood Books, 1996.

Richey, Russell E., Kenneth E. Rowe, and Jean Miller Schmidt. *The Methodist Experience in America: A History.* Nashville: Abingdon Press, 2010.

———, eds. *Perspectives on American Methodism: Interpretive Essays.* Nashville, TN: Kingswood Books, 1993.

Rockman, Seth. *Scraping By: Wage Labor, Slavery, and Survival in Early Baltimore.* Baltimore, MD: Johns Hopkins University Press, 2009.

Rohrbough, Malcolm J. *Trans-Appalachian Frontier: People, Societies, and Institutions, 1775–1850*, 3rd ed. 1978; Bloomington: Indiana University Press, 2008.

Rohrer, S. Scott. *Wandering Souls: Protestant Migrations in America, 1630–1865*. Chapel Hill: University of North Carolina Press, 2010.

Roney, Jessica Choppin. *Governed by a Spirit of Opposition: The Origins of American Political Practice in Colonial Philadelphia*. Baltimore, MD: Johns Hopkins University Press, 2014.

Ross, Steven J. *Workers on the Edge: Work, Leisure, and Politics in Industrializing Cincinnati, 1788–1890*. New York: Columbia University Press, 1985.

Rotberg, Robert I. "Social Capital and Political Culture in Africa, America, Australia, and Europe." *Journal of Interdisciplinary History* 29, no. 3 (1999): 339–56.

Roth, Randolph A. *The Democratic Dilemma: Religion, Reform, and the Social Order in the Connecticut River Valley of Vermont, 1791–1850*. New York: Cambridge University Press, 1987.

Rothman, Adam. *Slave Country: American Expansion and the Origins of the Deep South*. Cambridge, MA: Harvard University Press, 2005.

Rouleau, Brian. "Maritime Destiny as Manifest Destiny: American Commercial Expansionism and the Idea of the Indian." *Journal of the Early Republic* 30 (Fall 2010): 377–411.

Rowland, Dunbar, ed. *Mississippi: Comprising Sketches of Counties, Towns, Events, Institutions, and Persons, Arranged in Cyclopedic Form*. Vol. 1. Atlanta: Southern Historical Publishing, 1907.

Ruth, Lester. *A Little Heaven Below: Worship at Early Methodist Quarterly Meetings*. Nashville, TN: Abingdon Press, 2000.

Ryan, Mary P. *Cradle of the Middle Class: The Family in Oneida County, New York, 1790–1865*. New York: Cambridge University Press, 1981.

Sachs, Honor. *Home Rule: Households, Manhood, and National Expansion on the Eighteenth-Century Kentucky Frontier*. New Haven, CT: Yale University Press, 2015.

Saler, Bethel. *The Settlers' Empire: Colonialism and State Formation in America's Old Northwest*. Philadelphia: University of Pennsylvania Press, 2015.

Sassi, Jonathan D. *A Republic of Righteousness: The Public Christianity of the Post-Revolutionary New England Clergy*. New York: Oxford University Press, 2001.

Saunt, Claudio. *Unworthy Republic: The Dispossession of Native Americans and the Road to Indian Territory*. New York: Norton, 2020.

Scheiber, Harry N. *Ohio Canal Era: A Case Study of Government and the Economy, 1820–1861*. 1968; reprint Athens: Ohio University Press, 2012.

Schlereth, Eric R. *An Age of Infidels: The Politics of Religious Controversy in the Early United States*. Philadelphia: University of Pennsylvania Press, 2013.

Schmidt, Jean Miller. *Grace Sufficient: A History of Women in American Methodism*. Nashville, TN: Abingdon Press, 1999.

Schmidt, Leigh Eric. *Holy Fairs: Scottish Communions and American Revivals in the Early Modern Period*. Princeton, NJ: Princeton University Press, 1989.

Schneider, A. Gregory. "The Ritual of Happy Dying among Early American Methodists." *Church History* 56 (1987): 348–63.

———. *The Way of the Cross Leads Home: The Domestication of American Methodism*. Bloomington: Indiana University Press, 1993.

Schweiger, Beth Barton. *The Gospel Working Up: Progress and the Pulpit in Nineteenth-Century Virginia*. New York: Oxford University Press, 2000.

———. *A Literate South: Reading before Emancipation*. New Haven, CT: Yale University Press, 2019.

The Scotch-Irish in America: Proceedings and Addresses of the Second Congress at Pittsburg, Pennsylvania, May 29 to June 1, 1890. Cincinnati: Robert Clarke, 1890.

Scully, Randolph Ferguson. *Religion and the Making of Nat Turner's Virginia: Baptist Community and Conflict, 1740–1840*. Charlottesville: University of Virginia Press, 2008.

———. "'Somewhat Liberated': Baptist Discourses of Race and Slavery in Nat Turner's Virginia, 1770–1840." *Explorations in Early American Culture* 5 (2001): 328–71.

Seed, Patricia. *Ceremonies of Possession in Europe's Conquest of the New World, 1492–1640*. New York: Cambridge University Press, 1995.

———. "Taking Possession and Reading Texts: Establishing the Authority of Overseas Empires." *William and Mary Quarterly*, 3rd series, 49, no. 2 (April 1992): 183–209.

Seeley, Samantha. *Race, Removal, and the Right to Remain: Migration and the Making of the United States*. Chapel Hill: University of North Carolina Press, 2021.

Sehat, David. *The Myth of American Religious Freedom*. Revised ed. 2011; New York: Oxford University Press, 2015.

Sellers, Charles. *The Market Revolution: Jacksonian America, 1815–1846*. New York: Oxford University Press, 1991.

Semmel, Bernard. *The Methodist Revolution*. New York: Basic, 1973.

Shapin, Steven. *A Social History of Truth: Civility and Science in Seventeenth-Century England*. Chicago: University of Chicago Press, 1994.

Sharfstein, Daniel J. *The Invisible Line: Three American Families and the Secret Journey from Black to White*. New York: Penguin, 2011.

Shea, Daniel B., Jr. *Spiritual Autobiography in Early America*. Princeton, NJ: Princeton University Press, 1968.

Silver, Peter. *Our Savage Neighbors: How Indian War Transformed Early America*. New York: Norton, 2008.

Sirota, Brent S. *The Christian Monitors: The Church of England and the Age of Benevolence, 1680–1730*. New Haven, CT: Yale University Press, 2014.

Sleeper-Smith, Susan. *Indigenous Prosperity and American Conquest: Indian Women of the Ohio River Valley, 1690–1792.* Chapel Hill: University of North Carolina Press, 2018.

Smith, Craig Bruce. *American Honor: The Creation of the Nation's Ideals during the Revolutionary Era.* Chapel Hill: University of North Carolina Press, 2019.

Smith, Henry Nash. *Virgin Land: The American West as Symbol and Myth.* Cambridge, MA: Harvard University Press, 1971.

Smith, Timothy L. "Congregation, State, and Denomination: The Forming of the American Religious Structure." *William and Mary Quarterly,* 3rd series, 25, no. 2 (1968): 155–76.

———. "The Ohio Valley: Testing Ground for America's Experiment in Religious Pluralism." *Church History* 60 (1991): 461–79.

Snay, Mitchell. *Gospel of Disunion: Religion and Separatism in the Antebellum South.* Chapel Hill: University of North Carolina Press, 1997.

Snyder, Christina. *Great Crossings: Indians, Settlers, and Slaves in the Age of Jackson.* New York: Oxford University Press, 2017.

Sobel, Mechal. *Teach Me Dreams: The Search for Self in the Revolutionary Era.* Princeton, NJ: Princeton University Press, 2000.

Spangler, Jewel L. *Virginians Reborn: Anglican Monopoly, Evangelical Dissent, and the Rise of the Baptists in the Late Eighteenth Century.* Charlottesville: University of Virginia Press, 2008.

Sparks, Randy J. *On Jordan's Stormy Banks: Evangelicalism in Mississippi, 1773–1876.* Athens: University of Georgia Press, 1994.

Stanwood, Owen. *The Empire Reformed: English America in the Age of the Glorious Revolution.* Philadelphia: University of Pennsylvania Press, 2011.

Stark, Rodney. *The Rise of Christianity: A Sociologist Reconsiders History.* Princeton, NJ: Princeton University Press, 1996.

Stark, Rodney, and William Sims Bainbridge. *The Future of Religion: Secularization, Revival, and Cult Formation.* Berkeley: University of California Press, 1985.

Startup, Kenneth Moore. *The Root of All Evil: The Protestant Clergy and the Economic Mind of the Old South.* Athens: University of Georgia Press, 1997.

Stephan, Scott. *Redeeming the Southern Family: Evangelical Women and Southern Devotion in the Antebellum South.* Athens: University of Georgia Press, 2008.

Stout, Harry S. *American Aristocrats: A Family, a Fortune, and the Making of American Capitalism.* New York: Basic, 2017.

———. "Religion, Communications, and the Ideological Origins of the American Revolution." *William and Mary Quarterly,* 3rd series, 34, no. 4 (October 1977): 519–41.

———. *Upon the Altar of the Nation: A Moral History of the Civil War.* New York: Penguin, 2007.

Stout, Harry S., and D. G. Hart., eds. *New Directions in American Religious History*. New York: Oxford University Press, 1998.

Stowe, Steven M. *Intimacy and Power in the Old South: Ritual in the Lives of the Planters*. Baltimore, MD: Johns Hopkins University Press, 1987.

Sweet, Leonard I., ed. *Communication and Change in American Religious History*. Grand Rapids, MI: Eerdmans, 1993.

Sweet, Timothy. "What Is Improvement?" *Eighteenth Century* 52 (Summer 2011): 225–30.

Sweet, William Warren. *Religion in the Development of American Culture, 1765–1840*. New York: Charles Scribner's Sons, 1952.

———. *Virginia Methodism: A History*. Richmond, VA: Whittet and Shepperson, 1955.

Tadmor, Naomi. *Family and Friends in Eighteenth-Century England: Household, Kinship, and Patronage*. New York: Cambridge University Press, 2001.

Tanner, Helen Hornbeck, ed. *Atlas of Great Lakes Indian History*. Norman: University of Oklahoma Press, 1987.

Taves, Ann. *Fits, Trances, and Visions: Experiencing Religion and Explaining Experience from Wesley to James*. Princeton, NJ: Princeton University Press, 1999.

Taylor, George Rogers. *The Transportation Revolution, 1815–1860*. New York: Harper and Row, 1951.

Thompson, E. P. *The Making of the English Working Class*. New York: Vintage, 1963.

Tigert, John J. *A Constitutional History of American Episcopal Methodism*, 3rd ed. 1894; Nashville, TN: Methodist Episcopal Church, South, 1908.

Tiro, Karim M. "New Narratives of the Conquest of the Ohio Country." *Journal of the Early Republic* 36 (Fall 2016): 549–56.

Tomlins, Christopher. *Freedom Bound: Law, Labor, and Civic Identity in Colonizing English America, 1580–1865*. New York: Cambridge University Press, 2010.

True, Rodney H. "John Binns of Loudoun." *William and Mary Quarterly*, 2nd series, 2 (January 1922): 20–39.

Turner, Frederick Jackson. *The Frontier in American History*. New York: Henry Holt, 1920; Mineola, NY: Dover, 2010.

Turner, Victor, and Edith Turner. *Image and Pilgrimage in Christian Culture: Anthropological Perspectives*. New York: Columbia University Press, 1978.

Tweed, Thomas A. "After the Quotidian Turn: Interpretive Categories and Scholarly Trajectories in the Study of Religion since the 1960s." *Journal of Religion* 95, no. 3 (July 2015): 361–85.

———, ed. *Retelling U.S. Religious History*. Berkeley: University of California Press, 1997.

US Department of Labor, Bureau of Labor Statistics. *History of Wages in the United States from Colonial Times to 1928*. Bureau of Labor Statistics Bulletin no. 604. Washington, DC: Government Printing Office, 1934.

Usner, Daniel H. *Indians, Settlers, and Slaves in a Frontier Exchange Economy: The Lower Mississippi Valley before 1783.* Chapel Hill: University of North Carolina Press, 1992.

Valencius, Conevery Bolton. *The Health of the Country: How American Settlers Understood Themselves and Their Land.* New York: Basic, 2002.

Veracini, Lorenzo. *Settler Colonialism: A Theoretical Overview.* New York: Palgrave Macmillan, 2010.

Wade, Richard C. *The Urban Frontier: Pioneer Life in Early Pittsburgh, Cincinnati, Lexington, Louisville, and St. Louis.* Chicago: University of Chicago Press, 1964.

Ward, John William. *Andrew Jackson: Symbol for an Age.* New York: Oxford University Press, 1955.

Ward, W. R. "The Legacy of John Wesley: The Pastoral Office in Britain and America." In *Statemen, Scholars, and Merchants: Essays in Eighteenth-Century History Presented to Dame Lucy Sutherland,* edited by Anne Whiteman et al., 323–50. Oxford: Clarendon Press, 1973.

———. *The Protestant Evangelical Awakening.* New York: Cambridge University Press, 1992.

Waterman, Bryan. *Republic of Intellect: The Friendly Club of New York City and the Making of American Literature.* Baltimore, MD: Johns Hopkins University Press, 2007.

Watson, Kevin. *Pursuing Social Holiness: The Band Meeting in Wesley's Thought and Popular Methodist Practice.* New York: Oxford University Press, 2014.

Watts, Edward. *In This Remote Country: French Colonial Culture in the Anglo-American Imagination, 1780–1860.* Chapel Hill: University of North Carolina Press, 2006.

Weber, Max. *The Protestant Ethic and the Spirit of Capitalism.* Translated by Stephen Kalberg. New York: Oxford University Press, 2010.

Wells, Jonathan Daniel. *The Origins of the Southern Middle Class, 1800–1861.* Chapel Hill: University of North Carolina Press, 2004.

Wells, Jonathan Daniel, and Jennifer Green, eds. *The Southern Middle Class in the Long Nineteenth Century.* Baton Rouge: Louisiana State University Press, 2011.

Westerkamp, Marilyn J. *Triumph of the Laity: Scots-Irish Piety and the Great Awakening, 1625–1760.* New York: Oxford University Press, 1988.

Wiebe, Robert H. *The Search for Order, 1877–1920.* New York: Hill and Wang, 1967.

Wigger, John H. *American Saint: Francis Asbury and the Methodists.* New York: Oxford University Press, 2009.

———. *Taking Heaven by Storm: Methodism and the Rise of Popular Christianity in America.* New York: Oxford University Press, 1998.

Williams, Jeffrey. *Religion and Violence in Early American Methodism: Taking the Kingdom by Force.* Bloomington: Indiana University Press, 2010.

Williams, William H. *The Garden of American Methodism: The Delmarva Peninsula, 1769–1820.* Lanham, MD: Rowman & Littlefield, 1997.

Wills, Gregory A. *Democratic Religion: Freedom, Authority, and Church Discipline in the Baptist South, 1785–1900.* New York: Oxford University Press, 1997.

Winship, Marion Nelson. "The Land of Connected Men: A New Migration Story from the Early American Republic." *Pennsylvania History* 64 (Summer 1997): 88–104.

Witgen, Michael. "A Nation of Settlers: The Early American Republic and the Colonization of the Northwest Territory." *William and Mary Quarterly*, 3rd series, 76, no. 3 (2019): 391–98.

———. *Seeing Red: Indigenous Land, American Expansion, and the Political Economy of Plunder in North America.* Chapel Hill: University of North Carolina Press, 2022.

Wolf, Eva Sheppard. *Race and Liberty in the New Nation: Emancipation in Virginia from the Revolution to Nat Turner's Rebellion.* Baton Rouge: Louisiana State University Press, 2006.

Wolfe, Patrick. "Settler Colonialism and the Elimination of the Native." *Journal of Genocide Research* 8 (2006): 387–409.

———. *Settler Colonialism and the Transformation of Anthropology.* London: Cassell, 1999.

Wood, Gordon S. *The Radicalism of the American Revolution.* New York: Vintage, 1993.

Wright, Gavin. *Slavery and American Economic Development.* Baton Rouge: Louisiana State University Press, 2006.

Wyatt-Brown, Bertram. "The Antimission Movement in the Jacksonian South: A Study in Regional Folk Culture." *Journal of Southern History* 36, no. 4 (November 1970): 501–29.

Zaret, David. *Origins of Democratic Culture: Printing, Petitions, and the Public Sphere in Early-Modern England.* Princeton, NJ: Princeton University Press, 2000.

INDEX

Page numbers in *italics* refer to figures.

Adams, John Quincy, 167
African Methodist Episcopal (AME) Church, 126, 186
Ahlstrom, Sydney E., 60
American Revolution: and Anglo-American settler colonialism, 4, 24, 33, 36, 132, 196n37; and "imperial Protestantism," 20; and Methodism, 13, 18, 20, 22, 25, 182; and settler colonialism, 23–24, 33
Anderson, Benedict, 183
Andrew, James Osgood, 181, 189
Arminianism, 7–8, 22, 90
Asbury, Francis: on commercial society, 77, 119, 221n49; and evangelism, 15; and the growth of Methodism, 15–16, 22–23, 25–26, 33, 69; on holiness, 8; on localism, 8, 52–53, 183–84, 187; on Methodism as nationalizing, 25–26, 33, 37, 52–54, 186–87; on Native spirituality, 86, 88; positions held, 12, 20, 25–26; on preachers marrying, 112; on presiding elders, 45–48; on settlement, 8–9, 12, 69, 87, 118–19, 133, 161; travel, 46, 70, 86

Baker, Samuel, 118
Bangs, Nathan, 62–63, 188–89
Baptists, 134, 189
"Battle on the Wabash," 37
Beecher, Lyman, 85
Bigelow, Russell, 122
Blackman, Learner, 63, 70, 71–73, 76–79

Blair, William, 123–24, 128–29
Bonner, Frederick, 96–98
Bonner, Siney, 126
Booth, Ezra, 28–29
Boydston, Jeanne, 167
British migration to America, 18, 22–23, 136, 195–96nn25–26
Brooke, John C., 123–24
Brunson, Alfred, 118
Bunn, Seely, 68
Burke, William, 66, 94
Bushnell, Horace, 22, 24, 85, 186

Calhoun, John C., 89, 181–82, 185–86, 189
camp meetings, 39, 42, 52. *See also* revivalism
Cartwright, Peter: *Autobiography of Peter Cartwright,* 29–31, 55, 70; masculine image, 29–30, 55–57; as part of settler population, 29–32, 51, 56; work as circuit rider, 55–56, 63
Cato, 80
Chaucer, Geoffrey, 10
Christmas Conference (1784), 20
Church of England, 18–19, 21
circuit riders: and Arminian theology, 90; benefits from work, 2, 13, 129, 133, 136; composite occupational identities, 2, 13, 64–67, 82–83; connected settler society, 17, 23, 27, 30, 33–34, 56–57, 64, 83–85, 119, 183; experience of travel, 67–68, 70–75; first circuits beyond Appalachia, 34;

259

INDEX

circuit riders (*continued*)
  focused on white settlers, 78, 85, 126, 128; geographic origins, 61–63; as ideal of Protestant masculinity, 57–58, 66, 70; lifespan, 61–64; and Manifest Destiny, 57, 122–23; and marriage, 109, 111–13, 160; as mentally adventurous, 67–69; and Methodist social capital, 5, 10–12, 16, 49, 56–57, 85; methods, 3, 49; as objects of hagiography, 13, 35, 56, 60–61, 70; observations of the West, 76–81; pay, 64–65; as pilgrims and settlers, 13, 56, 67, 70–71, 85, 114, 151, 160–61; and postal service, 21–22, 120; relation to other roles in Methodist Church, 43, 44, 48, 51, 87, 108; sense of vocation, 82–85; spiritual formation while traveling, 72–73, 74–75; traveling distance, 43–44, 49, 52, 111; and John Wesley's design, 27; writings, 67–68, 69–70. *See also* Cartwright, Peter; Littlejohn, John
Claiborne, J. F. H., 105
Clay, Henry, 189
Coke, Thomas, 8, 20, 50
connectionalism: accessibility for women and minorities, 123, 124–29, 155, 175, 182; and the body of Christ, 10; in the early republic, 21–22; and letter writing, 89, 109–10, 121; limits of, 156–57; and power, 93–94; and the presiding elder, 89–90; and settlement networks, 3, 12–13, 17, 31, 53, 87, 93, 182–83. *See also* Methodist settlers; social principle, the
conquest of the West, 5
Cowper, William, 173–74, 176

Doctrines and Discipline of the Methodist Episcopal Church, 8, 49, 50, 123, 126, 137, 185. *See also* Asbury, Francis
Douthit, Samuel, 66
Dow, Lorenzo, 78
Dromgoole, Edward, Sr., 96–101, 120, 128, 164

Empire of Liberty: and Jefferson, 4; and Methodism, 17; and settler colonialism, 3–5

evangelicalism: in British Methodism, 19–20; and social exchange, 134–35; as US "principal subculture," 11; among women, 34–35, 58

Fairfax, Lord Bryan, 143–44
Federalist Papers, 52
Finley, James B., 35, 108, 115–20, 122–23, 127
Finley, James W., 116–17
Finney, Charles Grandison, 1, 18
French and Indian War, 5, 23

Garrett, Lewis, 66
Gatch, Philip, 91, 93, 96–97, 101
Gibson, Randall, 103
Gibson, Randall Lee, 106
Gibson, Samuel, 101–2
Gibson, Tobias, 92, 101–7, 129
Griffing family, 103–5

Haw, James, 34
holiness, 7, 64, 123, 200n108
humors, theory of, 74

itinerancy. *See* circuit riders

Jefferson, Thomas, 4, 23, 26
Jersey Settlement, 105
Jesus, 28–29, 115, 172, 186
Jones, John Griffing, 106–7
Juvenile Finleyan Missionary Mite Society, 127

Keys, James, 100
Knox, Henry, 37
Kobler, John, 185

Lakin, Benjamin, 66, 68, 73–76, 79–81
Langdon, John W., 185
Lindman, Janet Moore, 174
Little, Nathaniel, 121–22
Littlejohn, John: benefit from itinerancy, 131–34, 136, 141; Mrs. Bruce, 139; conversion, 136–37; death, 154; doubts, 138,

141; early life, 135–36; life as circuit rider, 136–41; as local preacher in Virginia, 133–34, 141–44; move to Kentucky, 144–46; neither Patriot or Loyalist, 213–14n4; network of, 140, 142–44, 146–47, 148–51, 152–53; relationship with money, 146, 150; relied on slavery, 146, 153, 220–21n48; and Monica Talbott, 140–42, 146, 150; tension with William Harrison, 144–45; ways of making a living, 133, 145–46, 147–51

Lord Dunmore's War, 36

love feasts, 49, 51, 184–85

Madison, James, 52, 183

Maley, George W., 119–20

Manifest Destiny, 57

Massie, Nathaniel, 94, 98

Matthews, Henry, 121–22, 128

Maxey, Bennett, 100

McCabe, James D., Jr., 55

McGuire, Adjet, 184–85

McKendree, William, 66

McLean, John, 94, 123

medical manuals (Methodist), 68

Methodism as American movement: camp meetings, 4, 39, 42, 52, 184; diverse beliefs about slavery, 14, 27, 88, 95–96, 223–24n66; evangelical, 11; focus on private affairs, 6; growth brought sectionalism, 187–89; growth in postrevolutionary America, 1, 15, 17–18, 25–26; language of love, 21, 43, 48–49, 65, 108–9, 116, 182, 184–85; Loyalist reputation, 20, 25, 213–14n4; and Methodist letters, 6; more movement than church, 2, 42, 192n6; "muscular Christianity," 55–60; origins, 18–20; as usually described by historians and others, 2–4, 56, 60, 132–33, 139–40

Methodist Episcopal Church (MEC): amplified acts of settlement, 12, 17, 20–21, 33–34, 53–54, 66, 127, 132, 182–83; break with Church of England, 143; as defender of respectable community life, 24–25, 113–14, 123–26; growth, 1, 15, 17–18, 22, 33, 37, 38, *40–41*, 92; in Kentucky, 24–25, 33–34, 39, 42, 44–45, 49, 91, 131, 188; localized as circuits shrank, 187–89; Methodist Protestant Church schism, 175–76, 184; in Mississippi, 13, 32–33, 42, 91–93, 106–8, 129; as nationalizing organization, 14, 26, 53, 182–84; in Ohio, 13, 33, 36–37, 39, 42, 49, 86, 91–94, 208n31; O'Kelly schism, 45, 152, 186; organizing, 12, 16, 18–19, 21–22, 31, 42–43, 53; postrevolutionary difficulties, 20, 25–26; as pyramid structure, 12, 44, *44*, 111; split over slavery and localism, 14, 181–84, 186, 188–89; in Tennessee, 32–34, 39, 42, 93, 188; in Virginia, 42, 49, 96, 208n25; *Western Christian Advocate,* 58; Western Conference, 32–37, 39, *41*, 42, 44, 61–62, 66, 91, 187–88; Western Methodist Historical Society in the Mississippi Valley, 58; wished to combat Catholicism, 53. *See also* structure of the Methodist Episcopal Church (MEC)

Methodist Magazine, 28

Methodist meetings: annual conference, 32, 37, 38–39, *40–41, 42–43,* 48, 52–53; bands, 50; class meetings, 50–51; conference minutes, 38, *40–41;* and gender, 50; general conference, 52–53; quarterly meetings, 51–52, 122, 187; types of meetings, *44,* 49–50

Methodist Quarterly Review, 70

Methodist Review, 70

Methodist settlers: and the civilizing process, 4, 16, 24, 26–27, 33, 59, 81, 107; concerned with security, 24–25, 36; disinterest in Native Americans, 5–7, 27–28, 127–28; and economic uses of networks, 31, 95–101, 108–10, 115, 119–20, 122–24, 126, 153; followed US military success, 16–17, 36, 90; growth in numbers, 33–34; identifying as pilgrims and pioneers, 4, 6, 10, 12, 42, 114, 161; in Kentucky, 131, 144–55;

INDEX

Methodist settlers (*continued*)
letter writing, 6, 88–89, 96, 107–9, 115–18; and the lives of itinerants, 61; many opposed deportation of Natives, 81; memorialize defeat of Native Americans, 30–31; in Michigan Territory, 117–18; in Ohio, 95–101; in Old Southwest, 92–93, 101–7; as participants in settler colonialism, 5, 12–13, 16–17, 27–28, 183; and personal uses of networks, 122–24; the place of education, 110–11; places of origin, 7; populist beliefs, 7–8; and presiding elders, 46–48; religion's influence on the everyday life, 6, 10–12, 16, 51–53, 87, 107–15; saw Natives as wasting land, 28–29, 42; as slaveholders, 102–3; social capital among them, 10–11, 31, 32, 108–15, 119, 124, 131–33

Methodist theology: Arminianism, 7–8, 22, 90; conversion emphasized individual experience, 136; love, 29, 49, 109, 128; original sin, 8, 113–14, 125–26, 163, 193n19; perfection in holiness, 7, 64, 123, 200n108; salvation not necessarily permanent, 68–69, 128; set apart from the world, 64, 128, 162–63; use of Old Testament, 29, 35

Methodist women: dissociation from economy, 167–88; hosting itinerants, 151–52, 157; lacking full benefits of MEC, 13–14, 124–26, 157–58, 193n30; leadership of early class meetings, 157; and Methodist networks, 34–35, 109, 112; and settlement, 157; and social action, 158. *See also* Mothers in Israel; Price, Ann Hulme

Miami Canal, 165

Miller, Perry, 68

Morse, Samuel, 15

Mothers in Israel, 14, 139, 157, 179

Native Americans: allegedly wasted land, 28–29; encounters with settlers and circuit riders, 23–24, 78, 127–28; genocide of, 4–5, 17, 194n8; Methodist criticisms of, 86; Methodist disinterest in, 5–7, 27–28, 127–28; military power, 36–37; perceived difference from whites, 29–30, 78–79, 80–81, 127–28; US military removal, 5–6, 16–17, 132, 194n8. *See also* settler colonialism

Northwest Indian War, 32, 36

Northwest Ordinance, 90, 95

Ogden, Benjamin, 34

Pelham, Peter, 98–100, 128

Pelham, Samuel, 96, 100, 128

pietism, 19

Pilgrim's Progress, 68, 137

Porkopolis (Cincinnati), 161, 167

postal service, 21–22

Presbyterians, 189

presiding elder, 12, 43–48, 87, 89–90, 95, 108

Price, Ann Hulme: attention to eternal matters, 162–64, 170–71, 174, 176; death of her child, 172–73; death of husband, 14, 156, 177–78; demands of marriage and motherhood, 158, 169–70, 173–75, 177; early life, 159; her house, 165–67; husband's business relations, 168; lack of help from MEC, 13–14, 157–58, 175, 177–79; life in Cincinnati, 160–61, 164–66; marriage to John Price, 159–61; and Mothers in Israel, 157; as pilgrim and settler, 160–64, 167, 171–72, 174, 178; social life, 171–72; support for husband's preaching, 159–60, 176; withdrawal from MEC, 175–76

Primitive Physic (John Wesley), 75

Quakers, 159, 174

republican ideology, 11

Republic of Letters, 88

revivalism: camp meetings, 39, 42, 52; characteristics, 10, 16; ecclesial and social function, 17–18; and Methodist quarterly meetings, 51; and Methodist success, 27; stoked by proper preaching, 118

Rush, Benjamin, 21, 55, 186

INDEX

sacred capital: and acts of settlement, 12; concept, 10–11; financial capital, 11, 131; product of Methodism's structure, 12, 16, 132–33, 182; race and gender determined access, 13–14, 178–79; social capital, 7–8, 11–13, 53, 131–35; and social exchange, 131, 134–35, 182, 213n1; supplanting Native spirituality, 86

Sale, John, 66, 96–98

Scott, Orange, 186

Scott, Thomas, 68, 93

Seaton, John, 107–15

Second Great Awakening: disturbed social order, 7, 10–11, 17–18; as Methodist event, 1, 18, 58; and women, 158

settler colonialism: and commercialization, 17, 25, 35, 67, 78, 81, 87, 213–14n4, 217–18n18; definition of settlement, 4; and the discourse of improvement, 164–66; effects on settler women, 158, 169; European-American migrations, 24, 33, 42, 91, 213–14n4; founded partly on Protestant religion, 27, 161, 182; after French and Indian War, 23–24; justifications from Old Testament, 29, 35; land seen as wilderness, 28–30, 35, 48, 56, 59, 71, 78; Manifest Destiny, 57; populated communication routes, 81; pro-settlement propaganda, 28; religion as bridge to new community, 134; in revolutionary America, 23–24, 33; and the royal proclamation (1763), 4, 23; settlers' bourgeois values, 23–24, 27; the unsettled classes, 156; view of Native Americans, 29–30, 127–28; the West as American Israel, 76–77; worked against Methodist union, 187–89. *See also* Methodist settlers

Sigman, John, 137

Sketches of Western Methodism, 9

slavery: and antislavery sentiment, 95–96; and division of the MEC, 14, 181–89; and forced migration, 132; influence in MEC, 13–14, 103–7, 181–82; and Methodist belief, 13–14, 27, 88, 95–96, 153; Methodist settlers as slaveholders, 102–3; in Mississippi, 107; power of biography, 57; slave-quarter churches, 126–27; slavery, 14, 181–89; and white morality, 126–27

Smith, Henry, 59–60, 69–70, 76, 82–85

social principle, the: allowed for differences on slavery, 14, 88, 116; in Asbury and Coke's writing, 8; the core of Methodism, 87; helped construct a settler nation, 183; and itinerant preachers, 10, 56–57, 64, 87, 133–34; localized and sectionalized America, 183–89; the power and problem of, 9, 86–87; produced sacred capital, 86–87, 96–101, 123, 183. *See also* connectionalism

Society for Promoting Christian Knowledge, 19

Society for the Propagation of the Gospel in Foreign Parts, 19

Southey, Robert, 57

Sprague, William Buell, 58

St. Clair, Arthur, 37

structure of the Methodist Episcopal Church (MEC): bishops, 45–46; districts, 43–45, *44;* the place of circuits, 43–45, *44;* presiding elders, 45–46; restructuring, 38–39, 42; vertical and horizontal elements, 20–21

Swayze, Samuel, 105

Sweet, William Warren, 2, 60

Talbott, Daniel, 138

Thompson, A. G., 68

Tiffin, Edward, 86, 93–94, 97–98

Tocqueville, Alexis de, 89

Treaty of Greenville (1795), 17, 37, 91, 132

Treaty of San Lorenzo (1795), 92

Turner, Frederick Jackson, 2, 35, 60

voluntarism, 17

Waddell, Charles, 124–26

War of 1812, 24, 36, 56

Washington, George, 21, 37, 100

INDEX

Watters, William, 138
Watts, Isaac, 162, 171
Wayne, Anthony, 37, 90
Wesley, John, 19–20, 25, 27, 57, 68, 75, 119
Western Conference (MEC), 32–37, 39, *41,* 42, 44, 61–62, 66, 91, 187–88

Winans, William, 92, 107–14
Worthington, Thomas, 93–94
Wright, John F., 58–60
Wyandots, 79–81, 116, 127–28

Zephaniah (prophet), 9

RECENT BOOKS IN THE SERIES
Jeffersonian America

Empire of Commerce: The Closing of the Mississippi and the Opening of Atlantic Trade
Susan Gaunt Stearns

Black Reason, White Feeling: The Jeffersonian Enlightenment in the African American Tradition
Hannah Spahn

Replanting a Slave Society: The Sugar and Cotton Revolutions in the Lower Mississippi Valley
Patrick Luck

The Celebrated Elizabeth Smith: Crafting Genius and Transatlantic Fame in the Romantic Era
Lucia McMahon

Rival Visions: How the Views of Jefferson and His Contemporaries Defined the Early American Republic
Dustin Gish and Andrew Bibby, editors

Revolutionary Prophecies: The Founders and America's Future
Robert M. S. McDonald and Peter S. Onuf, editors

The Founding of Thomas Jefferson's University
John A. Ragosta, Peter S. Onuf, and Andrew J. O'Shaughnessy, editors

Thomas Jefferson's Lives: Biographers and the Battle for History
Robert M. S. McDonald, editor

Jeffersonians in Power: The Rhetoric of Opposition Meets the Realities of Governing
Joanne B. Freeman and Johann N. Neem, editors

Jefferson on Display: Attire, Etiquette, and the Art of Presentation
G. S. Wilson

Jefferson's Body: A Corporeal Biography
Maurizio Valsania

Pulpit and Nation: Clergymen and the Politics of Revolutionary America
Spencer W. McBride

Blood from the Sky: Miracles and Politics in the Early American Republic
Adam Jortner

Confounding Father: Thomas Jefferson's Image in His Own Time
Robert M. S. McDonald

The Haitian Declaration of Independence: Creation, Context, and Legacy
Julia Gaffield, editor

Citizens of a Common Intellectual Homeland: The Transatlantic Origins of American Democracy and Nationhood
Armin Mattes

Between Sovereignty and Anarchy: The Politics of Violence in the American Revolutionary Era
Patrick Griffin, Robert G. Ingram, Peter S. Onuf, and Brian Schoen, editors

Patriotism and Piety: Federalist Politics and Religious Struggle in the New American Nation
Jonathan J. Den Hartog

Becoming Men of Some Consequence: Youth and Military Service in the Revolutionary War
John A. Ruddiman

Amelioration and Empire: Progress and Slavery in the Plantation Americas
Christa Dierksheide

Collegiate Republic: Cultivating an Ideal Society in Early America
Margaret Sumner

Era of Experimentation: American Political Practices in the Early Republic
Daniel Peart

Paine and Jefferson in the Age of Revolutions
Simon P. Newman and Peter S. Onuf, editors

Sons of the Father: George Washington and His Protégés
Robert M. S. McDonald, editor